MW01488370

Ellen M Tsagaris

Ellen M. Tsagaris, JD, PhD, has collected dolls since age three. She gives lectures, stages museum exhibits, appraises, and makes dolls. Dr. Tsagaris writes books and articles about dolls, including *With Love from Tin Lizzie; A History of Metal Dolls* and *A Bibliography of Doll and Toy Sources*. Her articles are found in Antique Doll Collector, Antique Trader, The Midwestern Journal of Victorian Studies and The American Journal of Play. She was also the doll collecting expert for About.com. She blogged for R. John Wright, Ruby Lane, and Antique Doll Collector and was a guest columnist for the Argus/Dispatch. She has won several writing awards and has appeared on radio and television programs.

Dedicated to my beloved husband, Dino Milani, who helped build our museum, my mother Clara Tsagaris and father Jim Tsagaris, my uncles Tom, Jim and George Fanakos, my grandparents, Steve and Marie Fanakos and Aunt Connie Fanakos. To Dr. Judy Little and to Miss Kitty Bangles, a doll collector and doll house enthusiast in her own right, who sat next to her mom and curled up next to the computer to provide inspiration and moral support. To Mr. Tuxedo Kitty who is the biggest toy enthusiast – animal or human – I've ever met. To our late, amazing kitty Emma Hatfield, who had her own doll collection named "Mouse". To our late, magnificent Daxie Kitty, who loved Beanie Babies, toys and shrimp. To our puppies; Killer, Smokey and Tiger, and to our late, great kitty, Mr. Opie, who lived to be 24 and who cherished an animal Muppet doll, a Victorian doll bed, and a stuffed cow doll. Also, in memory of Dr. Roald Tweet, who helped make this book possible, 1933–2020.

Ellen M. Tsagaris

THINKING OUTSIDE THE DOLL HOUSE

A MEMOIR

AUSTIN MACAULEY PUBLISHERS™

LONDON * CAMBRIDGE * NEW YORK * SHARJAH

Copyright © Ellen M. Tsagaris (2021)

All rights reserved. No part of this publication may be reproduced, distributed, or transmitted in any form or by any means, including photocopying, recording, or other electronic or mechanical methods, without the prior written permission of the publisher, except in the case of brief quotations embodied in critical reviews and certain other non-commercial uses permitted by copyright law. For permission requests, write to the publisher.

Any person who commits any unauthorized act in relation to this publication may be liable to criminal prosecution and civil claims for damages.

Ordering Information
Quantity sales: Special discounts are available on quantity purchases by corporations, associations, and others. For details, contact the publisher at the address below.

Publisher's Cataloging-in-Publication data
Tsagaris, Ellen M.
Thinking Outside the Doll House

ISBN 9781645361176 (Paperback)
ISBN 9781645361183 (Hardback)
ISBN 9781645365952 (ePub e-book)

Library of Congress Control Number: 2020925322

www.austinmacauley.com/us

First Published (2021)
Austin Macauley Publishers LLC
40 Wall Street, 33rd Floor, Suite 3302
New York, NY 10005
USA

mail-usa@austinmacauley.com
+1 (646) 5125767

I am grateful to my parents, James and Clara Tsagaris, for all their support and love through the years. May their memories be eternal. I would like to thank Dr. Roald and Margaret Tweet for their encouragement through the years, and for their many contributions to my collection. To my friend, noted author, doll artist, and expert, R. Lane Herron, for his inspiration and support which has never wavered. Also, I would be remiss in not mentioning the many collectors, friends, editors, dealers, and doll artists over the years who helped me learn what I know about dolls including Mary Hillier, Stephanie Hammonds, Jo Smith, Jenny Tellian, Carolyn Cook, Mikki Brantley, and Bernard Ravca. Thanks to our son, Mitchell Milani, who has tolerated dolls his whole life, and who supports our doll museum plans. My thanks to my writing teachers, including my dissertation director, Dr. Judy Little, and Dr. K.K. Collins, SIUC graduate advisor, my boss and mentor, H. Jefferson Powell, law professors David C. Baldus, may his memory be eternal, and Josephine Gittler. They taught me the nuances of all types of research. For all who have contributed to my collection and who have traveled with me to find dolls, and to those who attend my programs, read my blogs, and help with my exhibits. I would like to acknowledge the great writers who have come before me, especially R. Lane Herron, Laura Starr, Max von Boehn, John Axe, Chris Revi, Carl Fox, John Noble, Helen Young, Janet Pagter Johl, and Eleanor St. George. Thanks to the editors and fine people at Austin Macauley who have been my guides in this journey, and to Rachel Hoffman, my muse in so many ways in all things dolls. Finally, thanks to Anne Rice for her words on dolls, and to all the doll makers from the dawn of history, who make interest in dolls and this wonderful hobby possible.

Table of Contents

Epigraph

The world cannot move without women sharing in the movement. China compressed the feet of its women and thereby retarded the steps of its men.

Frances Ellen Harper

Preface

What culture doesn't have dolls? The truth is, I can't find any. Even countries where it is frowned upon to create human images and figures, allow their children to play with dolls. The dolls might be faceless, or even headless in some cases, but they are there. Elon Musk recently launched his Tesla roadster into space orbit, but Hot Wheels toys and a mannequin named Starman accompanied the roadster. Other toys have found their way to space as part of Astronaut's experiments, and a stuffed frog traveled with Christa McAuliffe on the ill-fated Challenger mission of 1986.

In *Interrogating the Meanings of Dolls*, Miriam Forman-Brunell writes that, "Dolls are ubiquitous cultural forms central to girlhood and young womanhood. Yet, understanding the historical and contemporary significance of dolls is a relatively recent development. The age-old trivialization of girls and devaluation of youth cultures led to the customary disregard of dolls as legitimate sources of documentary evidence even among scholars." (3)

Dolls really are everywhere. Everyone owns some type of doll, stuffed animal, holiday decoration, nativity figure, statue, action figure, robot, automaton, figurine, or mask. Anyone with three of any of these has a collection of them, like it or not. Or, as a good friend of mine who was also a noted authority on dolls, the late Mary Hillier used to write all the time, "Dolls are where you find them!"

And, we find them everywhere. Turn on any TV show or play a movie in your DVD player Blu-ray, and you will find any of the above objects as props. Articles about dolls pop up everywhere. The Internet is bulging with studies of Barbie, articles on Cabbage Patch Kids, advertisements on dolls, sites that sell dolls, doll blogs, doll videos, etc. There are even phobias connected with dolls and their cousins, automatons and robots. Mystery writers weave novel stories around them, and poets pay them attention in verse.

There is no house without a doll! Dolls touch everyone's life, one way or another. Even those who claim they have no dolls, or don't like them, have had a doll or doll related object in their lives. Here are some dolls and doll related objects that fit the doll theme, or what Lea Baten calls "The Doll Motif."

Basically, anything that is figural, portrait related, loved as a doll or toy, paper doll, or stuffed animal is, well, a "doll thing."

Here are some ways that dolls infiltrate and enrich our lives.

Toy soldiers and little plastic men, including railroad figures in all scales, are tiny dolls. Miniature figures are written about all the time in doll books, including the classics like Carl Fox's *The Doll* and Max von Boehn's *Dolls*. The Little Green Army Men from *Toy Story* fit the bill, so do the classic plastic Native American figures currently on display at The Museum of the American Indian.

Figurines, including the popular collectibles Hummels, Dresden, Lladro, Precious Moments, Cherished Teddies, Josef's Originals, Royal Doulton, and Lefton are, like railroad figures, dolls. Figurines are indeed figural, and many were made by factories that also made dolls, like Hummel, Royal Doulton, and Precious Moments. Figurines, especially Victorian bric-a-brac, are often found in doll collections. Hybrids include penny dolls, Frozen Charlottes, piano babies, and pincushion dolls.

Action figures: G.I. Joe and Big Jim appear in a lot of doll collections, so do Mego action figures, WWF figures, McFarlane toys, Stretch Armstrong, Major Matt Mason, The Universal Monsters, and more. The term "action figure" is just another term for dolls for boys. Yet, action figures are gender bending; girls love them and have their own versions like The Golden Girls by Galoob, She-Ra by Mattel, and Princess Leia of Star Wars.

Gingerbread cookies, chocolate rabbits and Santas, fancy cookies, Peeps, Sour Patch kids, Gummy Bears and other edible dolls and toys. Who among us has not enjoyed at least one of these treats? Who hasn't had an ice cream cone clown, or a pancake with a face done in raisins and berries? Edible dolls have a long history, dating to ancient times when dough figures were made to use in fertility rituals and other festivities. The Gingerbread Man has his own story and co-stars in *Shrek*. Doll cakes are very popular at parties even today. Sugar skulls and Marzipan figures are popular holiday items as well. The late artist Frida Kahlo was a doll collector, who also loved to collect sugar skulls.

Models: Models like Bride of Frankenstein, The Phantom of the Opera, The Invisible Woman, Dracula, and others are often an early introduction to doll-making for children and young adults. They even make an appearance in Stephen King's novel, *Salem's Lot*.

Stuffed animals and animal figures: Boys and girls love to cuddle and collect these. Vintage model horses and "My Little Pony" figures are very popular; Queen Elizabeth II and Princess Margaret had toy horses that they liked to "water" and put to bed each night. Teddy bears have been a hit for well over 100 years. Steiff has made all kids of animals, and all are lovingly collected and studied. Nearly every child in the U.S. has played with sock toys, knitted animals, Beanies, teddy bears, dinosaur figures, vintage Snoopy and Woodstock toys, and Noah's ark and farm animals. These are often given names, and characters like Mickey Mouse, Mighty Mouse, and Goofy are anthropomorphized.

Bobble Heads: These have their own museum, and their ancestors are bisque nodders. They have been props in *The Office* and other TV shows, and they are given away at sports events all over the world. Sports mascot memorabilia fit the category, too. People who would never think of themselves as doll collectors are avid collectors of these things.

Paper dolls, portraits, photographs, etc.: Paper dolls are often pictures of real people cut from magazines and made into dolls. Two-dimensional human images capture our attention and forge a relationship with those who see them the way dolls do. Think how many millions have fallen in love with *The Mona Lisa.* Anyone who has been fascinated by a painting or portrait has succumbed to "The Doll Motif," and a doll related object has touched his or her life.

Holiday Figures: Santa, snowmen, scarecrows, angels, witches, vampires, the ephemeral jack-o' lantern, the leprechaun, Cupid figurine and Easter Bunny toys are all examples of holiday dolls. There are many ornaments of these, and a lot of them are wooden which made the tradition of German Erzebirge toys. Nearly anyone who has celebrated Christmas has ornaments shaped liked dolls.

Added to these examples are advertising figures like The Cigar Store Indian, the old Holiday Inn mascot, The Little Midshipman, ships' figureheads, department store mannequins, and statues. Students of folk art and sculpture begin to notice soon that similar techniques are involved in doll making. Artists use lay figures and as models, and are influenced by dolls as were Marque, Picasso, Cornell, and Degas. Dolls are used in the medical and psychiatric fields as learning tools, and the fashion world uses them to create couture. Santos and religious figures are still important in many faiths. Early automatons and robots are very close relatives to mechanical dolls and vice versa.

Dolls are everywhere, and they touch every life. They are our storytellers, and as artifacts that live after us, our historians.

Foreword: The Doll Motif

Lea Baten in her book *Japanese Dolls; The Image and the Motif* refers to a doll motif, where figural art or the human visage influences and appears in art, sculpture, design, and drawing. The human form may be represented as a toy, an art object, an amulet, or something else needed for human existence.

For this reason, dolls have become important to studies of material cultural, to sociology, art, anthropology and archaeology.

Avatars have been compared to hand-made dolls and studied a though they were dolls. Liboriussen writes in *The Freedom of Avatars,* "Dolls and avatars are only truly understood through use." (4)

The idea of the doll motif is everywhere even today. One sees it in tokens left in cemeteries, especially on the graves of children. The current craze with Emojis and GIFS reflect it, as does the fad involving memes and Pokémon go, and anime. Doodles of all types, stick figures, rough cartoons of the human shape, all share in the doll motif, or this craze for anthropomorphized form.

Introduction: What Is a Doll?

Thirteen thousand plus, that is the number of dolls in my collection. This is an educated guess; it doesn't include the thousands of paper dolls, hundreds of doll books, countless miniatures, over 40 doll houses, shadowboxes, antique toys, art objects, photographs, statues, doll parts, doll clothes, and doll ephemera that make up my collections. If someone were to ask me if I played with dolls, I'd say, "Not as much as you think." I didn't play house with them or have that many tea parties. I liked to dress them and make clothes, but I used to stage plays for them where the dolls were the actors and I was the narrator. I also liked creating stage sets for them. I came relatively late to "playing Barbies," and the only reason I liked them was that the "bubble cut" doll of the early sixties looked like my mother. In fact, Barbie and Mom even had the same pink suit, and even similar proportions. Even if I didn't play with dolls, I was always around them, and I have collected them since I was a toddler. In fact, any type of portrait or figural object caught my interest, and I loved museums and art galleries as much when I was a little girl as I do now. This book tells the story, in part, of how I came to have so many dolls and why I still continue to collect them. In fact, I now have a brick and mortar venue for them, a nonprofit organization known as the American Doll and Toy Museum.

Maybe I can't tell you exactly how many dolls I have (because the number isn't that important to me), yet if someone were to ask me when I started to collect dolls, I could answer them precisely. I can pretty much pinpoint the exact moment. I was three, and sitting on the living room floor, just outside the kitchen at my grandparents' house. Everything around me was fashionably brown and burgundy, including the rug. Somebody, I think my mother, handed me two dolls. One was around 14 inches high, dressed in the costume of the "Amalia" or national women's costume of Greece. The doll had cloth hands and feet. Her black shoes and white stockings were painted on her legs. Her hands had stitched fingers. Her painted cloth face was stretched over a mask, probably of early plastic or Papier-mâché. Her painted eyes glanced sidewise, making her a little sly. Her wig was of brown, wavy mohair. Amalia was the first queen of Modern Greece. Along with King Otto, she was brought from Germany after the Greek War of Independence from the Turks in 1821. Amalia herself created the costume that is still worn today for parades and festivals anywhere in the world where there are people of Greek descent. Mainly, it is a long, light blue skirt with a closely fitted jacket of darker blue, and a red velvet tam with a long tassel. Under the jacket is worn a white lace blouse, studded with coins, which represent the woman's dowry. Amalia's costume was a combination of the Turkish inspired clothing worn by Greek women in the 1820s and the Biedermeir German fashions popular in her home country. Amalia and Otto ruled for several years, and then were ousted. They went back to Germany, and Amalia is buried in Munich.

The second doll was a 7-inch-Evzon, or kilted Greek soldier. These soldiers still perform a ritual changing of the guard in front of the Greek Royal Palace, even though King Constantine was dethroned over fifty years ago. This doll also has a painted face stretched over a mask and the sly, side glancing eyes. He wears a red velvet tam and tassel too, and pompoms on his red, pointed shoes. His hands are molded plastic, and he was meant to be a souvenir. I remember saying when I got the dolls, "I think I'll collect dolls!" and the rest, as we say, is history.

When I was handed these two dolls, I already had many others at home, including my first doll, a squeaky rubber doll dressed in a molded yellow bunny suit with a child's face peeking out from under the bunny ears. I also had purloined a Sudanese statue of a man wearing a fez and playing a drum that I called "The Little Drummer Boy." This 12-inch high figure had a mended foot, something I am responsible for, I'm afraid. There is a photo of me holding this figure, and wearing the mortarboard of my newly graduated Uncle George, whose property The Little Drummer Boy was in the first place. He had just graduated with his bachelors from Augustana College, and I was stealing the scene, doll, mortarboard, and all.

He and my Uncle Tom, both my mother's brothers, had created an impromptu collection of dolls for my grandparents. George loved to collect things, and when he went on a European trip with his father and my mother, he brought home many dolls, Greek vases, rocks, bits of marble, and artwork. My mother ended up marrying my father on that trip, but George, my grandfather, and the dolls came home.

My Uncle Tom was an MP in the Korean War. He brought home Japanese and Korean dolls, lacquered items, paintings, and statues of jade, porcelain, and soapstone. He brought children's books and paper dolls and toys for George, who was the youngest in the family and only a little boy at the time. Later, these became part of my collection. Tom worked in Peoria as a commercial artist for many years. He always came home to us over the weekend, and he always brought me a new doll. He also scouted for dolls in thrift stores and in museum gift shops. He could repair any doll or toy and make it look even better than new. I guess you could say he enabled me.

George had a lot of toys and I inherited many of them, including several robots, two large teddy bears, and a Lil Abner mechanical piano that I liked to dismantle. The figure of Lil Abner made a great whirly gig for my finger. George also had balls, jacks, marbles, tops, toy ships that fire torpedoes, little cars, and games. A few of these survived, but many disappeared when my grandparents moved to California. A few later went to my cousin, George's son, Steven. What did survive to come down to me was a handmade marionette George had created in art class.

Over the years, my grandparents and aunt and uncles sent me other dolls. My grandmother made them for me, and dressed them. She was a trained seamstress who loved dolls, more so since she didn't have any when she was a child. Her father died when she was six, and her sister, Voula, was around four. She and her sister wore black as mourning for their father even though they were just little girls. My grandmother Marie wore black till she went to Paris to marry my grandfather Steve. He bought her an entire trousseau on their wedding trip. When she and Voula were small, though, they worked by helping their mother sew, and went to school to learn sewing formally. In fact, both my grandmothers knew each other and went to school together in Kalamata.

My family collected other things, too. These collections included souvenirs, Christmas items, stamps, coins, books, plates, postcards, and decals. They had a lot of Native American items picked up on road trips out west, and rocks and shells from beaches all over the United States, Mexico, and Canada. It was normal for me to see tables and shelves covered with my grandmother's crocheted doilies and small dolls, statues, vases, and souvenirs of their travels. Glass cases full of curios were the norm in our family, so it was natural for me to want to collect something.

My mother collected charms, rocks, tea cups and saucers, the afore mentioned travel decals, postcards, and later, dolls. We looked for rocks in the Mohave Desert and elsewhere and even brought shells and rocks from Europe. Some of the shells she and her family collected on trips were embedded in cement in the sidewalk along their driveway. When our car broke down in the Mojave, my dad waved down someone who could call a tow truck for him, since we didn't have car phones or cell phones then. My mom and I would look for rocks. We're lucky we didn't find a rattle snake under one of them! Yet, during one summer biology field trip near our own Mill Creek, I turned over a large rock covered with fossils, and out slithered a small black and white snake. I screamed, and left the rock alone. I preferred the smaller specimens. It was my summer of snakes; while wading through a brook that same summer, what I thought was a deposit of mud suddenly took shape and rose as a large, brown water snake. Again, I choked back a scream and stepped out of the brook. Now, snakes and snake statues are one of my favorite sub collections. The student paralegal studies club I sponsored even adopted the python at Niabi Zoo. We nicknamed him Freddy; because of our sponsorship, Freddy got extra treats and toys. I have to wonder what kind of toys a Python enjoys, but even animals play and have toys. My dogs and cats would testify to that if they could. They have had their own toy boxes for years. As with children, animals often love to play with found objects. Annabelle, a late, great dog belonging to some friends, was a shepherd mix, with maybe a little wolf sprinkled in her ancestry for good measure. She had a fierce bark, and was fascinated with our son then aged six. When she barked, it sounded like she was barking his name! Her favorite toy was a small tree branch, not a stick or twig, a branch.

Just as Annabelle's branch was important to her, our families' things were important to us. Most dated from around the early '50s, when my grandparents moved back to Villa Grove, IL. My mother and all her siblings, but George, were born there. My grandparents, grandfather's brothers, and my great grandmother ran Fanakos Brothers restaurant and belonged to the Local Moose Lodge. In fact, the restaurant was on the first floor of a building that still houses the lodge. In 1938, my grandpa Steven took my grandmother, his mother, and their four children to Kalamata for what was meant to be a two-month vacation. He wanted to sell some real estate he owned, and show his family Greece. He hadn't been back in a long time. He and his brothers, and one little sister who later died, came to the U.S. as children. Their father came first, then my great-grandmother and her children. Later, her husband died, and she was left a young widow.

In 1938, a lot of families were leaving Europe. My family ended up getting caught in World War II. They nearly died on more than one occasion; in fact, their family in Villa Grove heard nothing from them for the duration of the war and thought they were all dead. My mother and her family survived the Fascists, Nazis, and later, the Communists. Uncle George was born there in 1942. They were stuck there till 1946, and came home by ship, and then train. My grandmother and George had to stay behind until their papers were in order. My mother left her favorite doll behind, even though she had brought it with her from Villa Grove. She gave it to one of her cousins. I remember she tried to get it back, but doll and cousin disappeared and haven't been heard from since. We replaced the doll, a lookalike Shirley Temple, later. Oddly enough, I lost two dolls to one of my cousins in Greece, too. I haven't heard from her, either.

The dolls collected after the war were important to my family, and symbolized their recovery from the nightmare they had lived for so long. My mother managed to save two small dolls that she dressed in dance costumes like those that she wore in Greek dance programs. During the '50s, tourist dolls and storybook dolls were popular collectibles. They were featured in TV shows including *The Danny Thomas Show*, *Father Knows Best*, and *The Andy Griffith Show*. Companies like Nancy Ann Dolls, Vogue, Effanbee, Madame Alexander, Hollywood Dolls, Duchess Dolls, Molleye E Dolls and others made these dolls, and it was status to have a doll collection. These dolls were made for little girls to collect, and there was even a Doll of the Month mail-order club. Plastic foreign dolls and storybook dolls were premiums at gas stations, or were available with box tops from various groceries.

The United Federation of Doll Clubs was founded in 1949 to accommodate the growing number of doll collectors. Previously, the UFDC was under another name, The National Doll and Toy Collector's Club (1937). Kimport Dolls in Independence, MO, home of Harry S. Truman, ran a business providing international, folk, antique, and novelty dolls to collectors. They advertised their dolls and wrote doll lore in a publication called *Doll Talk*. Kimport went out of business in the latter part of the 20th century, but they exist online as a pattern store, reflecting the first love and the first business of one its founders, Ruby Short McKim.

My collection increased during the 1960s, largely in part because we traveled so much, and because dolls were my favorite souvenirs. We went to Canada, Mexico, all over the United States, Greece, Italy, France, and Spain. On weekends, especially Sundays after church, we took Sunday drives, like so many other families. As our head of Travel & Tourism stated during a radio interview, the Sunday trips he took with his parents to local attractions, museums, festivals, communities, and outlying country towns were really history lessons. During these weekend drives, I learned a lot about local history and collected little dolls and artifacts that carried on the tales their point of origin told.

In Fantasy Land, in Gettysburg, PA (1965), I discovered antique dolls. Unfortunately, prices of dolls increased during the '60s as well. Barbie's debut in 1959 created an interest in 11 and 12-inch fashion dolls and their clothing, but Barbie mania had not yet hit the country. Antique dolls, however, were a different matter.

I attended my first antique show when I was seven, holding my mother's hand the whole time. It was a testament to a mother's love that she took me at all. She loved dolls of all kinds, and even won a contest dressing her kitten in dolls clothes and pushing her in a doll buggy when she was six. She didn't like anything old, though. She took after her mother in this. As much as she loved dolls, my grandmother threw out two antique dolls given to her by a neighbor for my mother and her sister. She was afraid that old dolls and old things brought sickness and bad luck. She'd fit right in today with the lunacy of the haunted object movement and the creepy doll fad. My first antique doll was a tiny, dead-white glazed china doll, about three inches high with black glazed hair and painted features. Her tiny Mary Jane shoes and socks were molded onto her feet. She is called a Frozen Charlotte, after a ballad where a young girl freezes to death because she wouldn't wear a coat on a 15-mile sleigh ride to a New Year's Eve Party. Apparently, she didn't want to wrinkle her gown. Lorenzo Carter, a blind folk singer of the 19th century made the ballad famous. Natalie Merchant has written her own version, "The Ballad of Frozen Charlotte," for her album, *Ophelia*. Carl Fox in *The Doll* has likened Frozen Charlottes to the Neolithic Venus figures. Also called Pillar Dolls, Teacup Dolls, *Badekinder,* penny dolls, Frozen Charlottes are popular today as items for art projects, jewelry, and shadowboxes. Thousands have been dug up on the sites of old doll factories in what was once East Germany. I have hundreds of them in various sizes, and even genders, including a "sexed" Frozen Charlie. Most are made of china, which is glazed porcelain, or bisque, which is not glazed. A few are made in Japan, and some modern reproductions come from China. Others are made of resin, wood, soap advertising McKinley for president, metal, glass, terracotta, and hard plastic. Most are immobile and nude. A few have wigs and painted clothing. My most unusual example represents a little boy riding atop a cigar. The whole toy is a whistle. I'm proud to say that such an example started the legendary doll collection of noted author and curator of the doll and toy collection for The Museum of the City of New York, the late John Noble.

Today, I doubt there is a household in America without a doll, statue, action figure, stuffed animal, figurine, or similar object. My friend, Mary Hillier, used to say, "dolls are where you find them!" How right she was. Her book *Dolls and Doll Makers* (1969) really stretched the definition of "doll." Dolls are related to portraits, photographs, moving images of actors, statues, human-shape buildings like The Statue of Liberty, busts of various types, all figural objects, puppets, marionettes, china figurines, human shaped bric-á-brac, Santos, androids, robots, and more objects that take on human attributes or resemble human beings.

Any object anthropomorphized can be a doll or companion. Tom Hanks has a soccer ball named Wilson in *Castaway* to keep him company. One poverty-stricken child in Victorian Edinburgh made a doll from an old shoe. Cosette treats a discarded footstool as a doll in *Les Miserables*, and Laura

Ingalls Wilder makes do with a corncob wrapped in a handkerchief named simply, Susan in *Little House in the Big Woods*. In their 1897 work, *A Study of Dolls*, G. Stanley Hall and Caswell Ellis discovered that children make dolls out of virtually any object, substantial or ephemeral, including old bones, cloth, plants, live animals, bits of glass, soap, yarn, even meat!

When I was a child, dolls were everywhere. Haymaker's Cleaners had shadowboxes in the wall that housed seasonal exhibits of now vintage Barbies dressed in outfits representing the four seasons. Our local Sears store displayed a doll in a hula outfit along with one of its washing machines; I don't know why. Leath Furniture, with its glittery sidewalks, displayed a doll and large plush poodle in its window. Several travel agencies displayed dolls from around the world in their windows, and near one law office, another storefront window displayed a 1960s' walking doll and two smaller dolls dressed as Halloween witches and ghosts, only they were there all year long. Bishops Buffet had a mechanical Mrs. Claus doll that wore different outfits for the season. The old Canal House Restaurant in Sterling, IL, had a 1960s' companion doll it displayed in vignette settings. The doll had a graduation gown and school desk, a Christmas tree, holiday outfits, a pumpkin, etc.

All over California, I saw dolls on display in restaurants and stores. An antique store in San Juan Bautista featured a very small doll museum that included a miniature Eden bébé and the Col. Harlan Sanders doll from KFC.

An old hotel in Galena had a large display case filled with antique dolls.

Our local Village Inn Restaurant decorates for each season with dolls and other items, including a Teacher Barbie and Santa dolls. One of our Thai restaurants has a whole collection of Siamese costume dolls, while our Japanese restaurants feature Geisha and Samurai dolls. Sometimes, there are hand carved dolls created from Japanese radish, including a Sumo wrestler and a Samurai.

A music store has a Barbie-size miniature band complete with detailed instruments.

There are large voodoo dolls made of burlap in Abernathy's in our downtown, and one dress shop displayed Walda porcelain dolls and Dutch celluloid dolls on their walls. Speaking of Dutch dolls, the seed stores used to have amazing displays of dolls from Holland, and the Belgian Consulate used to show a collection of dolls from Belgium in their window. Agencies for Latino citizens displayed Mexican dolls and Native American dolls. Countless private homes display dolls in their windows, and figural lawn ornaments in their yards.

In short, more of us are out there collecting dolls than we care to admit. Everyone has some kind of doll or stuffed animal, just ask the owners of the dolls above, or the drivers who travel in cars with Garfields on their window or stuffed animals or Beanies riding on their dashboards. I have seen dolls and stuffed animals on display with cars and planes at auto shows and air shows. Vendors sell teddy bears, action figures, small dolls, and miniatures at these events, but also at country fairs, street festivals, comicons, book fairs, teaching conventions, cultural fairs, art shows and quilt shows. I've found them for sale in army surplus stores, pawn shops, even gun shows and tool shows.

Interest in dolls and their various relatives is currently going strong. Perhaps, it's because dolls are portraits of those who made them. The Japanese and other cultures believe that dolls contain a piece of their makers' souls. For this reason, doll makers in Japan can hold Living Treasure Status, and there are temples devoted to dolls, where worn out dolls are taken to be cremated with great honor and ceremony. Japan has at least two major holidays where dolls play a crucial role, the March 3rd Hinamatsuri Girls Day Festival and the May 5th Boys Day festival. I first learned about these festivals by reading Rumer Godden's novels for children *Miss Happiness and Miss Flower* and *Little Plum*. Later, I read the 1956 *World Book Encyclopedia*, Volume D, which told even more about the Japanese doll holidays, as well as other cultural holidays involving dolls. It's still one of my favorite sources on the subject.

Anne Rice once wrote that when you loved dolls, you loved all kinds of people, too. *(Taltos)* I think she's right. After all, dolls are portraits of the people who made them, sometimes literally. They also express something of the artist's culture and taste. I've often thought there are at least as many dolls in the world as there are people, more, when you consider that dolls are duplicated and mass produced. This last point is driven home when we watch films like *The Toy Story Series* and *Small Soldiers*. In *Toy Story*, Buzz Lightyear sees himself replicated in huge numbers, and has trouble finding himself. His friends also have trouble telling him apart from the copies.

Chapter 1: It's a Small, Dolly World (After All!)

In a world filled with strife, political upheaval, and terrorism, we might all do better to start collecting dolls, especially dolls that sing. Even Khrushchev wanted to see Disneyland, and before he left the US, bought Vogue's Baby Dear dolls to take home to his grandchildren in the old USSR. This shopping trip took place after he banged his shoe on the table at the UN and threatened to bury the US without firing a shot. Maybe the UN gift shop was closed and he got upset?

Samuel Pryor, who as Pan Am Airlines VEEP traveled the world to buy dolls, always displayed his dolls mixed together, not segregated by country. Dolls standing in perfect harmony and rubbing elbows with different dolls, even "enemy" dolls, might inspire real humans to do the same things. I guess the same concept lies behind the Olympic Games, where recently, the two Koreas competed together, and Iran and Iraq marched together without incident. The Ancient Greeks even stopped wars to hold the games. Dolls have found their way to the Nazi Concentration camps, to the ruins of Chernobyl, to royal palaces, graveyards, plane crashes, shipwrecks, and even the rubble of 9/11.

Collections of international dolls were popular during the 1930s through '60s, especially for young girls. Walt Disney, through the 1964 World's Fair, capitalized on their popularity, and on the need for word peace and unity when he created the attraction that later became Disneyland's "It's a Small World."

The summer I turned seven, my parents and I took our first road trip to California to see my mother's family, but also to visit Disneyland. It was the first of several trips we would take over 20 years to both Disneyland and to Disneyworld. Of course, I was always on the lookout for dolls, and came away with quite a haul that Summer of Love. (By the way, I can say that I stood on the corner of Haight/Ashbury in San Francisco that first trip. My dad was particularly intrigued with the Hippies selling their wares and underground newspapers. My father was career military, in NATO, as an officer in the then Royal Hellenic Airforce, with the U.S. Airforce at Scott Air Base. Long hair was political heresy to him; he always wore a crew cut, no matter what. He had nothing but contempt for Hippies and war protesters, so imagine our surprise when we came out of a gift shop (holding dolls) and found my dad reading an underground newspaper he'd bought from, well, a Hippie. When asked to explain, Dad said, "He called me 'Sir' and asked me politely if I would like to buy a paper." Hmmph.

At any rate, I digress. After the whirlwind tour of Asian dolls in Chinatown, old Mexican folk dolls from San Juan Bautista, Native American Dolls from Nebraska to Colorado, and vintage baby dolls from the San Jose Flea Market, I landed in Disneyland. Disneyland, with its licensed characters, stuffed animals, animatronics, toy stores, antique stores, gift shops, and more, was an entire community of dolls and toys. Even the topiary trees were clipped into doll, character and animal shapes. The ice cream bars were shaped like Mickey Mouse's head; I found out later they were designed by the son of one of my mother's colleagues, the late Marilyn Kuhn. Her son also designed the Captain Crunch cereal character.

Everything about Disneyland fascinated me. If Gettysburg Fantasyland with its miniatures, antique dolls, and giant, talking Mother Goose inspired me, Disneyland completely overwhelmed me. It was my spiritual home in some ways. The animatronics were pure magic to me; I was even fooled by the Lincoln animatronic in the attraction "Great Moments with Mr. Lincoln." In the twilight of Victorian era exhibition hall that reminds one suspiciously of Ford's Theater, Mr. Lincoln nodded, breathed, made eye-contact, and gestured. I was sure it was an actor, maybe Hal Holbrook, playing the part. After all, we saw Ray Stevens and Phyllis Diller perform in Tomorrow Land, so why not? I was flabbergasted that he wasn't real, or that the animals in the Indian Village and the burning cabin in Frontier Land weren't real, either.

After Mr. Lincoln, we walked to the "It's a Small World Ride." The façade looked like a tinker toy village, all white and gold. Later, I found out that the gold decorating the structure was real gold leaf; evidently, it's cheaper to use real gold leaf than gold paint. Constantly having to repaint the façade with the paint is more labor intensive and expensive than covering parts of it with real gold. Plus, should anyone decide to murder one of the dolls by covering them in gold paint a la *Goldfinger*, the theme park itself would face legal liability. Gold is better. Who says "nothing gold can stay?"

In an interesting twist, Dr. Manfred Bachmann in his amazing book, *Dolls the Wide World Over* also discusses the Mr. Lincoln Attraction and Small World Ride.

The ride in Disneyland was brand new when we visited for the first time in 1967. It had enjoyed its debut at the World's Fair in 1964, at the UNICEF, (The United Nations Children's Fund), pavilion. Pepsi sponsored the ride.

Actress Joan Crawford played a role in convincing Walt Disney to create the ride for Pepsi. Crawford was the widow of Pepsi president, Alfred Steele. She thought the Pepsi Board of Directors was dragging its feet in deciding what kind of attraction to provide for The World's Fair. Also, Walt Disney was already designing exhibits for The State of Illinois, Kodak, Ford and General Electric. These other attractions were "The Carousel of Progress," "Great Moments with Mr. Lincoln," and "Circlevision." A company called WED enterprises had a mere eleven months to build the pavilion of international children that later became the Disney ride. Initially called "The Children of the World," "It's a Small World" was fabricated by WED at Disney Studios, and began life as a large mobile designed by WED's Rolly Crump. Crump designed the toys, props, and other figures later displayed with Small World in Disneyland.

Apparently, international dolls were a theme because of the UNICEF connection. Dolls were once a big deal there; my mother wrote to The United Nations Gift Shop enquiring about dolls on my behalf. She ordered a Chinese cloth doll created in Taiwan by artist Michael Lee. UNICEF products, including cards gifts were sold in traveling UNICEF stores, sold along with folk art paintings of children singing and holding hands wearing their national costumes, and more. Combine that with Trick-or-Treat for UNICEF, which combined Halloween, my favorite holiday, with foreign dolls, and I was hooked.

Possibly, because he loved animatronics or automatons and dolls, Samuel Pryor, former Vice President of Pan Am, and internationally known doll collector of more than 8000 dolls, founder of The International Doll Library Foundation, was in the process of negotiating an elaborate display of 2000 of his dolls for The Grand Pavilion of the 1965 World's Fair. Alas, negotiations fell through, and the dolls were not displayed, possibly because Pryor wanted only his doll showcased and no other displays in the Pavilion. Many years later, after Pryor's death, the dolls were auctioned. Among them was a large part of the collection of the late Janet Pagter Johl, whose husband Col. Max Johl, was a legend in stamp collecting. Johl wrote a series of books on doll collecting in the late '40s and early '50s that covered the entire history of dolls, collecting, and related objects, up to that time. She was the first president of The United Federation of Doll Clubs, the UFDC, and a reporter for *The Christian Science Monitor*. Her daughter, Jan Johl Weismann, told me that she was able to see her late mother's collection at Pryor's International Doll Library and was impressed with the display. Some of Pryor's dolls are pictured in *The Collector's Encyclopedia of* Dolls, Volume II, by Dorothy, Elizabeth Ann, and Evelyn Jane Coleman.

Back to It's a Small World, we rode little boats designed by Arrow Development into the ride; these and the platform surrounding the wooden palace have recently been renovated. Appropriately, safety instructions were broadcast in several languages as people entered and later exited the boats. Even now, though, clockwork dolls and characters exit the clock tower when the hour strikes and parade outside the palace and back into it when the hour strikes. These clock figures were inspired by the medieval clock figures of Europe and by antique automatons. During the Small World Ride, we sailed into room after room of dancing international dolls, each singing the song by Richard and Robert Sherman, "It's a Small World After All!" All in all, there were between 240 and 300 dolls on display, many with matching pets. They sang the theme song in their native languages and performed native dances to its music. The rooms were set up by hemisphere, then country. There was even a whimsical area with an underwater world representing the lost continent of Atlantis, where the dolls included mermaids, and where they sang as if they were under water.

The ride's layout and organization has influence in sphere we might never conceive. Law Professor Michael J. Higdon has written *It's A Small World: Using the Classic Disney Ride to teach Document Coherence* for WESLTAW's *Teaching Legal Research and Writing.* For the record; after my students and I read Professor Higdon's article, I used it, too, in my Legal Writing and Research Course.

The song itself is frequently called an earworm, yet not everyone agrees. Still, I shudder to think what Mark Twain would have done with it had he been able to tour "It's a Small World." We sang the theme song during the annual Christmas concert that year in the second grade; to us, it was more precious than The National Anthem. I still smile when I hear it, and one of the Disney-made musical replicas of the Small World Dolls that I own, plays it. Richard and Robert Sherman, who wrote the song and its lyrics, had worked with Disney for some time. They talked Walt Disney out of his initial idea to have the dolls sing different songs in their own languages; they warned Disney that the cacophony would drive away tourists. Disney was amenable to their ideas and asked for a song that could be easily translated into different languages. I always thought dolls were the perfect choice to sing the song; besides the long history behind mechanical dolls, automatons and robots, there isn't one country in the world or one civilization that doesn't have dolls. The inspiration behind the song's message of peace and brotherhood was the recent Cuban Missile Crises of 1962. "It's a Small World" could well be the most played song on earth; since 2014, it has been played around 50 million times worldwide just on the various Small World Disney rides. According to *Time's*

Caitlin Schneider, it beat "radio and TV estimates for *You've Lost That Lovin' Feelin'* and *Yesterday*, which were believed to have been played at least eight and seven million times respectively." (Wikipedia) It was also part of an album of songs from around the world; the St. Charles Boys Choir recorded the album as The Disneyland Boys Choir. I have my own 45 rpm record, still.

The dolls themselves were well-constructed and detailed. Each doll stood about three feet high. Marc and Alice Davis brought to life the dolls and their costumes. Blair Gibson worked with Disney to create their smiling faces. The color and style for the ride were the concepts of Mary Blair, who died in 1973. Blair worked on *Cinderella, Peter Pan* and *Alice in Wonderland*. She created a self-portrait as a small, older woman wearing glasses and riding a balloon. One thinks of Shakespeare playing bit parts in many of his own plays, and Barbara Pym inserting herself as minor character or inserting one of her books in the settings of her novels.

The Anaheim Disneyland Small World Attraction was the first; following it some years later was the Disneyworld Small World. Today, there are Small World Rides in Hong Kong Disneyland, Japan Disneyland, and French Disneyland. Each is a little different, and reflects the character and traditions of the host nation. In 1997 or so, the original ride in Anaheim and Orlando was made over so that now, Disney characters including *Ariel, The Little Mermaid* and *Alice in Wonderland* have been added.

As stated earlier, dolls and figurines have been made from the beginning, as have Christmas ornaments and other merchandise that reflect the small world dolls. Besides the musical porcelain doll I bought in Disney World in 1987 representing a French CanCan girl, I bought an eight-inch vinyl doll with the Small World, Mary Blair face dressed as an Irish girl. A music box my mother bought in the late '80s features the Egyptian doll on top of the music mechanism. Sears and other stores featured doll ornaments for Christmas 1968, made of plastic, wire and felt. They were in two sizes, three inches and seven inches, and they too, have the Mary Blair smiling face and wide eyes. Plush bean bag dolls were for sale at the Disney Store during the Beanie Baby craze.

International costume dolls were offered for sale at Disneyland in the Tinker Bell Toy Store. The selection in 1967 was staggering, and included dolls by English artist Peggy Nisbet and Sweden's renowned doll maker, Charlotte Weibull.

Mimi, a singing doll by Remco, in the early 1970s, is also a nod to "It's a Small World." Mimi was a tall, thin, blonde Barbie type doll, though she was bigger than Barbie. She sang "I'd Like to Teach the World to Sing In perfect Harmony" in different languages. This was Coca Cola's international jingle, sung on TV commercials by young people wearing various international costumes. Mimi came with different records that could be inserted into her body where a tiny record player would play them. She wore a purple beret, and a red and purple suit, but there were a few other outfits available for her, too. These were outfits representing Spain, Italy, Great Britain, Germany, France, and Israel. Here is a description of her from Dollreference.com: "1973 Remco Mimi doll, 19" tall, vinyl and hard plastic jointed body, long blonde rooted hair, painted blue eyes, battery operated, record player in body, sings the song, 'I'd Like to Teach the World to Sing' in several languages."

It seems even with dolls, their history, and Disneyland; we can't get away from the Cola Wars. Remember that Pepsi sponsored It's a Small World at the World's Fair, while Mimi sang the Coke song.

The little boat motif is used on other rides in Disney World and Disneyland. I'd love to take a world tour of Disney parks just to compare notes on how animatronics are used on the rides. In the late '80s, little boats were part of the Pirates of the Caribbean ride. We rode behind a particularly amorous teenaged couple. My dad splashed them with water every time the ride hit a dark spot.

Chapter 2: The Incident

It was September 1965, in Younkers Department Store, in Duck Creek Plaza. I was five. In those days, before Toys R Us, King Norman Toys, and now, Walmart, all the classy department stores had big displays of toys and dolls, especially after Labor Day. The toys arrived before the Christmas decorations in those days, and it was exciting to see what Santa might bring. I stood in front of a baby doll in a blue and white box. The box said she was a Vogue Doll, a very old company founded in part Ginny Graves, niece of the founder of Fuller Brush. Graves was from Medford, MA, the same town as Elizabeth Short, the Black Dahlia murder victim. Short bought *Gone with the Wind* paper dolls for a child named Mary Pacios, who later authored a book on Short called *Childhood Shadows*. Short was tortured and killed, and her bisected body dumped in an onion field along Norton Avenue in LA. She was only 22, and in a gruesome bit of irony, she was sometimes called The Broken Doll by those who wrote of her. To this day, her murder remains unsolved, but a Kewpie doll was found among her belongings after her death. Her body was discovered on January 15th, my mother's birthday.

The sweet little baby doll, with the pink and white organdy outfit and eyelet bonnet, was far removed from the grim corpse of a once lovely young girl. Called Baby Dear, she was originally designed by artist Eloise Wilkin, who illustrated Little Golden Books like *So Big*.

At five, I fell in love with Baby Dear, and began sobbing at how beautiful she was. I knew I couldn't have her, and that made it even worse. Usually, I was not a child to beg or cry for toys. I really didn't know what came over me. Somehow, my mom, dad, and I made it home. I went to bed, and cried myself to sleep.

The next morning, I woke up, and it must have been a Saturday; we didn't have the usual mad rush of trying to get ready, drink down our chocolate milk, get to the sitter, etc. Both my parents worked; mornings were hectic and stressful most of the time. Weekends were different, far more relaxed. My mom might scramble eggs, or make cinnamon rolls a la Poppin Fresh (who was also a doll). My mom called me in, and there, in her box was Baby Dear! I called her "Candy." It's still her name. She still sits on my bed. She's had many outfits, and my mom had to perform "surgery" to add stuffing once her body became limp. She has a crayon heart drawn on her chest; I decided Raggedy Ann was not the only doll worthy of a heart.

Candy has been to California and several other states, as well as Canada and Mexico. She was too frail to go to Europe in 1969; a Madame Alexander Pussycat baby went in her stead. Candy is my favorite doll, and will travel with me on my ultimate journey. She was an addition to what was already a growing collection, and she has many sisters, all variations on the Baby Dear doll, including some made by other companies. If dolls are considered an obsession, then Candy is a magnificent one.

Chapter 3: Ancient Dolls

No one could possibly know who made the first doll. As many have speculated before me, perhaps someone was walking along and found a root, a stick, a rock or piece of bone that looked like a human figure or face. From then on, human imagination took over, and primitive artists began to enhance the shapes they found into the first dolls, the Venus of Willendorf figures also called The Goddess Figures.

For a long time, it was believed that the stone age Venuses were only 40,000 years old or so. Now, crude goddess figures are being discovered that may have belonged to people that predated Neanderthal culture going back over 800,000 years. These are the Acheulean cultures, and the oldest site discovered is in Ethiopia, with another site from Tanzania, dating 1.7 million years. The oldest formed human tools come from this culture, which marked a change from simple hunter-gatherer behavior to a more complex human culture involving tools and the skills to use them.

There are modern artists who still make dolls and figurines this way; they pick up a found object and "read" its personality before enhancing it into a doll. And, dolls have been made from mandrake root for centuries because it resembles the human body. I have even seen ginseng root dolls created from natural roots in San Francisco. By the same token, the Loess dolls or Losskindel dolls are made of loam found in Loess, and the loam often appears to assume human form. In Max von Boehn's time, the 1920s, the Strasbourg museum had examples of these (25). As von Boehn has noted when commenting on the views of one Ernst Vatter and others, "If the genesis of the doll is sought for, it will be found…in a quality, which is shared alike by primitive races and by children – namely, the ability to discern human and animal forms in all sorts of freaks of nature" (24). In other words, primitive people and children saw human and animal figures in rocks, horns, bones, branches, and roots. Who among us has not looked at the clouds and seen shapes and figures of all kinds? Some even see figures in clouds, vegetables, potato chips, and toast. I suppose the Rorschach inkblot test might work on the same principle, but so does abstract art of all kinds. If anything, some experts argue that the shape of certain "figure stones" suggested the subject because of their very shape to Neolithic sculptures.

Whoever that first Neolithic artists was, however, s/he started something that will never die, and doll making was born. In a tradition, that is similar to many other religions including the Old Testament, the first dolls had no faces. They represented Mother Earth, and even then, it was taboo, apparently, to practice idolatry or to look upon the face of God, whoever God might be. There is one very rare example, the Venus of Brassempouy, with a scratched-on face; Jean Auel writes about it in her Clan of the Cave Bear books *(The Earth's Children Series)*. The little Venus figures come from the Ice Age. They date to the Quaternary period, with a civilization called Aurignacian. These people lived in the first half of the fourth Ice Age. These limestone Venuses continued to be made through the Solutarian through Magdalenian period, or about 30,000 to 50,000 years ago. New archaeological studies of these dolls indicate they may have been intended as children's toys from the very beginning, though what their research is for these conclusions is hard to tell.

The Venus of Willendorf hails from the Willendorf culture, near Krems, on the Danube River. She is only 11cm high. Max von Boehn postulates that the little figure was originally painted red. He believes other figures might have been painted as well. They are obese, and appear to celebrate fertility. Many believe that the figures were obese for other reasons, too. These scholars believe men preferred heavier woman, because many other statues similar to the Venus figures have appeared that also represent rotund women (29). Von Boehn presents figures from the late Neolithic periods that are tattooed, and these are from Rumania.

Another example is much later than the other prehistoric figures. One object, a pottery doll face from the Late Woodland Period, 600 A.D. has a rough profile of a human face, with wide eyes and a protruding nose. The face was found near Lake Huron, in Northeast Michigan. It may be a toy, because it was found with the remnants of at least ten pots that were probably toys. Of course, the pots associated with children could have been educational or ritual items, and other small pots found could have contained cosmetics or medicine. Or, they could have been toys. It will be hard for us to know.

The little face was buried with a crude stone drill and a pottery shard, and perhaps that drill, or one like it, made the doll's face. I can imagine the excitement the doll face created. I was nearly as thrilled myself when a dear friend sent me a tiny, Neolithic axe that she found on her property. On closer inspection, what appears to be a crude piece of rock or dirt is really an intricate object or tool used by someone before the dawn of time to go about his or her daily business.

More idols of the type von Boehn discusses appeared in the late Stone Age, for about 200 years. These were found in Europe, from Southern Russia, to Spain, through Moravia and Silesia. Others appeared in Serbia, Bosnia, and Bulgaria (Note that maps in the 1990s have reverted back to the configurations and countries von Boehn discussed in the 1920s and earlier). These figures have faces, though their faces are very crude. Their noses do indeed resemble the beaks of birds, and they are nearly always female. They are clay, and naked. Their arms are also stumps, as in the earlier Willendorf figures. Marble figures resembling "bird women" have been found in the ruins of Troy (von Boehn 19–23).

Greek dolls have been influenced by many cultures, mixing with, and creating doll simultaneously with, Greek artists.

Mary Hillier in *Dolls and Doll Makers* showed seated dolls with realistic faces and hair styles that resembled those on classic marble statues. These were missing arms, but obviously had jointed arms at one time. She called these theater figures, and it is unclear if they are toys or not. Ancient writer Xenophon allegedly discusses puppets in his works, and Plato's famous "Allegory of the Cave" from "The Republic" alludes to shadow puppets or figures on the wall.

Reproduction Kore tomb figures in my collection, one made in Greece, depict young girls before marriage, and are often 2 or 3 feet high.

Gorgeous ivory dolls wearing remnants of gold jewelry, and often found in little girls' tombs with scraps of cloth, were luxury figures, but many terracotta jointed dolls exist in the Benaki Museum and other European museums as proof that children's games of all types existed. When I was nine, I saw some of them myself at the National Archaeological Museum in Athens, and I actually cried from the emotional impact.

Maria Argyriades writes of dolls created during Byzantium, 330–1453 A.D. Bone dolls with etched figures, and large luminous eyes were popular. She quotes St. John Chrysostom, Archbishop of Constantinople and author of one of The Divine Liturgies of The Greek Orthodox Church, on the similarity between Christian dolls contemporary to him and ancient dolls. Doll makers still worked in clay, cloth, bone, ivory, and wood, just as they had 1000 years before. Dolls were still sold from workshops.

At the Monastiraki, I bought a black silk Greek doll head, and other souvenir dolls. We also saw antique German doll heads for sale. Argyriades pictures many papier mâché, wax, and bisque dolls, as well as Dresden German Christmas ornaments, wax angels, and other European toys popular in Greece during the late 19th and 20th centuries. She writes of these so-called "Type V" dolls as heads that come to a point, and date from the first to twelfth centuries.

They were inserted into cloth-stuffed bodies, and some had wigs. They remind me of half dolls of the early 20th century.

According to Argyriades, from 6th century on, writings talk about little girls' dolls and their importance. Pollucis Onomasticon mentions dolls in his work, (Lib. IX. 127). During this time, dolls were found in children's tombs, and Argyriades writes these are almost certainly toys. Pagan worshippers still had their idols at this time, and dolls were even found in the graves of Christian adults as symbols of adults entering the kingdom of Heaven as little children (Matthew XVIII, 3–4). Apparently, she writes there was a common Byzantine phrase cited by Phaidon Koukoules, "We're not playing with dolls." An interesting note is that the Empress Theodora treated her Holy Icons as dolls. I find this interesting; icons are meant to take the place of religious statues in the early church, yet at the same time, other citizens would have had idols and ritual figures as part of their worship. People do revere and address their icons as three-dimensional figures, and portraits and images like them are indeed cousins to the two dimensional and three-dimensional images we call dolls.

Chapter 4: Religious Dolls/Ritual Figures

These include Christmas figures, but could include Thanksgiving statues and dolls of Pilgrims and Puritans, Santos, African figures and dolls, Asian Ancestor Figures and Deities, Voodoo Dolls, Milagros, plaster saints, Crèche and Nativity figures, car dashboard figures, Biblical Action Figure Dolls, the Elsie Dinsmore Series, some Fetishes, even Kachinas and Inuit Figures or examples of Tlingit figural art.

Egypt has a long history with ancient religious dolls and figures, though not so much with modern dolls. Only recently have I been able to find any modern costume dolls, and some were Nubian women brought to me from a good friend's trip. Some trivia; on the other side of the Sphinx and the Great Pyramid lies a modern avenue, complete with fast food restaurants, including McDonald's. Two icons that span millennia are now neighbors. With the exception of one rare 1930s doll from Egypt that I found in an antique shop, it is hard to find dolls, though Ushabti are being reproduced, as well as jewelry and bone statues of Nefertiti, Tut, and others.

In the late '80s, I was able to find a pair of wooden dolls from Egypt at Disney's Epcot Center. I first came in contact with an ancient Coptic bone doll when I was seven, at the Rosicrucian Museum in San Jose. It was really a doll torso, but had a sweet face. I also saw the grave figures, or Ushabti, and wooden models with moving arms and legs.

There were Egyptian miniature rooms at our local museum, and a collection of small grave figures, too. I saw those when I was six, and began to read about paddle dolls and other figures when I was only nine, in Helen Young's classic, *The Complete Book of Doll Collecting*, and Mary Hillier's, *Dolls and Doll Makers*. These books made my 8th and 9th Christmases very special. I saw ancient Greek dolls in the museums in Athens and Delphi when I was nine, and I cried; they were very touching and even lifelike. I wanted them right away! Later, I reproduced them myself and looked for artist's renditions.

There are figures dating from Egypt that predate the 1st Kingdom and are well over 5000 years old. Many are made of faience, a type of clay composite, still available at craft stores today. I bought some when I was in school and made my own Ushabti pins from the powdery mixture blended with water to create clay. Others are made of painted wood that look as though they stepped from hieroglyphics. They have jointed arms, hold weapons, populate small rooms, and captain small boats, but these are tomb figures and not toys. Other figures are made of gold and precious jewels. Dolls in the ancient world literally saved the lives of people; witness the Terra Cotta soldiers of China. In fact, it was a Chinese emperor credited with the idea of using statues or small dolls to replace human beings in tombs. The population was dwindling from disease and too much human sacrifice; the little figures that would come to live in the afterworld were the solution. Also credited with the ideas is the ancient Japanese prince, Shotoku, known for his constitution.

My book, *A Bibliography of Doll and Toy Sources*, also has many sources for finding ancient dolls. Ushabti, once scarce in private collections, are now auctioned on a regular basis and appear on Internet sites and catalogs like Sadigh Gallery. Be advised, there are laws regarding the sale of antiquities and observe them before buying. One is the 1970 UNESCO Treaty. There are many good reproductions of these figures for those who want to add them to their collections. As long as they are clearly labeled reproductions, one can avoid ethical dilemmas and collect safely, and above all, legally. Other authors who discuss ancient religious dolls are Max von Boehn, Leslie Gordon, Janet Pagter Johl, Gwen White, and Carl Fox.

From the idols of Ancient Egypt, we move to Crèche Dolls, Nativities, Santos and Angels. My first memories of these dolls are of the vintage '40s and '50s nativities at my grandma's every Christmas. I fell in love with the miniatures then, and with their tiny stables strewn with miniature pieces of hay. One even played music, and it fascinated me. My first encounters with religious images were with the pictures my Uncle Jim showed me in my children's book of Bible stories, and of the icons we had at home and in church. Today, there are cloth models and even Playmobil stables and Holy Families to teach children these stories. When I was about five, and my grandparents and aunts and uncles moved, my mother took me to Woolworth's, and my collection of Nativities and religious dolls was born. These were made in Italy and Japan. Other names, incidentally for Nativities were, Crèche, Crib, Pecipio, Putz, etc. There were bins and bins of tiny plaster figures at the dime store, from one inch to six inches high, of The Holy Family, angels, shepherds, The Magi, lambs, donkeys, cows, and all sorts of animals.

Each year, we added to the set. I also had figures from my grandma's nativity, and later, my babysitter gave me her first set, bought at Woolworth's, in the early years of her marriage. I also got my first Holt Howard China Headed angels from her, really my first china head doll. I learned of the Neapolitan Crèches and Spanish Precipios from my friend Mary Hillier and her landmark book, *Dolls and Doll makers*, when I was nine. She also had pictures of antique figures made of cake and gingerbread, somehow preserved, of Ruprecht carrying off a naughty child. St. Francis of Assisi is credited with creating the first crèche. This was in the 13th century, but religious figures exist from Coptic Egypt, and paintings and sketches are even earlier. In the Catholic countries, from the time of St. Francis on, there were competitions among those who could afford them, to set up the most elaborate nativity. These were articulated dolls of gesso covered wood, carved ivory, plaster, precious metals, you name it. Some of the female dolls were built over cages like the fashion dolls of the 13th-19th centuries made of wood and gesso. These are popular today. The child's book, *Maria* and *The Museum of Mary Child,* talk of hand-carved religious figures like this, often mistaken as dolls. Rumer Godden's *The Kitchen Madonna* talks of another type of figure. An artist of these is featured in the excellent film *The Extraordinary World of Doll Collecting*, and in July Taymor's *Titus* (based on *Titus Andronicus* by Shakespeare).

Before Christianity, there were the Goddess figures, and the images that appear in early Judaism and Islam. Many of these appear in illuminations and mosaics. There are many representations of Buddha and Asian deities, the ancient world's Greco-Roman figures and statues, and of course, the Ancient Egyptian representation of the gods, often Ushabti. There are angel museums in Beloit, WI, and many avid angel and Christmas collectors and clubs all over the world. The Metropolitan Museum's Renaissance and 18th century angels, featured on magnificent trees also have many fans. Kwanza angels and African dolls associated with the harvest also appear, and there is a Diwali Barbie celebrating Festivals of the World.

I have more angels, Christmas dolls, and figures than I can count and I love them all. I have about 100 nativities from all over the world, some miniscule, others jewelry, some dolls with clothing, and of course, my Woolworth's figures that started it all. My doll houses all feature very tiny nativities, and I have a wax devotional doll, once in the Mary Merritt Museum. I was lucky enough to buy a bone and wooden figure at a recent Theriault's auction, and I have some 18th century wax and wooden figures. I am very fond of these Santos, and they join my elves, ornaments, blown glass, wax German angels, snowmen nutcrackers, and Christmas Peanuts figures proudly to honor the season in displays of dolls.

The Beloit, WI Angel Museum has thousands of angels, including a collection donated by Oprah Winfrey. They caretakers told me when I visited that they had other collections donated to them, but they didn't keep all the angels. They were also understaffed, so we couldn't go to the gift shop or little café. I was able to donate a copy of my book to them, and also bought one of their cookbooks. I hate these cases of Doll Interruptus. One reason I think personally so many doll museums are closing is that the professional idea of customer service doesn't exist to their owners. I remember traveling to Independence, MO to see Kimport Dolls. They were closed. Not long after, they were also out of business, though their granddaughter has resurrected the original quilt pattern business online. I was able to meet her about seven years ago, and we talked about what could be done with dolls salvaged from her grandparents' estate sale. I never heard from her, though, and I don't know what happened to the dolls.

Corn Dollies are ritual dolls with religious connotations. Many are circular in form. Even when I was very little, I was fascinated with circles. My hot pink hula hoop was the object of my affection at age seven. In school, I found studying spheres and circles intriguing, even in Geometry. My teacher was a stern woman, a former nun who struck the fear of God in our hearts, even in public school. She looked and dressed EXACTLY like The Church Lady from SNL. She once got into a "proof" war with my dad; via me as messenger, they went back and forth on how to solve a proof correctly. Ultimately, Dad won. Miss W, whose mother made dolls, had the grace not to flunk me. She was a lovely lady, just very stern in class. Yet, those circles attracted me, all the same.

Perhaps my fascination stemmed from the fact that circles are a symbol for the universal feminine. Triangles are, too, but circles represent the circle of life, associated with women and fertility.

Chapter 5: The Middle Ages, Renaissance, Baroque, 17th Century, 18th, and Early 19th Centuries

Images and portraits were important during the 1000 years or so historians designate as the middle ages. While much was written and created during this period, much was also lost. We depend on the art left, and on the writings of those who chronicled the period. In particular, we rely on Geoffrey Chaucer's *The Canterbury Tale* for an accurate description of the age. As Francis Beaumont said of Chaucer, "One gift he hath above all other authors, and that is by the excellence of his descriptions to possess his readers with a stronger imagination of seeing that done before their eyes, which they read, than any other that ever writ in any tongue." (Quoted in Loomis, "Introduction")

Games were plentiful, and some of the games children played are shown in the paintings of Lucas Cranach and others. These paintings portray children with toys and all kinds of dolls of their own. We learn about medieval pastimes by reading Chaucer, especially the descriptions of the pilgrims and their occupations. The tales assigned to them also let us know what they enjoy and loathe. For example, the Wife of Bath hates contemporary books that purport to explain women. The bawdiness of some of the tales indicates that love of play and recreation was alive and well, if a bit racy. A few dolls and toys have been found in plague pits, tossed in with their hapless owners, and one is described in the novel *Missing Melinda*, by Jaqueline Jackson. Manfred Bachmann shows medieval Leonard's Louts, soldiers on horseback of pewter and other materials, and discusses soldiers and effigies made for funerals and in remembrance which date from the medieval period.

French and German dolls which survive from the 13th, 14th and 15th centuries are mostly made of white pipe-clay, formed in molds. Some have a depression in the chest, which may have been meant to hold a coin and thus indicates that the doll was a gift, perhaps a christening present. Figures of people on horseback are common, whether knights or ladies, reflecting the pastimes of the wealthy of the period.

The Renaissance

Little girls are always appearing with dolls in Renaissance art. The sad, doomed Arabella Stuart holds an elaborately dressed doll in one portrait. A little Native American girl holds a doll dressed as a European aristocrat in a print said to date from Sir Walter Raleigh's ill-fated Roanoke Colony.

In her book, *Dolls,* Lady Antonia Fraser pictures a doll of the 16th century that belonged to Alicia Boleyn, a niece of Anne Boleyn. It isn't clear whose daughter Alicia was; Anne's brother, George Boleyn, Lord Rochford, was executed right before she was. His widow, Lady Jane Rochford, lost her head on the block with Anne's cousin and Henry's fifth wife, Katharine Howard. Could she have been a daughter of Mary Boleyn, that "other Boleyn girl."

A gesso-covered wooden doll also has a Tudor pedigree. It was once on display in the former Helen Moe Doll Museum, Paso Robles, CA. It allegedly belonged to Edward VI, the son of Henry VIII and Jane Seymour, his third wife.

A painted doll of clay with a molded hairdo caught in a net was found in a Rhenish house, circa 1530. One can't help but feel sorry for the child who lost her eons ago. If walls could talk, indeed. Early dolls like this seem to be more like figurines or mannequins. The *Hortus Sanitatus* features doll makers or puppet makers at work in a 15th century engraving.

That children played is undisputed; we have bits of their rhymes, game pieces, and descriptions even in Shakespeare's plays. We know that as a child, Joan of Arc danced around a maypole, and fashion dolls existed as emissaries of the latest styles. Anne of Brittany is said to have sent one as a gift.

Puppet shows and mechanical clocks had been around for some time, though these probably were not for children. Crèche dolls and Santos graced churches all over the world by this time, and were featured in religious ceremonies. Elaborate sculptures and figurines, including work in gold and silver by Cellini, and rumored automatons by Leonardo da Vinci, were the ancestors of many dolls and collectible items today.

The Baroque and 17ᵗʰ Century

The Bartholomew Fair was a huge event for decades in Europe, and elaborate dolls, ancestors of our carnival dolls, were famous. Some of these survive today. This is the era of The Old Pretender, Letitia Penn, and Lord and Lady Clapham, early dolls that survived and which were cherished as "collector's items" and as toys. It is the era of the Dutch and German baby houses or doll houses, and of toy villages like Mon Plaisir. These were the treasures of adult collectors, though at least one, Ann Sharp's Baby House, belonged to a child who catalogued her items of delight. For more, read Flora Gill Jacobs' books on doll houses. They are in my bibliography, *A Bibliography of Dolls and Toys.*

The 18ᵗʰ Century

During this time, dolls as fashion dolls and toys began to grown in number. There were some walking dolls, and many of the famous automatons were being made. In France, Pantin or jumping jacks were all the rage, and were supposedly so wildly popular that they were banned; less expectant mothers playing with them have abnormally shaped children!

So-called court dolls are attributed to this era; carved of wood, they represent 18ᵗʰ C. courtiers from the court of Louis XVI, but some stories claim they are really made in the early 20ᵗʰ c. They are anatomically correct, generally. Puppets were also very popular at this time, especially marionettes. Doll houses were being made, both for children and adults. Dolls are often called "poppets." Queen Anne, and actually, later Georgian dolls of wood are popular.

Wax dolls are being made, especially as religious and devotional figures, and some of these moves. There is an exquisite example in Mary Hillier's *Dolls and Doll Makers* of a wax mechanical. A little girl lies with eyes open on a flower covered bier. She has blonde hair, and a white silk dress. She is wax with inset eyes, and her lovely face and hands lift upward. When she is wound, she moves.

Toy soldiers are very popular, and soon, Maezel, inventor of the metronome, would devise the first Mamma dolls. There have been shops for toys in London since at least the 17ᵗʰ century, too. Baby dolls first make their appearance, and more and more dolls appear in art. George Washington left records of dolls and toys bought for his step-children.

Earlier, in the 17ᵗʰ century colonies, William Penn is said to have brought the doll Letitia Penn, a doll celebrity, as a gift for his daughter's friend. The story has since been questioned. 17ᵗʰ century cornhusk dolls or poppets played sinister roles in the 1692 Salem Witch trials, where dolls were more or less forbidden and seen as instruments of the devil.

I recently was able to reread Jacobs smaller classic *History of Doll Houses*, and was struck with the history incorporated in such a tiny volume. The book is about nine inches high, and is done in black and white. This is my second copy, but still retains the dust cover. Jacobs was curator of the Washington Doll House Museum for many years, till about the time she died at age 93, several years ago. She has written larger, color volumes about dolls and doll houses, and they are excellent histories as well. I missed out on one of these at a library sale; an older gentleman was buying it for 50 cents just as I walked in. Bad karma, that day.

According to Jacobs, miniature rooms, complete with furnishings and little dolls, have been found in Egyptian tombs. Tiny pieces of doll furniture and accessories have been traced to Greece and Rome, so she speculates there must have been tiny house at some point, too.

The fantastic Baby houses of Cabinets of the 17th century are legendary, and the tiny, hallmarked treasures of silver, copper, pewter, even gold, are works of arts in themselves with scores of collectors devoted to them. There are amazing books on miniature silver, alone. Some of these crossover as cabinets of curiosities, and I recommend *Cabinets of Curiosities*, reviewed on my Memoir and Pym/Bronte Blogs, as well. These cabinet houses are featured in the novel *The Miniaturist.*

Flora Gill Jacobs notes that the first doll house, of the type we might be familiar with, dates to about 1580, but of course, miniature soldiers and other tiny books and objects are older than that. She writes the best history of Ann Sharp's Baby House, c. 1691, of anything I've seen. This house was given by Queen Anne to her goddaughter, Ann Sharp. In 1967, when Jacobs wrote, the house was pretty much as little Ann left it, nearly 300 years before. The inhabitants wear name tags, and are precious Queen Anne wooden dolls, and dolls of wax. They are colorful and beautifully dressed, pink and pastels being popular colors per Jacobs' description. Little girls then must have loved the same color schemes as now.

There are nine rooms, with a top shelf that held gloves and shoes and other small objects belonging to Ann herself. There are tiny silver pieces and warming pans, a dog-turned spit in the kitchen, though dogs were missing, complete linens, wall paper, inlaid cradles, beds, you name it. It is a study of late 17th century life. The dollhouse is important as a time capsule, but also as proof that these elaborate objects were also toys. Then, as now, there are dollhouses meant to be played with, and others that were collector's items.

Here is a link to a blog called 18th century Notebook; maybe the best resource for 18th c. dolls I've seen: http://larsdatter.com/18c/dolls.html

Keep in mind that the Industrial Revolution brought changes to dolls and toys as well. My theory is that with the successful mass production of china and glass, in fact, all ceramics, and with the success of Josiah Wedgewood, china manufacturers were looking for new ways to use their raw product. Eventually, a billion china-headed dolls and more bisque and ceramic dolls and doll heads were born. Kestner and other German companies began in the late 18th century, and as cloth became commercially made, it was more feasible to make rag dolls and doll clothes, because the surplus of cheap cloth made the rag bag, and later, the flea markets we all love, so popular.

Early accounts of the Brontë children indicate that they had, as toys, wooden soldiers and dolls of wax. The famous stories the children wrote in miniature were based on the adventures of a group of wooden soldiers purchased for them as a gift. For allegedly impoverished children of the clergy, these were relatively luxurious toys. Paper dolls in Europe became the rage in the late 18th century and the vogue continued with sets like, "The History of Little Fanny" and "The History of Little Henry." Milliner's models with their elaborate coiffures and legends of being used as hat models or hat stands began to make their way into toy catalogs around 1820.

China figures began to be made in large quantities after the Industrial Revolution and many became dolls and doll heads in no time. Small china and bisque dolls became very popular with little girls.

There are many gesso-covered and ivory-Crèche figures and Santos from this time as well in Hispanic countries and colonies, and other countries in Europe and North and South America. Queen Victoria's doll collection of 132 dolls she and her governess dressed, are also legendary. These were tiny jointed wooden dolls with tuck combs in their lacquered hair. There is a great YouTube video about them.

Chapter 6: Puppets

Puppets have an ancient history, and much is made of them in literature, including *Don Quixote de la Mancha* and *Orlando Furioso*. Plato based his "Allegory of the Cave" from "The Republic" on Greek shadow puppets. Kariagioz has his roots in Turkey and Greece.

Indonesian shadow puppets and Thai puppets have their own plays and legends. Bunraku puppets from Japan had plays written for them, including the *Love Suicides of Anazaki.*

Punch and Judy have ancient roots and relatives in the Commedia dell Arte. Marionettes were used early on in morality plays to teach religion and the Nativity to a populace that often could not read or write, especially during the Middle Ages.

Often, when the puppeteer dies, so go the puppets. This was the case with Wayland Flowers, his potty-mouthed grand dame of a puppet, Madame. When Jim Henson died unexpectedly, a cartoon showed the Muppets hanging their heads around his empty chair. While Shari Lewis' daughter has become the voice of Lambchop, most of the other puppets are silenced, and the song that never ends has, indeed, ended. Lewis was an avid puppet and doll collector, immortalized by a beautiful Madame Alexander doll. Lambchop puppets, stuffed animals, pet toys, and dolls are still made. Lewis wrote a book for children on collecting called *The Thing Kids Collect.* It's a great book, and I recommend it as a means of interesting young people in antiques and collectibles.

With Captain Kangaroo gone, Mr. Moose and Bunny Rabbit are silenced. Who remembers Kukla, (whose name means "doll" in Greek and Russian), Fran and Ollie? Who remembers TV puppets Davey and Goliath, inventions of Art and Ruth Clokey? The Clokeys also created Gumby and Pokey, who are apparently immortal and exceptions to the rule. Their creators were the sister and brother-in-law of my beloved Milton and 19th c. Literature Prof, Dorothy Parkander.

My own intro to puppets involved a marionette troop that used to come to my grade school, and to the goatherds and goats in *The Sound of Music*, seen the afternoon after my first swimming lesson, where I nearly drowned. The puppets from the film are now in the MacNider museum in Mason City, IA, the home of Meredith Wilson who composed *The Music Man.* They were created by Bil Baird, a student of doll maker and puppeteer, Tony Sarg. Together, Sarg and Baird created the first Macy's Thanksgiving Day Parade balloons.

Chapter 7: Doll Clothes

Shopping for doll clothes can be fun, unnerving, and expensive. It isn't unusual to see doll dresses listed for over $1000 in doll stores and online. Paying hundreds of dollars for Huret or other fashion doll accessories is typical, and some Barbie outfits bring hundreds, even thousands, of dollars.

Some large dolls wear actual children's clothing. It is fun to search through rummage sales or vintage markets for clothes for dolls from the '40s to '70s. Some of my dolls even wear clothes I had when I was little. If need be, my mother would cut them down to fit the doll.

Baby dolls, especially life-sized ones, are fun to dress. If one sews, there are all kinds of vintage patterns for dolls made by McCall's, Vogue, and Simplicity. Individual outfits were sold in Woolworth's and other dimes stores and old big box stores like Zayre's, Turnstyle, and Topp's. Xavier Roberts dressed his original Little People in children's clothes he bought at yard sales and thrift shops. People who own Time Out kids by Faye Wine, Roberts' rival, do the same. In fact, yard sales, rummage sales, garage sales, consignment and thrift stores are terrific places to find clothes for dolls (and kids☺).

I enjoy shopping sales at high end department stores or the Marshall's/TJ MAXX chains for hats, socks, clothes, and shoes for babies and larger dolls. Reborn doll collector and artists do the same. Von Maur's and Dillard's have awesome sales on baby clothes, even the hard to find 0–3 months size.

One time, when I was about 17, I was in Kmart looking for booties for and old composition baby. I had on the peasant, smock type of blouse that was popular.

A woman walked up to me and began to ask me when the baby was due and gave some great advice on how to buy booties that don't wear out. My mother thought this was hilarious, but I was mortified.

Recently, I was in Von Maur's, buying baby outfits on sale for dolls I was dressing. The saleswoman finally asked me what I was going to do with them; curiosity got the better of her. She looked kind and nonjudgmental so I told her. As it turns out, a lot of people buy baby and toddler clothes there for dolls. We talked awhile, and she revealed that she had several tropical fish tanks. We had a fifty-gallon tank at my husband's office, On Guard Security, lest our kitties got tempted at home. They were, if you will, watch fish. Their names were Larry, Darryl, and Darryl, and the two shrimp, Mo and Shemp. I had fish through junior high school, and was passionate about them, and my goldfish and pet caterpillars and grasshoppers. I named my fish, e.g., Lady Strawberry and Lady Midnight, two female betas, Algy the Chinese algae eater who lived nearly three years, Sharkey the red tail shark, etc. We had snails, and plants, too. Our neighbor next door looked after them when we were on vacation and fed them. When the last little fishy swam away to fish heaven, we turned the aquariums into doll cases. Sometimes, I tearfully buried the fish myself under a pine tree in our back yard. I was over thirty when my Dad admitted that the rest were "buried at sea" via a good flush.

There were other things my parents didn't want to tell me that ended up being communicated with a doll. When I was seven, my mother miscarried a little girl. I had been lobbying for siblings for some time; I hated being an only child, and I longed for a sister. My mother had been knitting a light green baby layette, but she told me it was a birthday present for me and for the dolls. Later, I found out it was for the lost baby. We dressed an antique composition baby doll in the layette. I cried for days, but I cherish that doll. She is now a memorial to that little baby, but also to my parents, who have gone to be with her.

Antique christening gowns and baby gowns are perfect for antique bisque babies like JDK's Hilda, which are often very large. Little girls who love them can learn to knit, sew tat, and crochet to dress their dolls. I have a very large French bisque mannequin, artist made by Karen Rosenthaler that was once in The Festival of Trees a staple in my community for over 30 years. In fact, Cary Grant was here for the first, and later died, while I and many others were waiting go see his one man show. The lovely doll wears real Victorian clothes, but also my hat, blouse, and white fringed boots with beads in the acrylic heels that I brought from Spain. She and Tallulah, my department store mannequin, share some of my vintage outfits. My dad didn't know I had set up Tallulah when he went to check on something in my house. She scared him to death, which was hard to do. My dad was a military man, and as a child, survived the Fascists, Nazis, and Communists in Europe.

Vintage clothing, as Helen Young points out in *The Complete Book of Doll Making and Collecting,* is a great source of material and buttons for doll clothes. My grandmother and grandfather were married in Paris, February 12, 1927. He wrote to her, and she met him there, because he was a Greek expatriate and World War I veteran who could not return to Greece at that time. She traveled to meet him with the Mayor of Kalamata, their best friend. Tragically, the Communists hanged him during the Greek Civil War, just after

World War II. During that happy time in 1927, my grandfather bought my grandmother Marie an entire French trousseau. Her silk gown later melted, but my mom and I dressed dolls from the material, and made hankies, and Christmas ornaments, too. We saved every leftover scrap. My mom's gorgeous wedding gown was made for her, but it was rented. She saved remnants, and used these for dolls, too.

Chapter 8: The Miniature World

Small things spellbind us; as Alice said as she found herself small enough to fall into the rabbit's hole, "Curiouser and curiouser." Gulliver knew this; certainly Stuart Little and the Borrowers knew this, along with every author who has written novels about doll houses.

The more microscopic, the more amazing. Think of dressed Mexican fleas, once sold by Kimport, or carvings done on a human hair, that rest on the head of a pin. I think of E.O. Wilson's work with ants, how tiny and intricate, and busy their world is, and how complicated, as tiny, intricate, and complicated as a good doll house. Henry VII began a royal collection of minis that Queen Elizabeth II adds to even today.

Small dolls have a certain mini mystique; Queen Mary, owner of the fantastic doll house, knew this. She cherished and collected all types of miniatures. Allegedly, when she visited, families hid their treasures because if the Queen admired it they had to give it to her. Her wonderful doll house is full of treasures, including tiny volumes penned by famous authors like T.S. Eliot. They created mini books of their own masterpieces. Virginia Woolf, mentor and friend of Eliot, refused to write a small volume. As she writes in her journals, she thought it was a silly idea. I always puzzled over Woolf's refusal; she liked parties, dressing up, and well, frivolity. I would have thought the little book was right up her alley, especially since her friends were writing them. My theory is that she had some resentment against Queen Mary and the Royal Family. When Queen Mary was Princess May of Teck, she was engaged to the Duke of Clarence, grandson of Queen Victoria, owner and lover of dolls and dolls houses. Known as Prince Eddy, the Duke was meant to be Prince of Wales, and King. He was also suspected by some to be Jack the Ripper. Read Frank Spiering's *The True Story of Jack the Ripper..*

Prince Eddy's tutor was the uncle of Virginia Woolf. Some believed it was he who wrote the Ripper's letter. The royal family apparently had him locked up in an insane asylum after Prince Eddy died, relatively young. James Stephen, the uncle, starved to death in the asylum.

As luck would have it, there are Jack the Ripper dolls. One is part of the Six Faces of Madness series by McFarlane Toys. The others, all minutely detailed with accessories, are Elizabeth Bathory (two versions), Rasputin, Attila the Hun, Billy the Kid and Vlad the Impaler. Todd McFarlane found this way into the toy business after years of drawing doodles. I understand his method. My school and meeting notes are full of doodles, including little moppets resembling Joan Wash Anglund dolls, sketches of Anne Boleyn, elaborate trees, and during very boring meetings, entire families of paper dolls I would later take home and color. My students loved the Jack the Ripper doll. Preppy school girls would wax poetic over his tiny knife and leather apron. When given a choice of a film, they all begged me for *From Hell*. I have a set of miniature one inch, one-foot scale documents of the original Jack the Ripper case to go with the doll. I've often taught Ripper history; I compiled a booklet of materials for my students, and pointed out to them at M'Naghten, who gave us the M'Naghten Rule involving the insanity plea, was one of the detectives on the Ripper case. I wrote two stories about Ripperology, "Tigress", on Kindle, and another version for *The Legend of Tugfest*, which also included a doll. It was called "Scourge of the River." I read the story while a student at SIU, Carbondale, with the late poet, Lucia Perillo, and Gay Gavin, who like me, turned from law to literature. We all read stories and poems based on horror and violence against women. We didn't even plan it that way; it just happened.

Back to miniatures and doll houses, tiny dolls have always been favorites of mine. My grandparents used to fill a shoebox with them for me at Christmas. So did my Uncle George. I recently bought a small glass case for some of my tiny dolls; I was unpacking some of them, many were made by my friend Violet Page, who was a doll maker. These I put together and dressed. Others were tiny dolls, like a mini fur rabbit with red glass eyes, really tiny beads that I've had since I was maybe two or three. Another doll my mother knitted, only two inches high, he sits cross-legged, wearing a turban. Tiny bisque dolls, a Frozen Charlotte, a doll made of Kleenex with floss hair, something I made from a Kleenex I held during my Uncle George's funeral. Wood Erzgebirge miniatures from Germany, including a ¼ inch doll that lies in a wooden egg, all these and more were in my plastic shoeboxes. Each told a story, each one brought back memories.

Chapter 9: Masks

In *The Doll,* Carl Fox explores the many cultural meanings that dolls and related objects share in human cultures. He describes the New York brownstone of Irwin Hersey, noted statesman and collector, that is unassuming on the outside, but full of treasures on the inside. These treasures include masks hung on all of the walls, Inuit sculptures and dolls, Native American Dolls, fetishes, and musical instruments.

Like dolls, and other uncanny objects, masks can transform the everyday into the extraordinary. Once the wearer dons a mask, that person becomes someone or something else. Think of Jim Carrey's' role in *Mask*, and how his whole personality was changed.

Also, masks were used in Ancient Greek theatre to denote characters; we are familiar with- the masks of comedy and tragedy. Masks allow one person to play many roles, hence Joseph Campbell's work, *The Masks of God*, which explores different ways the Supreme Deity is viewed in comparative religion.

The Topeng theater of Indonesia uses masks, as does the Noh theater of Japan. Chinese opera uses them, as it uses opera dolls. The use of masks in ritual dance honoring one's ancestors began in the 15th century on Bali and Java, then spread to the rest of the Indonesian archipelago. Masks and dances adapted to changing cultural norms, so that new masks and their characters were created with the advent of Hinduism to Indonesia. Hindu religious stories were adapted to dance with masks. (Historyofmasks.net)

Masks are worn by characters of the Commedia dell Arte and by Mummers. They appear as props in some of Shakespeare's plays as well.

In Africa, masks were also used for ritual dances and other ceremonies. Other masks had more practical purposes and even served as passports that people wore when traveling among villages in different regions. An African mask inspired Picasso in his work with Cubism and also played a role in the creation of Joseph Conrad's *Heart of Darkness*.

Masks are used for fun, like Halloween Masks and Carnival Masks. Carnival masks originated from Venice, during the Carnival of Venice. Many were based on Commedia dell Arte characters. They were popular up till the 18th century. After Napoleon, when Venice fell to Austria, the city went into decline and Carnival was not celebrated for many years (TheMascherade.com). The carnival tradition morphed into Mardi Gras celebrations in New Orleans and elsewhere in the United States. Masks are worn then too, and as in Venice, are meant to disguise the wearer so that he or she can be someone else undetected. This theme was picked up in episodes where characters wear masks and live romantic fantasies in TV's *Cheers* and *Life Goes On*, and in the film, *Henry and June*.

Death Masks are a tradition in many cultures, dating back to the Ancient World. Two of the most famous are the death mask of Agamemnon and the death mask of King Tut. Both are made of gold, and Tut's is inlaid with lapis lazuli and other stones. Death masks were often taken from famous people and made arresting effigies for posterity. Madame Tussaud, who created wax works and whose museum is still going strong, was forced to model death masks from the victims of the guillotine. The heads were brought to her after each execution. At one point, she had to model the death mask of her childhood friend, Princess Mathilda.

Ski masks and the related balaclavas were meant to keep skiers and others warm in freezing weather, but they were later adapted to criminal use by those who wanted to rob, rape, murder, etc. The comedic stereotype of the cat burglar shows the burglar wearing a half mask, usually black. Where nothing else was available, criminals used stockings over their faces to distort their features, or made simple masks of bandanas tied over their faces, showing only their eyes.

Surgical masks are worn to promote a sterile environment in operating rooms. Similar masks are worn in public when someone does not want to catch a cold, or give one to others. These health-related masks are attributed to the plague masks worn during The Plague years. These are attributed to 17th century physician Charles de Lorme. Eventually, this mask became part of the Carnival of Venice, known as The Plague Doctor mask or *The Medico della Peste*. (TheMascherade.com)

During the Corona Virus Pandemic, surgical masks of all types have become cultural icons. Stores immediately ran out of them, and a cottage industry sprang up with people forced to stay home creating them from calico prints, coffee filters, and other materials. Online vendors like Etsy gave patterns to their sellers and encouraged them to make masks and sell them for those who couldn't get them in stores. Governors of various states mandated that anyone going out and entering an enclosed space had to wear them.

Sanders, construction workers, scientists, and others wear masks to protect them from harmful elements like dust or asbestos. Many people wear sleep masks at night to block out light. Some had painted, closed eyes on them. There are even tiny sleep masks for 11.5-inch fashion dolls of the sixties. Human sized examples were often props worn by men and women from TV shows and films of the '40s, '50s, and '60s. Make masks are mesh type objects worn to preserve one's make up.

Make up or mud masks are a paste that one puts on the face and allows to harden as a way of cleaning and conditioning the pores.

In film, masks are often part of elaborate make up used for special effects, like the early masks used in the original *Planet of the Apes,* sometimes criticized because some fans claimed they could see eye holes in the apes' masks. In *V for Vendetta,* a Guy Fawkes mask covers the protagonist's face the whole time.

In sports, masks protect the faces of players, especially in Hockey. In horror films, though, Jason Voorhees (*Friday the Thirteenth Series*) wears a hockey goalie mask to commit unspeakable slasher murders. Hannibal Lector in *The Silence of the Lambs* wears a cross between mask and muzzle to keep him from hurting his guards; it doesn't work very well. Arguably, the scolds bridle was a type of mask meant to punish women and making it impossible and painful for them to speak.

Masks are de rigueur part of a superhero's wardrobe. Heroes including The Lone Ranger, Batman, Robin, The Invincibles, the Green Hornet, Bat Girl, and The Flash, all wear masks. The idea is to hide their true identities, or course. Dumas' *The Man in the Iron Mask* has a hero who is imprisoned and forced to wear an iron mask to hide his true identity and deny him his claim to the throne.

Masks can conceal deformity. The Phantom of the Opera wears a half mask to cover his burn-scarred face, a Neil Gaiman character from *The Sandman, Dream Country*, Vol. III. wears masks to hide her deformed features. In Gaiman's retelling of *A Midsummer Night's Dream*, Shakespeare's troupe, The King's Men play before the real fairies and goblins, the play itself showcases. Gaiman says, "When the masks are lifted at the end, the actors revealed are not the same as the ones who put the masks on." A character from a Crypt Keeper script kills so she can remove the faces from her victims to create masks she can wear to hide her scarred visage. The Elephant Man wears a cloth over his face with eye holes, a crude mask that covers his features.

Homemade masks of paper plates, etc. are not made to hide as they are meant to transform. Simple white paper plates can become Jack O' Lantern masks with a little paint, glue, and glitter on Halloween. Add the right ears, and they can become cats or rabbits. Paper bag masks made the Unknown Comic a hit. I once made one into a portrait of Anne Boleyn for a Sunday school party. I really got into it, and took the mask home with me where we added an organdy scarf for a veil, jewels to line the "French Hood" headdress Anne introduced to England, and hair from a long Halloween vampire wig. I paired it with a lacy blouse and my mother's full skirted yellow prom dress. I still have that dress, and it did wonders for me many Halloweens. When I went to the party that night, I marched in the mask parade happily and proudly. I heard a whisper that I had won first prize. Then, at the last minute, I was disqualified. The Sunday school Superintendent suddenly remembered the "rules" said the mask had to be decorated only with paper. Disappointment notwithstanding, life masks are a popular school project to this day. Plain white masks of papier mâché or plastic are sold in craft stores so that children and decorate them, sometimes with found objects.

I have, in my collection, a homemade mask decorated with all kinds of seeds. An artist friend of mine created one from old cigarette butts. Grasses and straw are used to weave masks in Mexico and the Philippines. Also from Mexico, come wooden masks worn in dances, duplicated in miniature on wooden dolls that represent the human dancers. Gold masks and masks inlaid with jade and precious stones were important as death masks and religious object all over Ancient America. Currently, masks of decorated aluminum are made in all sizes in Mexico.

A mask from the Philippines in my collection has a shock of hair and facial hair derived from dried grasses. This mask grimaces in an open mouth grin; my husband makes me hide it. We have masks from Japan, the US, China, and Nepal hanging on our walls, but the grimacing mask really bothers him!

Miniature masks are sold as art objects or souvenirs and come from China, Africa, Nepal, Japan, and Mexico. Some dolls from Greece and Italy have faces that are cloth masks fitted over modeled heads. Other plush dolls, including a red plush Knickerbocker kewpie, have vinyl masks for face. Small porcelain doll faces are made into brooches and other jewelry and art objects. Other dolls from Germany and Poland have faces made from celluloid masks. The Polish dolls were very popular in the early sixties. They had wild-colored hair of orange, green, purple, and pink that matched their dresses and shoes. They had the celluloid mask faces and cloth bodies. Allegedly, First Lady Bird Johnson bought several. A public service announcement declared the dolls were flammable because of their celluloid faces. Now, they are hard to find. I have several of them, and nothing has happened.

Barbie and friends had outfits with masks called Masquerade in the early '60s. Harlequin dolls come with their own masks, as do dolls of the superheroes mentioned earlier.

Native American dolls of the Hopi, Zuni, and Tlingit people wear masks. The Tlingit were the original inhabitants of the Pacific Northwest. These cultures also have masks used as art of their ceremonies. The Tlingit also used masks in war. The Apache have dolls that represent dancers wearing black hoods with eye holes. The hooded spirits are the guardians and representatives of young girls, laughter, and medicine.

Halloween masks often are made to represent dolls, like Living Dead Dolls, Barbie, Muppets, decrepit Baby Dolls or Haunted Dolls, Strawberry Shortcake, Raggedy Ann, etc. A favorite in my collection is Judge Ito, from the O.J. Simpson murder trial (Actually, we have a Simpson doll, too). The Ito mask adorned the school skeleton at my old place of employment; he wore a black robe, and presided over our legal studies open house.

Collegeville plastic and antique cloth Halloween masks are sought after collectibles today. Many collectors like to collect entire boxed costumes when possible, or they hang the plastic masks on their walls as décor.

The best succinct history of the Halloween mask's origins is given in HistoryfotheMask.net:

"Halloween has originated from the old Celtic festival and even before that. In those times, a man painted a mask on their face with blackened ashes from the sacred bonfire and dressed up as fearsome beings. It was believed that this is the last night for the dead to have their vengeance before moving on so people wore masks and costumes not to be recognized, to scare away evil spirits and to prevent them from entering homes. They believed it was important to honor dead, so Halloween developed from Pagan ritual to Masquerade party night." (Historyofthemask.net)

Soon, people wore actual masks in an attempt to hide from the spirits that walked the earth. Masks eventually became entire costumes. For more on the general history of Halloween and related holidays, I suggest Ray Bradbury's *The Halloween Tree,* both the book, and the film, that he narrates. One of my students gave me the film many years ago. In my Diversity and Culture class, which I created, and in Humanities class, we studied holidays and festivals. I used to have scavenger hunts, but everyone got to draw for prizes each class. The prizes included books, food from around the world, candy, small figurines, toys, little books, and stickers. The stickers were prized, and students, college age and older, collected them and pasted them in albums. Steph, the student who gave me *The Halloween Tree* video, said that the film belonged to her two children, then preteen and early teen, one boy, and one girl. They said they would give me the film in exchange for a bag of the little toy scavenger hunt prizes and candies. I obliged with a very big bag. The appeal of toys and little dolls is universal and ageless.

Halloween masks also had origins in the beautiful masks during Renaissance masquerades and Carnival. Many Halloween traditions come from the Celts in Ireland. Irish immigrants brought them to the United States during the 1840s. (The History of the Halloween Mask.)

Costumes, and visiting houses for soul cakes was a Christmas tradition, but other churches, including the Greek Orthodox Church, had similar customs that took place around Easter.

By the Victorian Era, Halloween became a quaint festival for children that combined Harvest customs with Celtic traditions and traditions other immigrants brought with them. Many decorations and novelties were made during the Victorian era including masks.

By the early 20th century, parades, haunted houses and neighborhood gatherings were organized in the US for kids. Trick or treating became an established tradition during the 1940s. Costumes and masks were once again a way to fool the sprits. Centuries later, trick or treating became a child's pastime, just as many other traditions did. Many dolls and toys themselves, it is to be remembered, began as ritual artifacts and idols that fell into the hands of children

Collegeville, Ben Cooper, and Halco were popular makers of Halloween costumes that included plastic masks. (Vintage Halloween.) These were boxed, and have become very collectible. Cloth masks were made during the '20s through the '40s. Around this time, Dennison Party books gave ideas for costumes, parties, and masks using Dennison crepe paper and stickers.

Chapter 10: CPKs

Coleco first introduced these brain children of Little People Creator Xavier Roberts in the early '80s. They disappeared fast from toy shelves, even faster than Beanie Babies would ten years later. The original Coleco dolls had vinyl heads, needle sculpted bodies, and yarn hair. They came with dozens of accessories, pets, books, and more.

So great was the Frenzy for the Coleco dolls that people were knocked down and one woman broke her arm. Parents spent thousands on airline tickets to bring one of these dolls home, and one entrepreneur was selling mink coats for the dolls at $700 per coat and hat.

The original dolls were made of stocking material, and even the heads were soft sculptured. The cloth Little People made by Robert's own Appalachian Art Works came from a factory called Babyland General Hospital. Roberts and his staff dressed as doctors and nurses and each doll had a birth certificate.

The prototype dolls are little boys, and the early dolls all wore toddler clothes. Roberts lost a law suit to artist Faye Wine over the Little People. He alleged she copied his designs, but he lost the suit. Wine created the Time Out Kids popular in the '90s as well as the floppy eared bunnies you could make from McCall's patterns. She designed a lot of designs for McCall's for dolls, animals, toys, and clothes.

Cabbage Patch Kids were the first doll fad that I can remember. It was the first time that collectors couldn't find a modern doll anywhere. I confess that I never thought they would catch on. The first time I saw the original Appalachian Art Works kids was at a doll show that used to be held in Aledo, IL. Aledo is synonymous with doll collecting in our area because it was the location of the first doll show held in the Quad City area, a geographic designation that encompasses four cities, three in Illinois and one in Iowa. Several surrounding communities are also included. Aledo, Illinois was once the home of Lifetime Career Schools, now on line. Among the correspondence courses one could complete, was a course in doll repair, designed by Aledo's own Ola Finch.

Aledo has long been visited for antique shops and quaint festivals like the annual Rhubarb festival.

CPKs were everywhere; I have one friend with over 300 of them and everything that goes with them. I still find them, but sometimes, the boxed examples are rather pricey. I've had my moments with them. They tend to disappear at the local thrift stores as fast as they appear. I found two of the prototype little boys handmade by Roberts at his hospital for under $60, around $30 in one case. Two of the actual children from Appalachian Artworks were only $75. At the time, the original dolls sold for $600 to well over $1000. It was one of the luckiest finds I'd ever had. CPK collectors have taken flak from the first. I had a folder decorated with them that I kept law school notes in. It was a way to lighten an otherwise grim experience. A fellow student took issue. Apparently one of our classmates had given up a child for adoption. For some reason, her friend took offense on her behalf. As for my classmate who gave up her baby, well, she spent the bulk of her legal career handling adoptions for other people. Until then, I didn't think a doll could rile anyone up.

Faye Wine

Faye Wine created dolls during the 1970s, roughly parallel to the creation of the Cabbage Patch Kids by Xavier Roberts. Her Blossom Babies were very similar to the early soft sculpture CPKs, but more on that similarity later. She also created patterns for McCall's and other companies for Time Out Kids, floppy eared bunnies, grandma/grandpa dolls and more soft sculpture characters.

I'm sure you would all recognize her dolls just as I did, but you perhaps are not familiar with the artist's name, just as I was not.

Ms. Wine was a former dog groomer, breeder, and boarder. She and her husband raised Shih Tzus and were AKC handlers for many years. Just for that, I have to like her. We had a Shih Tzu named Tiger at my family's house in California, and my best friend at school, now deceased, also raised them. They are such beautiful, yet happy little dogs. But, as Wine noted in an article about her written in "The Evening Independent," August 14, 1978, caring for the Shih Tzus, Pomeranians and miniature schnauzers was a lot of work. It was rewarding though, because she won 19 Best of Show awards in the US, Bermuda, and Canada.

While she was a 4-H teacher who sewed, Wine did not make dolls. She got interested because her sister, who did sew dolls, invited her to a doll show. There, Faye Wine saw many dolls, but none that excited her or, as Charla Wasel writes in her "Evening Independent" article, "Nothing that would inspire ecstasy in a child or grown up. And Fay Wine thought she could do that."

Ultimately, Wine did.

Her first doll was very small and was called Jenny. Making Jenny apparently gave Wine confidence, so she created a life-sized version. Soon, she began making soft sculpture "sock" dolls that were far more detailed than any regular sock doll could be. She created a life-sized doll called "Granny" that was her mascot. So life-like was Granny, that many passersby at craft and doll shows tried to talk to her and asked her about prices for the other dolls. Granny wore old calico and vintage spectacles that once belonged to her creator's grandmother. She had real hair, and real fingernails.

Wine lived in Largo, Florida, and sold her dolls there. She prowled craft and fabric stores to get ideas, and learned to make embroidered face and painted face dolls as well as soft sculpture ones. She opened a shop in her garage Christmas 1977, and did very well. It was called The Hen's Nest Orphanage. She called the soft sculpture Blossom Babies "Little People" and bestowed a name on each doll. According to Wine, each doll had its own personality, and she called them Little People because to her they were; she even spoke to them at times.

Here, of course, is where she got into trouble with Original Appalachian Artworks and Xavier Roberts. Or rather, McCall's Patterns got into trouble because of her.

Faye Wine designed many doll patterns for McCall's, including the Little People, the faceless Time Out Kids popular during the '80s and '90s, and the floppy bunny dolls we can still find today at craft sales, hobby shops, and thrift stores. Her designs were incredibly popular, even if not everyone knew her name.

Not everyone was enchanted with Wine's dolls or success. Original Appalachian Artworks sued McCall Pattern Co. in 1986 in Georgia, where Wine had sold some of her dolls.

Prices for Faye Wine items on line are reasonable, but respectable. On Etsy.com, Cloe's Closet offers a '90s Time Out Kids 36-inch Doll pattern for 12.00. The Pattern Shop features a Stuffed Bunny and clothes Pattern for $11.99, while Pattern Depot sells McCall's 691 Vintage Bunny Clothes for $7.00. Faye Wine's large Snowman Greeter's Pattern McCall's Crafts 9446 sells for $5.95 from tealductoo or $6.00 from johnmark1, as number P400. The Kitchen Cow Vacuum Broom Toaster Cover Patterns old by vintage such goes for $10.00. EveryPicTellsAStory sells a Blossom Babies Pattern for $6.00. Faye Wine's Bear Dolls, Clothes and Bag Pattern sell for $4.00. McCall's 5652/P349, 1991 Halloween Costume Pattern for real children and parents sells for $8.95 from Lovnthisstuff. A four-foot-tall shopper Doll Pattern, uncut, is $5.00 by the shop DaisyandErma.

Wine's versatility is staggering. She also did Red Hat Society hat, purse, and corsage patterns, Christmas and holiday figures, a PIGS Weeding Party, reindeer, more doll clothes, patriotic dolls and folk dolls.

On eBay, completed time out dolls sell from $39.00–$69.00. I wonder if my mother-in-law will read this. Uncut Time Out Kid cloth bodies that need stuffing and finishing sell for $12.99 or so.

A completed Blossom Baby type doll sells for $31.50 on eBay. A 20-inch bunny doll sells for around $19.99. A 27-inch Bunny was offered at $29.99. Another of unspecified size sells for $39.99 on eBay.

Chapter 11: Living Dead Dolls

Now created by Mezco Toy Company, these gruesome little toddlers were the brainchild of two friends who purloined dolls the mother of one of them used to make angels. There is nothing angelic about these wildly popular little ghouls, some of whom are inspired by real people. Dahlia (aka, Beth Short, the Black Dahlia murder victim), Erzebet Bathory, Lizzie Borden, and Edgar Allan Poe were real people.

I used to be able to find them at Spencer's Gift, but not now. Hot Topic had them for a while, and I've been lucky finding things at thrift stores, like a game, some lights with the dolls' heads. Now, you have to look online; Amazon has a good selection.

These little plastic monsters attract people who otherwise pay no attention to dolls. That's a plus. On the minus side, they encourage the whole creepy doll garbage.

When I bought my first doll in its coffin box, Bride of Valentine, a little girl that I often saw at yard sales, and the neighborhood antique shops, was standing next to me at Spencer's. "Oh," she said very seriously, "they come alive at night!" When I told my mom about what the little girl said, my mother thought she had LDD envy!

Chapter 12: Bobble Heads

People who wouldn't be caught dead with other dolls are manic about collecting bobble heads that have their origins in ancient ritual figures from India and the orient. Bisque Nodders from Germany and Japan of about 100 years ago are also distant relatives. Some, like the John Wilke's Booth bobble head offered by Springfield, IL's Lincoln Museum, are very controversial. They have enjoyed a real Renaissance, and even have their own museum of 6000 strong in Wisconsin.

Bobble heads made of a mix of plaster and papier mâché were made in Japan during the mid-sixties. They were sold at gift shops and novelty stores. Early examples represented sports figures, but there were kissing bobble heads of Chinese couples, and tiny hard plastic "kissing" dolls from Hong Kong that had magnets in their heads. There is a famous set of Beatles bobble heads from the '60s that came in the papier mâché material and in a small, four-inch hard plastic version. Today, bobble heads appear in shows like *The Office* and on insurance commercials. They are popular giveaways at sports events, and have once again become coveted collectibles. Once, I could have bought a whole basket of them of $6 at a yard sale; I kick myself because another woman grabbed them before I could make up my mind. On a challenge, I made a couple Anne Boleyn bobble heads out of Play Dough. I think they are cute, and pick up one or two here and there. I have the Bix Beiderbecke and Buddy Lee examples that I enjoy very much. In dolls, as other things, variety is the spice of life.

Chapter 13: Space Toys and Dolls

Artifacts and toys of exploration have been around for centuries. Space toys certainly fit into this category. Perhaps the oldest toy in the world is the doll; its form dates back at least 40,000 years to the prehistoric Venus figures. Toy boats, complete with tiny sailors, were around in Ancient Egypt, and later in Greece, Roman, and elsewhere. The Travels of Marco Polo, and then Columbus, inspired even more travel related and nautical artifacts; even Shakespeare caught the fever with The Tempest. (O Brave New World that has such people in it!) Jonathan Swift parodied both toys and travel with *Gulliver's Travels* and his scathing essay "A Modest Proposal." By the time of the Conquest of Mexico, books on travel, some fake, and toys reflecting the love of the ocean and the age of exploration were popular all over Europe and in the New World that was slowly being populated.

Ancient Inuit culture involved small boats filled with tiny figures that were a talisman for safe voyages. The Whaling industry inspired literature for adults and children that spawned children's books and toys, including Herman Melville's *Moby Dick* and Rachel Field's *Hitty*. Other souvenirs besides toys emerged, including Sailor's Valentines, small items embellished with shells, macramé objects, ships in bottles, and scrimshaw.

Pirates created a whole new nautical culture and mythology, and they, too inspired toys. Of course, they, and other ancient sailors have always navigated by the stars, sun, and moon. They also followed the flights of birds and the patterns of swimming fish. For more on the exploits of ancient sailors, I recommend my all-time favorite, Thor Heyerdahl's *The Ra Expedition and Kon Tiki*.

Space is indeed the final frontier, and Space toys are the cultural artifacts of that exploration; people collect alien action figures just as little girls collect dolls in international costume. Think the intergalactic beauty pageant of *Lost in Space*. *Star Wars* is also permanently in our culture as part of a US Military defense strategy, and lest we forget, former Vice President Dick Cheney was called derisively by his opponents, "Darth Vader."

While Leonardo Da Vinci and others experimented with the idea of flight through scale models and life-sized machines, it is not exactly correct to call

Leonardo's efforts toys. Even earlier, artists had been portraying *The Zodiac* and the constellations in art and sculpture. Plays, songs, poems, dance, all forms of art, portrayed the heavens as each culture saw them. The Druids and Celts, in particular, are credited with early attempts at astronomy. According to some scholars, Stonehenge was an ancient observation point of astronomical events.

Really the first space toys arrived on the scene shortly after Buster Crabbe first portrayed Flash Gordon in the 1930s. The first space toys documented was probably the ray gun made of lithographed cardboard that was a premium, created in 1933. By the time Orson Welles scared the pants off of everyone with his Halloween broadcast of War of the Worlds, theories of aliens abounded. The alleged alien crash and autopsy in Roswell, NM, gave us the iconic, emoji like alien with green skin and oval bug eyes. Early in the 1940s Three Stooges Episodes had the goofy boys cavorting with alien women aboard a ship.

Dr. Who, the oldest running TV show in history, gave us a whole host of new aliens, including The Dalek, and the space mobile of all space mobiles, The Tardis. Even today, grown-ups drive around with bumper stickers that read, "My other car is a Tardis."

By the '60s, the Space Program was in full swing; dogs, monkeys, humans, all went to space to explore. As art always imitates life, so toys imitate society. Space toys and Martians were inevitable. The brave exploits of the Gemini, Mercury, Apollo, and Shuttle astronauts caused more and more space toys to be created. In the early '60s, Americans gathered their children at school to watch the launch of each mission, until in July 1969, the Eagle finally Landed, and the US planted a flag on the moon. I was in Greece with my family, visiting, and we watched that one giant step-for-man take place on an old set in the middle of a relative's living room.

NASA, by now, was a household topic of conversation. In fact, even today, they sell toys at their souvenir stores and online. The National Aeronautic and Space Museum has its own collection of over 2000 Space Toys. The University of Iowa's Old Capitol Museum has an exhibit dedicated to Prof. James van Allen which includes space toys and models.

The first doll in space was Stargazer Lottie. She spent 264 days on the International Space Station as the guest of an English astronaut. She was designed by a 12-year-old girl. ("Doll" Wikipedia).

Popular TV shows including *Lost in Space, Bewitched, Star Trek, It's about Time* and *I Dream of Jeannie* featured astronauts. Toys and spinoffs from these shows including dolls, costumes, and lunch boxes featured the characters. *The Jetsons* that took their cue from The Flintstones, made us all want to have a Rosie Robot and to fly around in our own flying saucers. *The Dick van Dyke show* featured a toy saucer in one episode, and an entire show developed around Martians, *My Favorite Martian* with Bill Bixby and Ray Walston.

Star Trek Movies, spinoffs, conventions, and cartoons made the show even more popular in toy form. Hallmark began making space ornaments. A friend of mine had for sale in her shop an original costume. I was lucky enough to meet Leonard Nimoy at a doll house show in San Jose, and he signed an autograph for me. I complimented him on his role in *A Woman Called Golda*, and he actually beamed with surprised pleasure. No wonder he wrote *I am not Spock*. The Mego Star Trek figures have become iconic; they have come with their own bridge.

Not to be outdone, Barbie has appeared at least three times in astronaut garb, once in pink lame, and once as part of a Star Trek Barbie Gift Set. G. I. Joe appeared as an astronaut several times, and at least once, he had his own Mercury 7 capsule. Major Matt Mason and Johnny Apollo soon joined him, along with an entire fleet of robots. Some of these are made in Japan and bring over $40,000.

The original *Star Wars* movie in 1976 created a whole host of collectible toys, including 12-inch figures. Some of these are worth thousands of dollars if found in original packaging, including the Yak face action figure and the Jawa with a plastic cloak. Really popular are Lego sets, including Jabba the Hut's palace, which became controversial because some felt it looked like a mosque when complete. Queen Amadula appeared as a series of dolls, action figures, an inflatable chair, a coke bottle, and a pizza box.

During the '80s, *Battle Star Galactica* had its own toys, and so did *Mork and Mindy* and *Alf. Out of this World* featured Doug McClure, the Marlborough man, and Hanna Barbera never stopped its cartoons with the Martian.

By the '90s and early 2000s there were many more *Star Wars* movies, apocalyptic space movies including *Deep Impact* and *Armageddon*, several more *Dr. Who*, *Highlander*, and *Stargate*, an Egyptian themed Sci-Fi classic that seemed to step out of the pages of the 1970s' cult classic paperback, *In search of Ancient Astronauts. Small Soldiers* featured alien dolls in several dimensions. *The Terminator* and *Total Recall, Men in Blank, Mars Attacks, Space Jam Toy Story I-IV, Lost in Space, Space Balls*, all had their toys.

TV Shows like *Big Bang Theory* and *That '70s Show,* and *The Goldbergs* featured many of these space toy dolls and collectibles as props.

A new American Girl doll based on an Astronomer has caused a bit of controversy. Lucianne Walkowicz of Chicago has sued Mattel, parent company of the American Girls claiming that Mattel stole her likeness and played with her name to create their astronaut/astronomer American Girl doll. Walkowicz has worked with NASA and is a TED senior fellow at the Adler Planetarium. The doll at the heart of the lawsuit is named Luciana Vega. Walkowicz has researched Mars exploration as well as the constellation Lyra, which contains the star Vega. Like Walkowicz, Luciana Vega wears holographic shoes and purple streak in her dark hair. For more, see Ed Trevelen's article at etrevelen@madison.com.

Scientist Katharine Walker of *Hidden Figures* was immortalized as a Barbie doll recently, just a year or so before her death.

Like the astronauts they often represent, dolls have blazed a pathway to the moon and beyond.

Chapter 14: Barbie and Fads

In 1959, a mother and daughter were vacationing in Europe. In a Swiss airport, they saw a German doll called Lilli. Lilli was a 3D representation of a German cartoon character that was created to appeal to men. Lilli would have been very happy frisking among the pages of *Playboy* or *Hustler*. She was reputed to be a call girl or worse, but she still had that bouncy little pony tail, stylish outfits, and accessories. Lilli's kitchen rivals anything later dolls had. I still wonder if that was made for men to play house with, or a subversive way for their wives to get them to cook. Bild Co. made Lilli.

But I digress.

The mother and daughter in Switzerland were Ruth and Barbara Handler. Ruth, the mother, was one of the founders of the Mattel toy corporation, which began in the garage of one of the partners and which originally made ashtrays and knick knacks out of Lucite. Ruth Handler bought two of the Lilli dolls; one for her, and one for Barbara. She took the doll to sculptor Jack Ryan, once married to ZaZa Gabor and she described what she wanted, showing the dolls. Ruth was impressed by how her daughter and her friends played with paper dolls. She started to wonder if a paper doll figure could be made 3D so that little girls could play with them and dress them in extensive wardrobes.

By 1959, she had her doll, and it was called Barbie, after her daughter, Barbara Millicent Roberts, her full name. Soon, in 1964, she was joined by a clean-cut boyfriend named Ken, named for Ruth and Elliot Handler's son. Ken's last name is Carson.

The rest is doll history. Numerous friends and siblings have joined Barbie over the years, including Skipper, Scooter, Midge, Rickey, Alan, Tutti, Kelley, Chrissie, Stacey, etc. Barbie has run for president, been a teacher, astronaut, vet, doctor, stewardess, artist, fashion model, and who knows what else!!! She has been a talking doll, supersized, a gymnast, starred in movies and movie sets, been a bride many times over, and all at a youthful, eternal sixteen. Her parents, who must be in their nineties by now, seem to produce a new infant sibling every year or so. There are Barbie pets, boats, cars, airplanes, stages, theaters, etc. Holiday Barbies have been a tradition since 1988, but there are dolls in Gone with the Wind outfits, Wizard of Oz outfits, mermaids, fairies, Harley Davidson, Samurai dolls, dolls of the world, and many more.

Barbie has starred in her own movies, including a version of *The Nutcracker*, and as one of the 12 Dancing Princesses, based on Mark Twain's *The Prince and the Pauper*, about Henry VIII's son by Jane Seymour, Edward VI.

She is a pop culture icon with a place in both *Toy Story* and *The Smithsonian*. Artist Andy Warhol even did her portrait. *Barbie Nation* is a documentary about Barbie that includes two middle-aged women with their own S&M doll house. Erica Rand's *Barbie's Gay Accessory* discusses Barbie's history and her role in the gay community.

Chapter 15: Creepy Dolls

Francis Shaffer and other philosophers have written that when times are dark and financially difficult, people turn to the occult and to horror in general. Dystopias and apocalyptic societies tend to be cathartic when the real world is scary. Since 9/11, these stories seem to proliferate. Zombies are once again popular and not just for Halloween. There is even a restaurant chain called Zombie Burger, complete with Zombie baby dolls and animatronics. Haunted houses with doll rooms are all the rage right now, too. One of the best is Terror at Skellington Manor, Rock island, IL.

During the '60s, warm and fuzzy monsters found their way into TV sitcoms and into our living rooms. *Bewitched, The Addams Family*, which even featured an Iron Maiden and a headless doll called Marie Antoinette, *The Munsters*, with Eddie the werewolf child and his werewolf doll, *Milburn the Monster, Sabrina the Teenaged Witch* and *The Groovy Goulies and Sabrina, Count Chocula, Caspar the Friendly Ghost* and Glinda the Good Witch of Oz took the fear out of the horrible creatures that were the stuff of horror literature.

Dolls per se were not considered creepy. The only creepy dolls around were Halloween props and models of the Universal Studios Monsters. Something changed over the last 40 years, and dolls became the subject of horror films. One of the earliest citing of a creepy doll occurred in The Twilight Zone episode "Livng Doll" where Telly Savalas met an untimely end at the hands of Talky Tina, an evil Chatty Cathy type. Before that, dolls made a few supernatural appearances in silent films and in *The Bad Seed* with Patty McCormack, but they were only props. Voodoo dolls were around, but they were considered a joke in many circles, or a cute souvenir from New Orleans.

By the time the late '70s rolled around, dolls were starring in horror movies, including *Chucky* from *The Child's Play* series and Stuart Gordon's *Dolls*. A spooky doll appeared in *Night Gallery*, and another homicidal poppet chased Karen Black around in *Trilogy of Terror*.

Books parodying dolls and doll collecting coincided with reality shows like *Hoarders* and *Clean House*, which lumped collecting into various mental disorders where people couldn't part with garbage bags full of dirty diapers. As the world began to spin faster by the light of its iPhones, collecting anything fell out of fashion, but dolls fell into disfavor. What Rilke observed about 100 years before in his essay "Puppen" about bisque dolls with their staring eyes was interpreted to mean that dolls were weird and creepy. The Uncanny Valley study of 1970 by Masahiro Mori which focused on the uncanny nature of dolls didn't help.

The same people who exhort us to simplify and hold on to the memories, not the stuff, advocate ironically, the use of dolls in memory therapy. It's sort of like concept of one of the hearsay exceptions in The Federal Rules of Evidence; you can use just about anything to refresh a witnesses' recollection of an event.

Of course, if we didn't take peoples' collections and possessions away from them, we wouldn't have to rent dolls to remind them of who they were when they are imprisoned in a tiny room at a nursing home, with nothing to call their own

Dolls, the Uncanny Valley study went, were not alive, yet not quite dead. They were more than inanimate objects. Freud, too, had addressed this topic in his essay "The Uncanny" where he addressed stories of dolls and statues coming to life, like E.T.A. Hoffman's The Nutcracker Prince and Coppelia. I should mention that Freud, who often is made as a doll, also had his own collection of ancient artifacts that included dolls and figurines. *Newsweek* Magazine, once part of a series of companies that owned my former school, had a photo of them, and they toured the country in the late '80s, including a display done at Stanford University. There are photos of them online now. Indeed, many are "creeped" out by automatons and mechanical dolls, even robots, because they look alive, and can breathe and talk, yet are not. *The Stepford Wives* by Ira Levin, who also gave the world *Rosemary's Baby*, drove home the point about the fear of soulless robots taking over our homes. The fact that these robots were made by Disney do not make the Stepford wives any less sinister.

Broken dolls, cracked composition babies, old bisque dolls repurposed to look like monsters, these all contributed to the creepy doll craze.

In a San Clemente neighborhood, in 2014 or so, a woman was horrified to discover that the dolls she left on neighbors' porches as gifts were collected and taken into custody as one cop put it, because the gated community feared they were some fetish project that was the work of a pedophile. They couldn't just be a surprise for a little girl who liked pretty dolls. In fact, not many little girls seem to like dolls at all. Everything is an online game played on a phone, a movie character, or a soccer game. Play dates and after school activities take up the time books and toys used to. Dolls, once the cherished companions of childhood, are now tossed aside and sold at yard sales, or just ridiculed. It is both stylish and faddish to declare "dolls are creepy," even if the speaker is only six or seven years old. A commercial for Halos citrus features a little girl escaping from the house of weird twin sisters who have a large doll collection. So much for imagination and creativity, it's apparently frowned upon.

Monster High and Living Dead Dolls made it okay for dolls to be creepy. MH defined different in a positive way; there is even a Lady Gaga MH doll because like The Gaga, she was born that away. As an aside, Lady Gaga apparently follows one of my social media sites; she was dating someone who was a neighbor to my boss at one of the magazines where I wrote about dolls.

Living Dead dolls, now made by Mezco, were the brainchildren of two young men who got ahold of some dolls the mother one of them was dressing as angels. Original dolls can bring thousands, and new series quickly sell out. Some represent real people like Elisabeth Bathory or Edgar Allan Poe; others are ghosts, vampires, fictional characters, or monsters. They come as plush, 9-inch gruesome toddlers, voodoo dolls, bears, tiny lights Halloween Costumes, or games. More adults than children seem to like them, and each doll comes in her own coffin. My favorite may be Frozen Charlotte, a dead white baby doll with an icy crack on her face. I'm also fond of Eggzorcist, a demonic Easter Bunny, Valentine's Bride, Dahlia, and Lizzie Borden. (Liz Borden is sometimes my pen name, and is also one of my family nick names. I also adored my idol Elisabeth Montgomery in the part of Lizzie Borden. Go figure.)

Chapter 16: Black Dolls

The setting was Naples, Fl, March, 2018. Theriault's Auction was having another of its famous Marquis Auctions of high end, i.e., expensive antique dolls. Featured were dolls from Samy Odin's Musée de la Poupée, and his personal collection. These were fantastic dolls in their own right. Odin, an expert on dolls and former owner and curator of the Museum in Paris, had decided to close in 2017. He remained a frequent contributor to antique doll publications.

Also featured were the dolls of noted author Myla Perkins, who wrote two books on black dolls, *Black Dolls*, Vols. I and II. These paperback books were collector's items in their own right, and could sell for nearly $140 each on eBay. I met a local collector and politician who told me he had spoken to Perkins about his own collection of Black dolls; I also had both her books. She was featured in *Ebony* and other magazines, and had a significant number of dolls by Leo Moss, black doll artist of the early part of the 20th century. Moss was a handyman and itinerant worker from Macon; many of his dolls had tears molded on their papier mâché faces, and had names like Mina, Lillian, and Carrie. A male doll wearing a suit is supposedly his self-portrait. The late Mrs. Lenon Hoyte had Leo Moss dolls, and Lillian was featured in a photo study of her dolls, *Who Won Second Place at Omaha?* Mrs. Hoyte's dolls were auctioned off; her museum, Aunt Len's, once located in Harlem was closed. An off Broadway play about her and her dolls was popular for a while, and tours would go by and point out the home where she had her museum. She must have had 5000 dolls crammed into her brownstone; what I would say is a good start. As she said, "Clutter is clutter a mess is a mess. We are not a mess." I have to agree.

As with most rare and unusual dolls, Moss dolls were copied. At least two artists did so honestly, and one was a friend of the Moss family. Let me emphasize that, there are Moss children and grandchildren, and while the stories of his wife running off with a Caucasian business man and taking with them his designs may be legend, the man and his family, and dolls were real.

When I was little, Ralphs' Antique Dolls from Missouri, owner Ralph Griffiths, used to come to the Masonic Temple antique show, once hosted by the local Women's Club. Now, the building is called Skellington Manor; it hosts weddings, special events, and mystery dinners. In October, Skellington Manor becomes the most amazing haunted house, with state-of-the-art animatronics, and yes, dolls everywhere, including an eclectic collection in a room called The Baby Doll Room. I love them, and the manor is my spiritual home when it comes to dolls.

Back to Ralph G., he was very pricey, but brought dozens of dolls. My mom's student, now a successful romance writer named Kim Cates, also loved dolls and we would run into her at the shows. I was good for a tiny penny doll one year, and a Petit Colin celluloid baby another. I wanted a tiny German bisque doll with red hair and class eyes dressed in a baby dress, but in 1969 or '70, $125 was too much for us to spend. I also have an original printed bag from Ralph's. Everyone knew of him, and he was quite popular, though his dolls were expensive. Allegedly, Ralph hired someone to replicate Moss dolls by building them over old composition dolls. Hence the rumors, that all moss dolls were fakes. I never saw anything, though, that looked like a Leo Moss doll in his booth at the Masonic Temple show.

Social Media was abuzz with rumors when Theriault's announced the auction. Some collectors sold their Moss dolls, at a loss. Others scoffed that the whole thing wasn't real. Debbie Garret, noted expert on black dolls, had also written about Moss, and documented dolls from the Moss family.

I had seen a great exhibit on black dolls belonging to Deborah Neff on loan from the Mingei at the Figge Museum, Davenport, IA. Moss dolls were there, along with the doll that had been X-rayed with a photo.

Moss made dolls through the early '30s; it is possible he used broken dolls to build on. It isn't unusual. In fact, another Neff doll with a cloth face had been built over a tin head metal doll, the kind I wrote on in *With Love from Tin...A History of Metal Dolls.*

The dolls that were at the Florida auction sold for thousands of dollars. Ultimately, the black Leo Moss dolls brought over $60,000.

Apparently, most collectors did not believe the rumors. Had they not done well, Mrs. Perkins and Theriault's would have had a law suit for tortious interference with a business opportunity. My take is that people don't research their opinions well enough, and that some are racists. Some can't accept that an untrained artist like Moss, who was black, could produce such amazing dolls. To them, his talent had to be a fraud. It sets my teeth on edge when I hear collectors deprecate dolls of color with comments like "I don't care for them," or "I'm not interested in that." We don't have to collect every doll in the world, but we should be interested in all of them for the sake of research.

Whoever made them, Moss dolls are well-modeled, and wonderful in person. The little girls with their tears, the little boy with his tongue sticking out, are precious. They almost seem alive in their expression. Black dolls are historical and wonderful; they have their mention in *Brown v. Board of Education* (1954), when Justice Thurgood Marshall discussed a study involving children playing with black and white dolls. Black dolls and African dolls are as diverse as their makers, yet I hear many collectors scoff, "I don't care of those." I was able to get a Coleco CPK during the height of the CPK frenzy because my mother walked into a display of black CPKs in K-mart no one was buying. She overheard one clerk say to another, "I don't want those; no one wants them." We did. I still treasure that doll. At another auction, I was able to buy black oil cloth dolls and Native American dolls. It was a tiny town, but the auction was packed. I am bad at auctions, and didn't think I stood a chance. But, my husband said, "Remember where we are. These people only like white dolls." Sure enough, the black and Native American dolls came home with me.

Karen B. Kurtz has written in "Collecting Black Dolls: A Walk-through History," that, "The Study of Black dolls shows how different groups perceived the dolls, and they (the dolls) often reflected the changing values of society." (1) As with other rag or cloth dolls, it is true that women worked with what (1) they had, often piecing together scraps from the family rag bag. Laura Ingalls Wilder, for example, describes how Ma made dolls for her and Mary, especially the famous Charlotte rag doll, in *Little House in the Big Woods*. Today, there are replicas made of Charlotte, and least one I have in my collection has won a prize in a local competition.

Many early black dolls were important in Southern oral history narratives. Slave women sewed them from bits of cloth for their own young children, though time for leisure may have been limited, and for children of the plantation owners. It's not unlikely that these children played with each other. Helen Keller writes of playing with the black children of the then emancipated Keller servants in her autobiography, *The Story of my Life*.

Black rag dolls and other black dolls appear in the hands of children of both races in photographs collected by Deborah Neff. The Neff collection is now subject of a forth coming documentary and has been traveling first the US, and now France. It was first displayed at the Mingei Museum. Dolls have been recovered from underground railroad sites, and a small doll appears in the film *Amistad*.

Chapter 17: Native American Dolls

My earliest and happiest memories are of road trips my family and I took out west. We traveled Route 66, but at age six, I was too small to appreciate Jack Kerouac. I only knew the TV show, and its theme, *Get your kicks on Route 66!* And get my kicks, I did! My first Native American doll, or Indian doll as we used to call them, came from Ft. Cody in Nebraska. Before that, I only had a few beaded miniatures and plastic souvenir doll made in Japan that came from local Powwows or museum gift shops. We used to have them at our own Putnam Museum, and at the Hauberg Indian Museum, which once had its own collection of dolls at Black Hawk State Park. I was in love with Grand Island and Ogallala, Hastings, and other small Nebraska towns because they all seemed to have their dolls. Front Street had the amazing gift shop with very expensive Sioux dolls made of buckskin and cornhusk, china reproductions, Dresden figures, and more plastic dolls dressed as Native Americans. In the 19th c. vignettes, there was a case with antique toys, including a china-headed doll, black-haired with a flat, Mary Todd Lincoln style coiffure. I took a picture of her one year. Alas, by 1985, the last time I was at Front Street, the doll was gone. A little pile of dust rested where her feet once stood.

The Hastings House of Yesterday had its own collection of dolls, and there is a photo of me at age ten, standing in front of a magnificent case of antique and vintage dolls. It became our family Christmas card that year. Again, by 1985, the dolls had been thinned out, and many exhibits had changed.

Grand Island had a museum near our Holiday Inn with a large antique German bisque doll sitting in a buggy. This was the Stuhr Museum of the Pioneer Home. I think the doll was a Kestner, with blonde hair and a white dress and bonnet. From there, I brought home a pink-painted, upholstered doll chair made from a soda can. Now, these tin-can doll house furnishings are themselves desirable collectibles. The Grand Island Holiday Inn also had a great dinner buffet, and a painting commemorating a local incident where two boys escaping two assailants were riding on the same horse. The boys were shot by the same arrow. It pierced one boys' body to impale itself in the main rider's back. Both children survived.

Ft. Cody was an authentically fake fort, with Manikins trying to climb the walls, and life-sized Indians shooting arrows at them. My first Native American doll was called "Sioux Princess" and was a 7.5-inch Dress me doll, brown skinned, hand dressed in buckskin, beads, and feathers, with a baby or "Papoose" on her back, also of hard plastic. She was dressed and distributed by Carlson Dolls, that once allegedly sold the Mary McAvoy Skookums dolls and Minnetonka Moccasins. I fell in love with that doll. I had seen other little plastic souvenir Indian dolls at my grandmother's house, but I hadn't had my own before now.

We picked up many Native American dolls between Grand Island and San Jose. We found wonderful Carlson dolls, including some 24-inch examples that were too pricey for my allowance, but I found a lot of the dolls representing different Native peoples from five inches to about 12 inches. The company dressed its dolls in the US and went out of business around 20 years ago, but many of the dolls can still be found with original tags. They also made Inuit dolls, Hawaiian dolls, and historical figures like The Sprit of 76 and George Washington. The Little America Resort had a large selection of them and other dolls. Disneyland and Knott's Berry Farm also had terrific selections.

In Gallup, NM, and Flagstaff, AZ, I found many Navajo dolls; some were handmade cloth figures, a few of Navajo women sitting at their looms weaving tiny rugs. A large cloth man came from Indian City, a business founded by Native Americans to sell Native American art objects. Members of the Tribes could get discounts.

My first Kachina was from Nebraska, and was called "Navajo Love God." At around five inches in red and blue with a yellow feather, it was crude and turned on a lathe. You could tell because of the triangular piece cut out of its skirt. I loved him, but he was a far cry from the "real" Hopi and Zuni Kachinas carved from cottonwood root and signed by their makers.

Traditional, ancient Kachina dolls are hand carved in one piece, hands close to their bodies. Yei figures, or flat dolls given to babies, are small and colorfully painted. During the mid-'60s–early '70s, Large, fantastic Kachinas depicting dancers were carved with arms and feet simulating dance movement. They wore real jewelry, feathers, leather breech cloths, and in some cases, gingham shirts and blue jeans! Early dolls had eagle feathers. When it became illegal to use eagle feathers, because eagles were declared endangered species, we saw whole glass cases marked off limits in galleries and souvenir shops because he Kachinas had the Eagle feathers and could not be sold. I have no idea what happened to them, or if the feathers were removed later. Jesse Walter Fewkes first wrote a seminal book on Kachinas, but it has been attacked and discredited by Native American writers. John Wayne and Senator Barry

Goldwater collected Kachina dolls. So did my University of Iowa College of Law Civ Lit Prof, Allan Vestal. We had a nice talk about them one day in his office after I told him I was having hard time with Rule 4 of the Fed Rules of Civ Pro.

True Kachinas are probably Hopi and Zuni, but similar figures do exist in the Navajo and Apache culture. The Apache mountain spirit is depicted as one of my Kachinas, and though he seems menacing with is black hood, he represents and protects young girls, marriage, medicine and laughter. Mudheads and striped Zuni figures are the clowns, and the female corn maiden is a favorite of mine. Some Kachinas are too sacred to represent. Others are given to children after special ceremonies. I have some stylistically carved as art objects, representing Long Hair Kachinas. I also have sweaters, purses, and jewelry decorated with them, as well as prints and books.

The maker of the Maria pots was into dolls, and learned to dress and sell them before she made pottery. Helen Cordero created the famous Story-teller dolls, a figure with lots of little figures attached, while the main figure tells "stories."[1]

Zuni fetishes of all kinds are popular with doll and miniature collectors. I used to find terrific one's in a store in St Charles, IL, along with other examples of Native American Dolls and jewelry. It was my mothers' favorite place and mine.

I used to see life-sized Skookums mannikins in museums like The Hauberg and in Cavanaugh's antiques, formerly of Dubuque, but no more. I found lots of Skookums dolls and knockoffs out west. Some were celluloid, and came from Wisconsin Dells, mint, as old store stock. Little babies were meant to be attached to postcards and mailed and came from Wyoming.

As the song "Cherokee Nation" by Paul Revere and the Raiders implied, some stone bisque Indian dolls made in Japan with plastic clothes of "pleather" were sold as souvenirs during the '40s and '50s. I have some of these as well. A friend and I used to play the guitar and sing this and other songs at school and club gatherings in 8th and 9th grade.

Now, elaborately dressed Native American dolls made in China by Cathay House and other companies are sold in Indian stores, at Native American Shows sometimes, and in dolls shows. Artists like June Goodnow made

---

[1] Actor Robert Clary of Hogan's Heroes dressed French dolls for extra money for his family. Apparently, Louisa May Alcott did, too, and astronomer Maria Mitchell liked sewing doll clothes. Convicted Murder Susan Atkins stole doll clothes from the Woolworth's in downtown San Jose I used to go there, to, but I paid for my doll clothes.

authentic examples, and Pocahontas by Disney encouraged an interest in Native American dolls and cultures. Native American Barbie did the same and inspired knock-offs. I see some of these objects at high prices occasionally; though not authentic, they are a variation on a theme. German doll makers like Armand Marseilles also made brown bisque Indian dolls, and these are sought after by antique doll collectors.

In Old Spanish Town, Albuquerque, I found a doll shop, and many amazing dolls from Spain and Mexico as well as Native American dolls. Some were less than an inch high, carved Kachinas. Some were made of silver. One set had its own miniature Kiva. I always had a field day, and collapsed happy and sated for a wonderful dinner at the restaurant La Placita. My mother loved Old Spanish Town; I would help her pick out miniatures for the Christmas Piñata party she held for her Spanish Classes each year at Rock Island High School.

I bought kits to make traditional dolls for infants; these were made of yarn, beads, and ands simple materials. We bought one in Winnemucca, Nevada. I also bought a carved Indian doll of a woman there; she was a miniature of the life-sized statues that decorated their town. A traditional Big Nose doll came from Wyoming. From the Grand Canyon lodge, came Zuni beaded dolls and tiny figures and baskets of woven horsehair.

I wanted a buckskin doll very badly, but they were very expensive. Even today, there are entire magazine issues devoted to traditional Native American dolls. I finally made my own out of an old purse. I studied and did the beading, and attached a bird feather my mother picked up in Mexico. I found other examples later at The Field Museum in Chicago, and at doll shows. At one Wisconsin Dells museum, I bought a wonderful Apache doll. From Peoria, came a faithful replica of an Iroquois faceless doll of cornhusks and cloth. The River Museum in Peoria has a nice example of a Native American doll and some other artifacts. Unfortunately, that museum would not accept a collection of several thousand dolls a dying woman tried to leave to them. The woman's collection began when she lost her only child and her husband gave her a doll to help ease her grief.

Over the years, I found figurines, more Kachinas, Cherokee cornhusk dolls, Canadian Inuit dolls of skins and soapstone, Inuit carvings of stone and bone, Canadian handmade cloth dolls and artist dolls dressed in leather, Navajo Sand paintings, Navajo women made of porcelain and plastic, dressed in Navajo velvet. I used to see these women dressed like this shopping in stores. One doll I had even had contemporary material for a skirt that decorated with pink teddy bears. My mother was shocked; she wanted me to buy something more traditional, but the real women wore calicos like this with their hand-woven shawls and velvet blouses. I dressed one Anne Boleyn doll I made in rust-colored Navajo velvet, too.

I painted many Native American dolls and statues later in ceramics courses, and bought the Indian doll from the stamp series, too. Indian dolls, or Native American dolls, encompass figures from South America, Mexico, and Central America as well. I found native dolls from Brazil of Rubber, from Venezuela, and from Argentina, some made of grasses and other plants. Pre-Columbian statues and heads are also part of this grouping, as are the precious objects Anne Rice wrote of in *Merrick the Vampire*. I loved Carlos Fuentes' short story "Chac Mol," about the blood thirsty Toltec rain god statute that came to life in his new owner's home and took over his identity. In the last scene, the statue Chac Mol answers the door wearing his owner's bath robe! I had the chance in 1981 to meek Carlos Fuentes, and to shake his hand and complement him on "Chac Mol." I think it gave him pleasure to hear, and he laughed and said in Spanish, *"Tu tienes que olvidar Chac Mol!"* ("You need to forget Chac Mol!") There I was, just returned from Spain, a college senior, in a black and white pinstriped school dress with a red bow, white collar and cuffs, the only time I've ever felt star struck by celebrity. We were at Knox College, with my Spanish teachers, my International Law teacher and his wife, and a few students. My law prof actually became QC Poet Laureate at one point, and his wife was from Spain. She still teaches at the same places I do from time to time.

The Ancient Nampa Figurine of Idaho, a few inches long of clay, may be the oldest doll of all time. It was found in a stratum of earth where most artifacts are about three million years old. Since its discovery in 1889, many argue the figurine **is** a fake, but others deny it and argue it is real. The mystery is it would have been impossible to plant it as a fake at the level it was found.

As Dr. Bachmann has pointed out in *Dolls the Wide World Over,* many cultures have these spiritual figures, some sacred, some protective, that are often given to children after special ceremonies. Cultural that seemingly have nothing in common with each other have dolls that stand in for lost twins, or are protective spirits. The Ashanti have the dolls made with big heads and carved foreheads meant to ensure intelligence and beauty. The dolls are given to young girls, who often carry them on their backs till they have families of their own. Often, the dolls are kept even after children are born. Bachmann writes of similar African dolls, passed from generation to generation that may not be sold or thrown out lest their former owners suffer death or misfortune. In some parts of Africa, if a child dies, a doll replaces it as its twin. The very idea of the doll makes them into our image, either literally or figuratively. The Kachinas are similar to the Santos and guardian angel figures that are found in

Christian homes all over the world. Russia has Santos figures carved in wood, and they appear in Bachmann's book and in my friend Mary Hillier's book, *Dolls and Doll Makers*.

Nabor kids are carved Nunis designed by a doll artist from Alaska. They have large eyes and are carved from wood. Nunis are small; one-piece wooden dolls, with large eyes, and dressed in scraps of fur. Some appear on key chains.

One notable Native American doll of literature is the little souvenir doll Humbert. Humbert bought his teen aged paramour in *Lolita* by Nabokov.

The late Edwina Mueller, founder and editor of *Doll Castle News*, frequently called on her readers to donate dolls, toys, and stuffed animals to schools for Native American Children. I am happy to say that my former club at school continued the tradition for as long as they existed. Now, I carry it on by sending money, but we have sent toys, small dolls, books, and clothing to one of the schools Mrs. Muller used to mentor for some time.

Chapter 18: The Doll-Making Industry Begins

Following the era of the ancient dolls, Europe became a major hub for doll production. These dolls were primarily made of wood. Primitive wooden stump dolls from 16th and 17th century England number less than 30 today. The Grodnertal area of Germany produced many peg wooden dolls, a type of doll that has very simple peg joints and resembles a clothespin. A page from the 15th century book, *Hortus Sanitatus* shows doll or puppet makers at work making heads of wood or some kind of composition, a substitute for wood. Composition is a collective term for mixtures of pulped wood or paper that were used to make doll heads and bodies. These mixtures were molded under pressure, creating a durable doll that could be mass produced. Manufacturers closely guarded the recipes for their mixtures, sometimes using strange ingredients like ash or eggshells. Papier mâché, a type of composition, was one of the most popular mixtures.

In addition to wooden dolls, wax dolls were popular in the 17th and 18th centuries. Munich was a major manufacturing center for wax dolls, but some of the most distinctive wax dolls were created in England between 1850 and 1930. Famous makers were Montanari, Pierotti, Peck, and Vargas. Anna Morandi, an 18th century anatomist featured in the blog "Morbid Anatomy" created life-sized wax figures for anatomical studies called "Venuses." She also did a detailed self-portrait. Mme. Tussaud escaped the French Revolution where she was compelled to model the heads of those recently guillotined. She fled to London, and the first Tussaud's wax museum went into business. It, and many others around the world, is still operating.

Wax modelers would model a doll head in wax or clay, and then use plaster to create a mold from the head. Then they would pour melted wax into the cast. The wax for the head would be very thin, no more than three mm. One of the first dolls that portrayed a baby was made in England from wax at the beginning of the 19th century.

Porcelain became popular at the beginning of the 19th century. Porcelain is made by firing special clays in a kiln at more than 2372 degrees Fahrenheit. Only a few clays can withstand firing at such high temperatures. Porcelain is used generically to refer to both china and bisque dolls. China is glazed, whereas bisque is unglazed. Germany, France, and Denmark started creating china heads for dolls in the 1840s. China heads were replaced by heads made of bisque in the 1860s. Bisque, which is fired twice with color added to it after the first firing, looked more like skin than china did.

So popular were china heads, and it has been estimated that over 1 billion were made between the years 1830 and 1940. The two World Wars drastically affected the doll industry.

The French "bébé" was popular in the 1880s, and it has become a highly sought-after doll today. The bébé, first made in the 1850s, was unique from its predecessors because it depicted a younger girl. Ironically, one of the most popular of these dolls was modeled allegedly not after a little girl, but after a portrait of a little boy, who would later become Henry IV of France. Called the Jumeau Triste, or Long-faced Jumeau, this doll was supposedly the favorite of Buffalo Bill Cody. I saw an example at The Cody Museum in Wyoming during the 1970s, that he is said to have bought for his daughter. I have artists' versions of this doll, and my husband photographed one of them for the LeClaire Museum in Iowa. LeClaire was the birth place of Buffalo Bill. I gave the photo to the museum, but never heard from them. They do have a doll collection. Many years later, I edited and contributed to a book of host stories called *The Legend of Tugfest*, published by 918studio. There were 13 stories, and Mike Wolf of American Pickers did the forward. All proceeds benefited the museum.

Until the bébé was introduced, most dolls were representations of adults. Although the French dolls were unrivaled in their artistry, German bisque dolls became quite popular because they were not as expensive. Kammer & Reinhardt introduced a bisque character doll in the 1900s, starting a trend of creating realistic dolls.

For centuries, rag dolls were made by mothers for their children. Rag dolls refer generically to dolls made of any fabric. Cloth dolls refer to a subset of rag dolls made of linen or cotton. Commercially produced rag dolls were first introduced in the 1850s by English and American manufacturers. Although, not as sophisticated as dolls made from other materials, rag dolls were well-loved, often as a child's first toy. Izannah Walker and Martha Chase were noted makers of cloth dolls. Beecher Babies, created by Julia Ward Beecher were soft sculpture dolls that became popular. Beecher was related to Julia Ward Howe "The Battle Hymn of The Republic", and Harriet Beecher Stowe, *Uncle Tom's Cabin.*

Doll-making did not become an industry in the United States until after the Civil War in the 1860s. Doll production was concentrated in New England, with dolls made from a variety of materials such as leather, rubber, papier mâché, and cloth. Celluloid was developed in New Jersey in the late 1860s and was used to manufacture dolls until the mid-1950s. German, French, American, and Japanese factories churned out cheaply produced celluloid dolls in mass quantities. However, celluloid fell out of favor because of its extreme flammability and propensity to fade in bright light.

After World War II, doll makers experimented with plastics. Hard plastic dolls were manufactured in the 1940s. They resembled composition dolls, but they were much more durable. Other materials used in doll manufacturing included rubber, foam rubber, and vinyl in the 1950s and 1960s. Vinyl changed doll-making, allowing doll makers to root hair into the head, rather than using wigs or painting the hair. Although most dolls are now mass-manufactured using these modern materials, many modern doll makers are using the traditional materials of the past to make collectible dolls.

Chapter 19: Paper Dolls

Before I start, let me note that this is the best site I've found for paper dolls and their history, plus it has lavish illustrations; The Paper Collector. http://thepapercollector.blogspot.com/

It is a blog, but I like the beginning of research with blogs; I find most are written by people who are passionate and who care. This one is no exception.

Paper has existed for centuries, and was probably invented by the Chinese. Though, the Ancient Egyptians had papyrus, and others wrote on vellum. Rare medieval manuscripts and illuminations were painted by hand in monasteries by talented monks; the famous tome of these is *The Book of Kells*, represented in artwork done for Colleen Moore's Fairy Castle.

Early paper could be traced to the Papyrus plant, known as The Paper Plant. Thor Heyerdahl wrote about creating a boat of Papyrus in *The Ra Expedition*, which was also made into a film. I remember when my dad took me to see it on a Tuesday night; I had a reprieve from the infinite math homework I was assigned. Ancient Egyptians wrote hieroglyphics or papyrus, and their scrolls and paintings were really early versions of books. Papyrus was as valuable to the ancient as paper, with its rag, linen, plant content would be later. Heyerdahl writes of the controversy surrounding his voyage; many thought a papyrus boat could not make the journey, but he proved it could.

In fact, even today, paper is becoming scarcer. Paper dolls have shot up in price, as has all ephemera. I was discussing this fact at the "megamansion" estate sale my friend was having. She had amazing paper, some photos, books, pamphlets, ledger books, sheet music, lithographs of little Victorian girls, prints, at very reasonable prices. I play the music, and use the rest for research and collage projects. In this paperless world, many things are recycled, which is good, but some, like paper dolls and old catalogs, should be preserved for future generations. I recently bought a Betty Furness kitchen gadget, and was reminded of Ms. Furness and the tour of her designer closet that she gave on *The Today Show*. It was always on or near Christmas Eve, and she wore a red and green tweed designer suit for the holidays. In one segment, she also talked about what would be collectible in the future. She suggested saving ads, or even ad inserts, with unusual graphics or products by placing them in the bottom of a hope cedar chest.

Books and paper were rare and prized in Europe. Wealthy people posed with their libraries, showing that the more books they owned, the wealthier they were. The book *A Gentle Madness* describes famous book collectors, all wealthy, who had "rock star" status. Sor Juana Ines de la Cruz, a 17th century Mexican scholar, mathematician, poet and writer who was also a child prodigy and a nun, kept a library of 2500 books and manuscripts in her cell. She is often painted with them. For her talent and genius, she was famous in both Spain and Mexico, and was the granddaughter of the viceroy of Mexico. She died from the plague at around 45, while nursing others who were ill Early manuscripts that have survived by Cervantes, Byron, Keats, Wordsworth, and other 15th-19th century writers show that they conserved paper, saved old manuscripts, wrote on scratch paper, and wrote all over the page, turning it upside down, writing on margins, etc. Paper was collected and sold at rag and bone shops, and would not be thrown out. Our modern-day recycling hearkens back to this era.

Wealthy people were often painted in front of their books and libraries; because they were wealthy, they could afford such things. Wealthy noblewomen were shown with the trappings of education, including their books. Books and paper were sacred to women writers, who often suffered, if not died for their art. For wealthy woman, they could only speak freely when facing death, or if they could claim insanity. Paper, pen, books, and in the case of artists like Artemisia Gentileschi, canvas, were very nearly religious objects.

In Japan, origami has long been a treasured art. Figures of paper have often represented the souls of the departed and were used in ceremonies where they were thrown into water at the end. Paper figures are burned in similar rites in Malaysia. Paper scrolls play a role in the Japanese Milky Way festival, as described by Rumer Godden in her story of two Japanese dolls, *Miss Happiness and Miss Flower*. There is a paper doll in love with a lead soldier in Hans Christian Andersen's "The Steadfast Tin Soldier."

As we know them, paper dolls were created in the 18th century, more as amusements for adults than children. Indeed, Mary Hillier and Helen Young have written that 19th century jointed pantins originated in France. "Pantin" is another French word for a puppet or marionette. The pantins were made like jumping Jacks. Supposedly, a law was written prohibiting them, lest pregnant women give birth to deformed children because they played too much with the paper dolls themselves. These jumping jacks still exist. Shackman reproduced the original Polichinelle varieties, but they are also made in wood. Often, they come from Germany or Italy. I have a rare, X-rated-one done in metal involving a couple with 1920s' style hairdos. This is a family book; I'll leave the rest to your imagination.

Paper dolls were often hand tinted, and represented fashions of the day. There are fashion plates made of ivory, very thin, where images of hats and wigs are laid over a head to try out the latest styles. There are examples of these in the Cincinnati Museum of Art.

The books of foremost authority R. Lane Herron also feature great articles on paper dolls, as do the books of Janet Pagter John and Clara Hallard Fawcett. Mr. Herron was the first authority to write on and publish about paper dolls.

By the time *The History of Little Fanny* and *The History of Little Henry* came around, lithography was being used in books and paper, and paper dolls could now be lithographed and mass produced. Fine examples exist from the 1820s to 1890s. Paper dolls, often printed on both sides, where used to advertised products, so that Lion Coffee and other companies used them as others did trade cards. There is also as set featuring Queen Isabella and other European queens that dates from the Columbian Exhibition.

There will be more on the handmade varieties that abound, some in 3D, as well as a word on paper toys and printables, as well as, paper doll houses. For those who crave more, I recommend Marilyn Waters' *The Toy Maker site,* Jim's Mini *Printables and* Marilee's *Paper Doll Page.*

England, according to Loretta Holz in *The How to Book of International Dolls,* takes credit for being the first to produce "true" paper dolls in about 1790. These were printed in sheets, ready to cut out, featuring the latest fashions, intended for adults; Yet, our earliest records of China and Japan show paper dolls were used in religious rituals where images were hung on trees, perhaps during The Milky Way Festival, and sometimes thrown into bodies of water with prayers; China, I think, also takes credit for inventing paper as we know it.

In any case, these sheets of paper dolls came to the US by 1840, and with *The History of Little Fanny* and *The History of Little Henry*, became children's toys. Holtz writes that by the 1850s on, paper dolls of famous people were all the rage, and there are examples of Jenny Lind and Maria Taglioni in prized collections, like the former Mary Merritt doll museum collection. If you have the auction catalog, you will be able to see for yourself.

Firms like Raphael Tuck, which was still producing greeting cards in the 1990s, began to create lithographed dolls, and commercial concerns like McLaughlin and Lion Coffee made historical dolls for the Columbian Exposition, especially of Queen Isabella and other historical figures. By the '20s, there were many homemade dolls, like those Laura Ingalls Wilder talks about, and celebrity dolls like those of Mary Pickford became popular. These were extremely popular between about 1930–1970, with *Gone with the Wind Dolls* (bought for a little friend who later wrote about her by Elizabeth Short, the Black Dahlia murder victim), and represented every major actress from Gene Tierney to Shirley Temple to Lucille Ball and The Partridge Family. Many were made by an artist named Queen Holden, and others were printed by Whitman Publishing. Three-dimensional dolls like Barbie, Raggedy Ann, and Cheerful Tearful also had paper counterparts. Some doll had joints, or houses, other were magnetic and had wigs. The scouts had many varieties of paper dolls, and Lettie Lane, Dolly Dingle, and Betsy McCall began to appear in magazines. ODACA is an organization for paper doll artists, and *The Paper Doll Quarterly* and *Paper Soldier* were publications that featured them. Many doll magazines had paper dolls, and some like *Doll Castle News* still feature them.

I have many, many examples, from miniatures to nearly life-sized manikins. Some are handmade, and even done on my computer. Virtual paper dolls exist online for doll play, and there is software for creating them.

Chapter 20: Asia

Dolls from Asia have played a role in doll-collecting for thousands of years. In fact, the largest toy museum in the world, including dolls, is in Penang, Malaysia. Puppets have been a crucial part of Japanese culture for centuries, as shadow puppets, marionettes; and Chinese theater dolls have been important in China and its provinces. Door of Hope dolls are favorites with collectors, as are the many Japanese dolls, including Friendship dolls, Dogun figures, Netsuke, Hinamatsuri dolls, Ichimatsu Ningyo, Bunraku, Karakuri, Kokeshi dolls, Hakata dolls, Kabuki figures, Boys' Day figures, Satsuma china, nesting dolls, Samurai of all kinds and more.

Alan Scott Pate is clearly the expert in these matters, and his website and online store are a virtual museum for those who love Asian dolls. A recent auction by Theriault's also featured a stellar collection of Japanese dolls, and their Love, Shirley Temple auction showcased a life-size doll sent to Temple by the children of Hawaii.

Indonesia has carved dolls, tourist figures and shadow puppets, some of carved wood, some of paper, and some of buffalo hide.

Dolls are very popular in India, and there are several museums there, including Shankar's International Doll Museum in New Delhi.

Vietnam has a history of dolls as well. Thin plastic dolls in traditional dress were popular souvenirs during the Vietnam War. Our local newspaper, *The Rock Island Argus*, had a picture of one of these dolls being searched at an airport for bombs.

There are dolls shops today in Vietnam that create artists, BJD type dolls as well as traditional dolls in costume. Older Vietnamese dolls are made of cloth stretched over wire or composition.

Singapore provides lovely tourist dolls.

Thailand has a tradition involving puppets and dolls of all kinds. Some are interesting china heads glazed in blue and white. Others are realistic figures of clay molded over wire. They are created in special schools. Dancing figures of all kinds are also made in schools and are usually mixed media, primarily cloth over wire. Other costume dolls are also popular, and there is even a Thailand Barbie.

Malaysia has paper and papier mâché figures on a stick that is meant to be burned in sacred fires. Malaysia also provides gorgeous costume dolls of cloth and vinyl dressed in silk.

China may very well lead the toy making industry, with its own manufacturers and importers, and American and other international companies that make their dolls in China.

Toy making in China is controversial, to say the least. The lead paint scare of 2007/2008 made many collectors rethink their choices, and allegations of Chinese goods, including toys, being produced by "slave labor" have fueled the fire. In fact, the late Madame Mao allegedly made dolls while imprisoned. Ironically, as a young actress, she starred in a production of Ibsen's *The Dolls House*.

Gunther van Hagen, a German pathologist living in China has created mummified figures out of the bodies of real humans with the skin removed to show the skeleton muscular structure. They are posed realistically, and his art, as it were, has caught on in China. A traveling exhibit of similar figures by other artists showcases the figures, and there is controversy that some of the figures are the bodies of those executed by the Chinese government. These macabre statues stretch the concept of dolls' relationship to corpses, as explored by Rainier Marie Rilke and others.

Chinese tomb figures from antiquity, as well as the Han soldiers from the emperor's tomb have become iconic. The soldiers are reproduced in all media, even resin and metal, and appear as garden ornaments or small figurines. There is even a novel dedicated to them, called *The Emperor's Tomb*.

Cousins of dolls, both sacred and profane, abound in China and other parts of Asia. The largest statue in the world represents Buddha, and there are dozens and dozens of statues and figurines of Buddha and the Seven Immortals available. Some are made of precious metals, jade, and precious stones. In shrines all over Asia, Buddha statutes are honored by dressing them in clothes and making offerings of food and milk. In this, the statues are like the early Santos of the Catholic Church that were joined with real hair, glass eyes, and clothing. Offerings of food and flowers were often brought in tribute to them as well.

Old ivory dolls are now considered contraband. Some dolls of bone include the doctors' ladies that represent a nude woman reclined on a couch. A maid would take the doll to a physician and point out where her mistress' ailments were.

Janet Pagter Johl writes of a doll from China carved out of cake of ink. I have block of tea carved this way that represents a pagoda. Figural objects made of graphite that double as pencils are available today.

Currently, China makes BJD dolls, souvenir dolls, especially from Tibet and Taiwan, figurines, and expensive life-sized "living dolls" for adult entertainment. The Chinese manufacture toys for North Korea, including tin toys of tanks and little guns.

Many stuffed animals and tiny crocheted figures are also made in China. These dolls and figures first began to arrive after President Nixon's historic trip to China around 50 years ago. China also makes Japanese dolls in the traditional style with gofun at a fraction of the price dolls in Japan would cost.

Dolls exist in Afghanistan, but it is hard to find them. I have male and female examples dressed in traditional costumes, standing on a wooden base, with inscriptions on them. One male doll is dressed in a style similar to Osama bin Laden with rifle in his arms; he dates from the '50s. Dolls in many Islamic countries are allowed as toys for children, but are not to be collected. As collectors' items, having them is considered forbidden idolatry. In fact, the Taliban blasted the faces off of gigantic statues of Buddha, carved into mountain sides. Attempts are being made to restore them, even as I write.

A recent news story about ISIS talked about a school where young children practiced beheading people on dolls. Such brutality is not new; Mary I of England, aka Bloody Mary, practiced her role as queen by beheading the blooms off flowers.

South Korea makes dolls of wood, of wire and silk, and ceramic. They make their own stuffed animals, brass figures, bobble heads, and play dolls. There is a whole shopping district dedicated to toys and to children reminiscent of the Nuremburg Toy Fair. Many stuffed animals are also made their, and are also called "dolls."

North Korea imports toys from China, particularly war toys. North Korean children usually cannot afford the toys imported, and play games, when they can, that don't involve toys or equipment. One North Korean blogger alleges that a toy factory in North Korea produces 100,000 dolls per day, but there is no source for the statistic. Another YouTube video shows a North Korean toy store, loaded with strollers, children's clothing, western and traditional, plastic toys and animals, stuffed animals, and other things similar to Hello Kitty! Yet, this store is just a staged setting; no one in North Korea can afford the goods there, though by our standards, they are cheap and tawdry.

As with everything else, toys are regulated by the whims of Kim Jong Un, the "Dear Leader" or Dictator of the North. Recently, he posed with two "unauthorized" stuffed animals confiscated by his minions.

I am not sure how true this is, but the film *Team America* which features marionettes and miniatures, showed a scene where the late dictator of North Korea, Kim Jong Il, posed with his collection of Hummel figurines.

Dolls of all kinds are popular in the Philippines, as well. Many are cloth over silk and wear traditional attire. Lovely stone bisque dolls dressed paper clothing similar to the Japanese kimono were imported to the US during the late '80s.

March 3rd is the day of the Hinamatsuri or Japanese Doll Festival. For great histories of this wonderful holiday involving tiered displays of special dolls, peach blossoms, and blessings for the health of young girls, read *Miss Happiness and Miss Flower* by Rumer Godden, friend of Tasha Tudor, who was so kind to me when I wrote my dissertation. Godden had her own real Japanese doll house, made to her own specifications. Heiress Huguette Clark had several heirloom quality Japanese doll houses that she planned to the tiniest authentic detail. My friend Mary Hillier has excellent information in her *Dolls and Doll Makers*, and Alan Scott Pate and Lea Baten are also excellent sources and noted authors on Japanese dolls of all types. I have a foldout Hina set that dates to the Korean War and other Korean and Japanese dolls my Uncle Tom, an artist, brought from Korea.

Tom was a big contributor to my doll collection, and taught me to paint in oils. He repaired all sorts of dolls, and brought me one every weekend. He was a graduate of the School of the Art Institute, and very talented.

My introduction to Japanese dolls came early; I wasn't even in kindergarten when I became familiar with the many dolls and artifacts Uncle Tom brought home from The Korean War. He gave me many of the dolls he brought, including Miss Kyoto, a lovely ichimatsu example named for the city she came from. Later, my family and I brought many fine Japanese dolls from California. One baby is a friendship doll type many were Kokeshi or Hakata dolls. I looked many years for Hinamatsuri dolls; I finally found some at miniature shows, museums and in California, at antique stores. Store owners told me that Japanese families simply would not part with their dolls; this I was told in the late '70s. In the early '80s, my father went to Japan. The businessmen he visited sent me dolls as gifts, and Dad brought many more. He couldn't find the Hinamatsuri dolls, though; the store owners told him they had never heard of them.

By the time I read *Miss Happiness and Miss Flower*, I was hooked on Japanese dolls and was creating my own Japanese style houses for some of my impossibly tiny dolls. I was so excited, that I drew a Geisha doll on a kite for second grade art. My teacher and acquaintance of my mother from Delta Kappa Gamma, was scandalized. She made me tear up my gorgeous kite, doll and all, in front of the entire class. I was confused and humiliated, but at some level, I knew she thought Geishas were just bad women, or prostitutes. I got good grades from my teacher, but she loved embarrassing me. She called me her "little Greek girl" who had trouble counting money for math lessons because she played with her dolls at home. Hello! Again, I was seven. Another day, she made me trade a Mercury dime I had for a Roosevelt dime. She told me the Mercury dimes were "no good." I was indignant, but felt I had no choice. I was an early coin collector, too, and I knew Mercury dimes were desirable. My worst humiliation was on show and tell day. My friend, Wendy, brought a large Hummel figurine of a chimney sweep to class. Our teacher became ecstatic; she waxed poetic on Hummels. I thought Hummel meant figurine, or little doll. None of the other kids really knew what they were. At the time, Hummels were very popular collectibles. The next show and tell, I brought a Josef's Original figurine, thinking it was a Hummel. Miss D corrected me in front of the class, emphasizing the inferiority of my little figure. Now, Josef's are in vogue, and Hummels are an object of ridicule in some quarters. My mother was incensed. I know she had words with Miss Dl, but there wasn't much we could do. She was recovering from a heart attack, not her first. We weren't supposed to do anything that upset her. I think it made her into a resentful tyrant. The first quarter of school, her oldest sister, Mrs. Edna Dixon Garrett took the class. We loved Mrs. Garret, who showed us photos of herself wearing button down shoes and who told us stories of teaching in one-room school houses her first year. Her only child, a girl, died at five. She drove from Sherrard, and had enough love for all of us. I scared her without meaning to when I fell out of my desk and nearly hit the chalkboard ledge. She was afraid I'd broken my neck.

Next, we had the oldest sister, Miss Ruth. She had a class snowman jar that magically filled with candy after we put our heads down to nap. Miss Ruth was strict but fair, and had genuine affection for us. We learned well from her and we respected her. Miss Ruth lived with Miss D on the family farm in Viola. It sounded perfect, and I wanted to move there. The farm had been started by their father, and Ruth and Miss D live there with a gentleman called "the handyman."

The handyman went to dinner with them at The Gay Nineties and other restaurants. He was there to care for Miss D and "tuck" her in at night. He was an integral part of their lives. If we kids thought it was a little strange that the hired help had such personal access to his employers, we didn't say anything. Later, I read in Miss Ruth's obituary that "the handyman" was actually one of their older half-brothers.

Back to Japanese dolls, destroyed Geisha doll kites, notwithstanding. Japan has a long history of doll and idol making. The prehistoric inhabitants of Japan lived about 16,000 years ago. Figures called Dogu made of clay date from about 2500 B.C. According to the British Museum, "Dogu are from the earliest-dated tradition of pottery manufacture in the world, dating to the prehistoric Jomon period, which began 16,000 years ago. Most of the figures in the exhibition are from about 2500 BC to 1000 BC (the Middle and Late Jomon periods) and show the development of the sculptural form over time." There are some excellent examples of Dogu in The Milwaukee Public Museum, Milwaukee, WI.

Paper figures are associated with other holidays in Japan and there are temples devoted entirely to dolls, where worn out dolls are cremated. There are famous museums, including The Yokohama Doll Museum. Also, there are many schools where doll making is taught. Hakata is known for more contemporary clay dolls and wooden Kokeshi are currently very popular. There are also dolls representing Anime characters, Takara Barbie, Hello Kitty! Domo, Robots, Iron Japanese Figures, Bunraku

Japan's history of doll making dates to ancient times, and doll makers are often honored as living national treasures. The Friendship dolls sent to the US in 1927 have their own fascinating history, as do Kokeshi dolls, Hakata Clay dolls, Warrior Dolls, play dolls, Morimura Brothers bisque heads, celluloid dolls, paper dolls, and Takara dolls, robots, and anime figures. There are even shrines where beloved, but worn dolls are taken to be cremated. Many American doll and miniature museum feature impressive displays, and Kogura of Japan Town, San Jose, California, sells complete sets and individual dolls even today.

Anime, Blythe, Big Eye Dolls, Sailor Moon, Takara, Bandai, Manga: Japanese Anime characters have influenced dolls all over the world, and western culture, including Googlies, big-eyed dolls, and Margret Keane big eye paintings have, in turn, influenced Japanese art. One of the first dolls to adopt the big-eyed look that is still very popular in Japan is Kenner's Blythe.

I got my first Blythe in 1972 for Christmas. I love her because she reminded me of the big-eyed children of Margaret Keane and others. My room was full of these paintings, and there are even a couple big eyed dolls by other makers, Miss Gooch and Lonely Lisa by Royal Dolls, an eight-inch Japanese version of Lonely Lisa, a big-eyed Harlequin that matched the one in my painting, at least two other prints, and many, many cards that I bought Big-Eyed Children at the now defunct retail chain, Turnstyle. Years later, my Aunt Connie ran into Walter Keane, Margaret's ex-husband in Carmel. He was selling cards, and he autographed several for my Aunt. She then sent them to me. He told her he had painted the original portraits on which the cards were based, and this was in the early '90s, after the Keane's had divorced, and Walter's art fraud was exposed. Anyone who has seen *Big Eyes* knows that it was Margaret who painted the big-eyed children and animals!

Paintings of big eye children were everywhere; we used to eat at a local restaurant called Ben's Gourmet, and it was full of them, some more adolescents than little kids. I loved that wide-eyed look, but it is not unique to Keane's characters.

Googly eye dolls were made by Oscar Hitt, Kestner, Armand Marseilles, Freundlich (US, of composition), and many unknown Japanese firms. I have a pair of French bisque characters dressed in Alsace Lorraine costumes with the Googly look. Lenci dolls often have that characteristic, wide-eyed stare, as do their competitors from Italy, France, England, and Spain, where certain Roldan characters sport the look.

Small Portuguese costume dolls by Elena have those beguiling saucer eyes, so do carnival dolls, often called Kewpies, and flappers or Betty Boop characters from the '20s and '30s. Clara Bow figures and dolls have the cute, bee-stung lips and wide-eyed flapper look.

Chloe Preston was an artist who specialized in big-eyed cherubic children, and my friend Mary Hillier wrote a book about her art and dolls. It was to be her last book. I remember how proud and happy she was that it was published.

Rose O'Neill, a trained, fine artist and early suffragette, gave us her Kewpies and other characters, and they made the wide-eyed look iconic.

Anime has a following entirely its own, with drawing sets, action figures, original art, even a Manga Barbie portrait and Manga versions of *Jane Eyre* and *Wuthering Heights.* There are movies, like the ones mentioned and Ghosts in the Shell, which is about a set of robot dolls, and *Sgt. Frog*, which spoofs the Japanese Doll Festival in one episode.

Chapter 21: Doll Prices

With the current economy, I wonder a lot at prices in the antique market, especially the doll market. Antique dolls began to get really expensive when I first got interested in them, when I was about six or seven. I saw my first German bisque doll at Fantasy Land in Gettysburg when I was about five, and then my next group at the Folk Festival we used to have every summer at one of our junior highs. I was hooked. My first old doll was **a** Nancy Ann bisque in her box, given to me by my babysitter. Her daughter played with them, and her mother had saved them. She had other dolls, too. There was a ball-jointed doll with a sweet face, not bisque, about 14 inches long in an organdy dress that I loved, a tiny silk wrapped wire doll, a little hard plastic, probably Irwin, in a crocheted dress, and several Dress-me dolls and Nancy Anns. The Nancy Anns were in a trunk, and I can't even tell you how many there were, but Sandy, the daughter, was the baby, and had everything, so there were probably at least fifty.

Mrs. G., my babysitter, was in her late fifties, but she seemed so much older to me. I think the styles of the day didn't help. My mother was about 12 years younger at the time, but she looked like she could be Mrs. G's daughter. The next time I had a chance to see old dolls was our first trip to California in '67. The San Jose flea market was full of them, and my first big Arranbee compo baby came from there. It was "Little Angel," and her red dress was melting, its gilt polka dots fading. We kept the dress; one of my vintage cardboard Halloween skeletons is wearing it, but Little Angel had had a wardrobe of baby dresses, and now wears a vintage christening gown. I saw very old Mexican dolls that summer and boudoir dolls were going for 25.00, a fortune. We did buy a '40s composition doll from Mexico, and her dress didn't even resemble the once bright China Poblana costume, but her composition body and mohair wig were near mint. She wore her hair in braids on top of her head, like my mother did as a teen, and like I did once in a while. After I read Rumer Godden, she became Mrs. Plantagenet, and though not in scale, is still the real mother of my dollhouse family.

That fall, we went to the now defunct Women's Club antique show at our old Masonic Temple. The dolls were to die for. We were a paradise for big dealers, including Ralph's Antique Dolls. Prices were discouraging, but there were French bebés and fashions for under $100.00. They would soon climb to $600, then $1000, then the price of a mortgage. My first real antique doll came from that show, a tiny china Frozen Charlotte, named of course, Charlotte. We were thrilled, thought that $6.00 was a lot of money for us to pay. My mom made her tiny dresses, and she still has a gilt sleigh with upholstered pillows she sleeps in. That Christmas I read all about her in Helen *Young's The Complete Book of Doll Collecting*. This was my second doll book. The first was *Dolls* by John Noble, a 7th year birthday present. The third was written by my friend Mary Hillier, still a classic work, *Dolls and Doll Makers.* These were people who thought outside the box, and as a result, encouraged me to do so too, as a collector.

Now, antique dolls' prices have held steady, but they can still cost well over $100.000, far more than that in the case of the famous Albert Marque that was just sold, I have to wonder who sets these prices, and what do they want to accomplish? Every good collection and antique shop when I was growing up had a variety of bisques, china heads, French bisques, and nice miniatures. They weren't priced out of the market yet. Collectible dolls didn't exist, and vintage Barbies cost under $2.00, and I could buy cases of them with clothes for less than that. Shackman and a few ladies like my Aunt Rose made reproductions, but Emma Clear reproduction dolls were already in a league of their own. Foreign dolls and Mme. Alexanders made up the collections of lucky little girls, and Shirley Temple was about the only compo doll people seemed to want. Paper doll collectors were just getting started.

Modern dolls were a collecting after thought, but I kept my babies, figuring they would in time be valuable. I was right. Pat Smith's books on modern dolls, beginning in 1972, began to identify modern dolls and also to set prices, which also began to rise. These prices have begun to bottom out, and I have been able to replace the few dolls that did get given away (when I believed as a child that poor little children went to The Salvation Army for toys), and yesterday, I had a real moment of serendipity. One of those Salvation Army giveaways found her way back to my collection. I recognized her right away, and she came back home for fifty cents. She was at a local flea market, absolutely filthy, a 12-inch hard vinyl doll, made by Eeegee in the sixties. She was one of the dolls my uncle used to bring on weekends. She was still wearing the one-piece yellow flannel PJs that belonged to one of my Uneeda dolls that had a Styrofoam body built over wire. She hadn't traveled far. I'd like to think some of her bad condition was due to being well loved, but who knows?

What if all doll prices dipped, and they were no longer playthings of the rich? What if all dealers banded together and said no doll would be over

$1000? This is real fairy tale thinking; many people, including friends and acquaintances of mine, make a living out of high-end dolls. But, as Helen Young used to say, there are collections and accumulations. It bothers me that museums close, and it bothers me even more that they de-access their permanent collections, either for money, or because they are like antique stores in decline. I know of at least one collection often written about that has all the rare bisques, all-pristine, none under 15 thousand dollars in value, most worth more. After seeing pictures of about ten of them, they all looked alike to me. The old celebrated collections Johl and St. George wrote about no longer exist. Everything is too specialized, and the variations on a theme begin to merge together when I look at them. Advanced collector now means a millionaire or a dealer who can afford to buy and sell in movie star circles, though there are some movie stars who collect who prefer stuffed animals, modern dolls, reproductions, or artist dolls. Not even billionaires and millionaires always want to shell out fortunes for one doll. Collector and dealer are not interchangeable. Both are fine titles, and they can run into each other now and then, but not everyone collects to sell.

Veteran authors and collectors who owned dolls that were worth thousands were horrified that that dolls were costing five, ten, one hundred thousand dollars. Even new dolls for children often begin in the $40.00 range, and American Girls can run parents into thousands of dollars if they buy everything to go with the dolls, which now cost close to $100. Tonner, Wright, Iaccono, Deval, Ortiz, and other artists are out of the price range of most collectors. And, the motto is no longer, "Buy what you love," but "Buy what is a good investment." Well, personally, I say contribute to your IRA, buy bonds, invest in CDs, mutual funds, your 401k, or even play the Market, albeit prudently. Dolls are not an investment per se. Plunges in the secondary market have shown that interest can wane, and speculating can be dangerous.

Collections are meant to be kept for them to vest, any collections. Quick turnarounds among dealers in all antiques are fascinating to observe, but are they setting a good example? Who knows? I love *Antiques Roadshow*, but a good yard sale is getting harder and harder to find because of the show. People check and compare prices to The Roadshow's, and everyone now checks out eBay and Etsy before pricing their items. It isn't just about getting rid of stuff anymore. I love eBay and Etsy, but good antique shops, even malls are few and far between. I love books on quirky antiques and collectibles, but once one is written (and I include mine in these comments) prices just go up and up. Why do we write, I ask, to boost prices, corner markets, or inspire others to follow in our footsteps?

Also, there is often a glut in availability because anyone can put dolls on computer auctions. Even I get jaded sometimes, and rare doesn't mean what it used to mean. Any more, I think it is rare if I can't find it on a computer auction, or in a book!

But, let's look locally. Dolls in all types of condition, made of all materials, disappear off the shelves our local thrift stores and rummage sales. I see people grabbing CPK dolls, and Alexanders of all types do very well at doll shows and estate sales. Doll parts do well on online auctions, and broken, dug up bisque heads are popular no matter what. A & AM 370 and 390 dolls are pooh-poohed by some dealers, but they sell very quickly, again, in any condition. I've seen many people proudly show them at lectures as their family heirlooms, and the rest of the audience ooh and aah about them. Grown men have tried to buy foreign dolls and Dress-me dolls out from under me everywhere I go.

The new, super expensive ball jointed dolls are becoming status items; I see Generation Xers carrying them around, and Living Dead Dolls and Goth dolls are attracting new doll collectors in the same tradition that Barbie, CPK, Raggedy Ann, and Precious Moments dolls attract them.

Hummels are also ridiculed, but they are still desirable to most people, and selling well. They are still expensive, and still do well in antique malls where I live. I still love them. My mother and I collected the ones with dolls and toys, but we managed to gather quite a few others, including dolls, plates, and other Goebel figurines.

My experience with pricing collectibles shows several different findings. First, whenever someone writes a book about something, that item begin to appear I more antique show and flea markets, and prices go up.

Next, prices vary in different parts of the country, and even in the world. I watched a rare Cobo Alice dolls show up on the British Antiques Road Show priced at around $60. In the late '80s, I saw one at the Pheasant Run Antique Show in Chicago Land price at over $700. In England, the doll wasn't that thrilling. Antique Japanese dolls in the San Francisco Bay Area cost far less than they did in the Midwest in the late '80s, if you could find them east of San Francisco.

When Pat Smith wrote her first volume in the Modern Collector's Dolls series, prices even for rare dolls were usually under $100. By 1980, some of the same dolls were bringing over $1000. The so-called Hawaiian Shirley Temple was listed at around $75 in the early books, then, she was listed at over $1200 a few years later. Now, she is turning up on eBay for between $275–$600.

Smith believed that dolls should be sold at 40% over what the dealer paid for them. It is just a guideline, but it seemed to me that it made sense. Also, modern dolls often arrived in played with condition. They needed refurbishing, and there were many articles in magazines like *National Doll World* and *Doll Designs* that showed how to re-root doll hair, re-wig dolls, make clothes and shoes from patterns, and clean vinyl dolls. Refurbished dolls brought a lot of money, sometimes more than the doll would bring in good condition.

Some blame online auctions for the demise in the modern and vintage doll market, though such dolls do well on Etsy and Amazon.com. It is true that many collectibles that were hard to find now flooded the online auction market. For example, Marilynn Ross's Dark Shadows novels were one very hard to locate and were highly collectible; In the late '90s, I was able to locate almost an entire set for a very low price through online sales sponsored by the former Hobby Central on AOL.

Lots of collectors still buy at doll shows; for a while it seemed that doll shows might die out, but attendance has been good at the big NADDA shows, and at our local shows. I have done well at shows, but one dealer friend, and shop owner I knew in California, believed that dealers brought their junk to shows. Some collectors only bought at auctions, or through ads in magazines like *Doll Reader* or *Hobbies*, both now out of publication. The COVID 19 pandemic has forced many shows online.

Popularity of dolls changes, too. For a while, it was Madame Alexander, vintage or new. You couldn't buy them in stores or for a while, directly from the company. Now, they appear discounted at places like T. J. MAXX, and you can buy directly from the company. At Estate sales, Alexanders that sold for over $300 pop up for $15 in their boxes.

At one point, I saw A&M 370s and 390s selling for as much as $800 in antique stores. Now, I see them at doll show and in online auctions for under $100. My advice is to ignore the doll snobs and buy them. They are beautiful antiques, and now are over $100 years old. They aren't going to be made again, and their numbers are finite.

At one-point, carded Mego action figures and dolls were bringing hundreds of dollars, and some were over $1000. White's Guides and ToMart's Guides to Figures listed even uncarded figures at prices from $25 to over $100. Prices have dropped significantly on these now.

Difficult economic times do affect doll prices, as they do the prices of other collectibles. These things are, after all, luxuries, not necessities. And, money is money. One woman at an auction was telling me she remembered when $30 for a doll was a lot of money. "But, you know," she said to me. "That's still a lot of money." Trying to explain doll prices to non-collectors is hard. They can't understand the differences among dolls, or why anyone would pay good money for a bit of ceramic, wood, cloth, paper, etc. One visiting Swedish couple once told me that it was crime to spend $700 on a doll when people were starving. Yet, Sweden has a healthy population of doll collectors, and after all, it could be said it is a crime to spend millions of dollars on a painting when people are starving.

Rare dolls will always bring high price, like the Jumeau mold. 201, one of two known in the world that bought $225, 000 or the one of a kind K&R character girl that brought nearly $400,000 for Bonham's nearly 4 years ago. These dolls usually travel and change hands among the same group of dealers and wealthy collectors.

Emotional value also plays a role in pricing. We attach more value to things that are nostalgic in nature. Also, those who buy collectible dolls, mad to collect, not for play, often feel they should get more than what they paid when they sell. The secondary market fluctuates wildly on these dolls. For example, Precious Moment items flooded the market a few years ago; now, except to die-hard Precious Moment club members, they aren't worth much. Avon bottles and objects were once very hot; today, you can find them for a few dollars or less at yard sales. A few really enthusiastic collectors do cover Avon, however, and prices can go up at conventions of Avon lovers.

I tried to price a group of Byers' Choice carolers at $100 for ten figures, with about half being the small figures or animals. Oh no, the lady said, they're worth more than $100. Her sister did pay about $75 each at an expensive gifts shop, but prices on eBay, Etsy, Amazon and Ruby Lane are all over the place. Individual dolls go for between $29 and $80. Groups of ten large dolls can be $350. Starting bids, with zero amounts bid yet, start at $19.99.

Collect what you love, rearrange, repair, and read, read, read about your dolls. Kudos to *Doll Castle News* for keeping up the tradition of catering to an audience of those who love dolls and for not emphasizing money and price. We love the family heritage behind them, and the fact that they love all types of dolls, for just as there are all kinds of dolls; there are all kinds of people.

According to Jan Foulke in *The 16ᵗʰ Blue Book: Dolls & Values*, these factors are important in evaluating dolls: marks, quality, condition, body, clothing, total originality, age, size, availability, popularity, desirability, uniqueness, and visual appeal.

Chapter 22: Africa and the Middle East
Fullah, Saudi Arabia, Egypt, Iran

African dolls are as diverse as the continent itself. For a great photo study, try Pam and Polly Judd's *Asian and African Dolls.* In *Dolls of the World*, author/illustrator Gwen White has written of African dolls the following, "A varied array of dolls comes from Africa. Some are playthings, others are made for fertility reasons and many have their shape and features, or rather the lack of them, influenced by religion" (55).

At one point in my teaching career, I designed a course called Diversity and Culture. One exercise I used involved African dolls and masks. I would bring dolls made in Africa and arrange them on a table. The objects I brought were diverse; they were made of bone, wood, cloth, metal, gourds and other materials. No two were alike, nor were they all one dark skin tone. Africa is a large continent filled with diverse populations, all with different customs and languages. Next, I brought black dolls from the West, created by Europeans and Americans, for the most part. These, in contrast to the diverse African doll and masks, were basically white dolls painted black. The costumes, materials, and sizes were varied, but the dolls were basically white dolls, generic figures painted black.

As far as the countries of Africa, each one assigns a different meaning to their dolls. For example, The Sudan has long created dolls with magical and supernatural associations. Long necked dolls with heads of clay or beeswax are sold by "witches" to women who want to have children (White 56). These dolls are heavily decorated with charms and ornaments and are ten to fifteen inches long.

Gwen White writes in *Dolls of the World* that some peoples of Central Africa create crude dolls from lumps of wood because a too realistic doll might be too "uncanny" and scare its child owner (56). Similarly, the Achewa people made dolls of a couple of pieces of wood bound with cloth. These are called spirit dolls because they are supposed to be home for the spirits of the dead.

In the Congo, where some of my cousins grew up, iron dolls are made for chiefs, not as children's playthings. Spirit dolls exist there, too. Some dolls are made of cassava root, and little girls carry them on their backs. The Ashanti

Dolls of Ghana, carved from wood with large heads, serve the same purpose; they are the ideal of beauty and intelligence and little girls carry them on their backs ensure their babies will be smart and beautiful.

Many dolls involved in initiations and ritual come from Africa. These are often made of gourds, or wood decorated with beads. The Ndebele people of South Africa created doll made entirely or heavily decorated with beads. Other dolls are fetishes or idols, meant to be used in religious or medical rituals.

In Nigeria, dolls are made of wax, grassy material, and wood. In Senegal, large wooden dolls are also carried on the backs of their owners, indicating a desire for marriage and children.

Leather dolls are made in special shops in Morocco, and dolls of wrapped wire representing water bearers are traditional. The mother-in-law of a friend sent one of these dolls home to me with her daughter-in-law. In turn, I sent her a blue silk scarf. The doll is very special to me; it bonded a universal friendship.

Modern dolls from Egypt include a wishbone and wooden bead doll from the '30s, wooden dolls with heads that turn, Ushabti replicas, and elaborate costume dolls. Bronze and clay figures of Egyptian deities are also made. Nubian dolls of a clay substance are made at home and sold to tourists One of my former professors recently brought one back for me. See the section on ancient dolls for more on dolls from Egypt.

Middle East: Part of the Middle East is located in Africa. According to White, headless dolls, or those with no faces found in ancient graves belong to Hebrew children (55). She notes ancient Jewish dolls found all over the world had no faces because Mosaic Law forbids portraying the human face. In what reads like a retelling or allusion to The Golem, the Prophet Mohammed stated, "Every representation of this kind of faces would be placed before its author on the Judgment Day, and he would be commanded to put life into it, which not being able to do, he would be cast for a time into Hell" (55). Emily Jackson writes in *Toys of Bygone Days* that one of the wives of Mohammed was only nine when she joined the Harem, and that she brought her headless dolls with her.

In Betty Mahmoody's memoir of how she escaped from Iran, *Not without my Daughter,* she talks about buying toy dolls for her young daughter. She regrets they had to leave behind the little girl's faded bunny when they fled. I have several costume dolls from Iran, Afghanistan and other Moslem countries. Dolls may not be popular, but they do exist as toys and as souvenir dolls.

Saudi Arabia: I once read that Barbies in Saudi Arabia had to wear the Burka as they lined store shelves. Dolls, as toys are allowed; collectible dolls are frowned on. Ironically, the Saudis just made Sophia, a sophisticated android, a citizen of Saudi Arabia. In December 2003, Barbie, was declared immoral. The same year, import bans were put on dolls and teddy bears. A few years ago, a teacher was arrested for naming the class teddy bear Mohammed.

Things seem to be more liberal in Saudi Arabia today. There is a YouTube Video called "Saudi Arabia Doll" where a blond mechanical doll in a pink dress is walking. A Saudi company is selling a variety of dolls and stuffed animals, including babies that look like the baby dolls Cittitoy has made for a long time and Minecraft plush. The toddler dolls by various companies have blonde hair and look very western. One, a QA Baby Doll is described as "Doll with a soft and cute design • Fun game for your kids • Feature Talk with the child • Troy stories • It can record conversations." (Saudi.souq.com)

In 1999, a Barbie type doll called Fulla was created, and made her debut in the Islamic countries in 2003. I have a dentist Fulla wearing the Hijab. She is described this way in Wikipedia:

Fulla is the name of an 11½ inch Barbie-like fashion doll marketed to children of Islamic and Middle-Eastern countries as an alternative to Barbie. The product's concept evolved around 1999, and it became available for sale in late 2003. (1) Fulla was created by a UAE manufacturer from Dubai called NewBoy FZCO. Fulla is also sold in China (where it attracts children of the Hui minority), Brazil, North Africa, Egypt, and Indonesia, while a few are sold in the United States. Although there had been many other dolls in the past that were created with a hijab, such as Razanne and Moroccan Barbie, Fulla surpassed them in popularity due to launching alongside a marketing campaign aired on the then-popular television channel Spacetoon. Fulla is a role-model to some Muslim people, displaying how many Muslim people would prefer their daughters to dress and behave. (Wikipedia).

Chapter 23: The New World

In Argentina, Evita Peron was known for gathering poor children and treating them for a day to expensive dolls, toys, and other treats. She allegedly stockpiled thousands of dolls as compensation for the toys she never had.

All of North and South America is known for pre-Columbian idols and statues, some made of jade and gold or silver. Elaborate masks also come from this part of the world. Each country has its own particular dolls. Haiti is known for Voodoo dolls, but also for folk doll and dolls with plaster heads and traditional costumes.

Frida Kahlo and Diego Rivera are the subjects of dolls, but he collected figurines and she loved dolls. She became injured in the now infamous bus accident that destroyed her health because she left a toy on another bus and was returning to retrieve it when the accident took place. She bought dolls in Paris at the Paris Flea Market, and also liked to buy dolls that needed repair. Some of her dolls are on display at her home, Casa Azul, even today. Frida immortalized some of the dolls of Mexico in her painting "Four Inhabitants of Mexico." Mattel recently released a Frida Barbie to a lot of controversy started by Selma Hayek the actress who played her in the film *Frida*.

Woven dolls from Peru surfaced around 20 years ago in all sizes. These were made to look like ancient grave dolls, and they were constructed with very old materials. Some rumors associated with the dolls claimed the cloth actually came from ancient graves. Costume dolls with clay heads and woven clothes also come from Peru. Gwen White created her own sketches for her books on international dolls, including *Dolls of the World*. She has sketched flat wooden dolls carved from dark wood with metal eyes that seem to be a combination of Kachinas, the gigantic heads of Easter Island, and Native American totem pole figure. This doll was part of the British Museum Collection (White 9). Another very unusual Peruvian doll resembles the dolls of the Plains Indians. It is made of what whites call "fawn canvas" and has a human air wig of long, dark hair. Its features are stitched and it wears a blue gown trimmed with white beads arranged in pairs. The beads are sewn in the shape of a collar around the doll's neck. This doll is 13.5 inches high and hails from the Bethnal Green Museum.

Very usual dolls of the Choroti people are clay with tattooed features. These resemble ancient Greek figures with similar tattoo designs and small clay dolls from India that are used in various festivals (White 40). The tattoos indicate the age of the doll. They are among the people of the Chaco, of which there are several tribes. Other tribes, the Lenguans, make toys from ostrich bones including dolls (50). White shows wax dolls from the Chaco peoples. The Choroti inhabit parts of Paraguay (Google.com search). They also lived in Argentina (Delcampe.net) and Bolivia (White 50). The Chaco is a great plain that borders Argentina, Bolivia, and Paraguay, and means Great Hunt (50).

Girls' schools in Ecuador during the '20s taught little girls to make dolls and miniature linens and table cloths for doll houses to demonstrate their skills. My mother gave me one of these tiny stockinette dolls and set of bed linens and mini sweater that fits an eight-inch doll, as well as an embroidered table cloth with tiny napkins. They were given to her by another teacher.

Brazil has interesting dolls made of rubber, and also souvenir dolls wearing regional outfits. Dolls representing Carnival as well as masks are popular, too. Various edible dolls come from Brazil, as well as dolls made of straw, clay, and bone (48).

Dolls with wire armature bodies, including tiny worry dolls, come from Ecuador and Guatemala.

Chapter 24: The Nineteenth Century

Rachel Engmann gives an accurate and concise description of the European doll making industry:

The Thuringian doll industry produced more dolls than anywhere else (Angione, 1969; Hamlin, 2004) due to large nearby clay deposits required to make porcelain. For example, in 1844, the German firm, Voit and Fleischmann reported producing 360,000 heads. Another unnamed company was reported in Harper's Bazaar as producing 1,000,000 dolls (Pritchett and Pastron, 1983). The German firm, Simon and Halbig, founded in 1869 supplied heads to both German and French companies (King, 1984; Sherer, 1992) such as Jumeau and François Gaultier. Dolls/figurines were extremely heterogeneous in form and quality, varying in size, material, hairstyles and clothing (Hamlin, 2004). Made of glazed and painted porcelain, sizes ranged between three inches to much bigger dolls, around 40 inches tall, dressed in fashionable dress of the time.

The Thuringian doll industry was dominated by domestic producers who employed fewer than five employees, often composed of family members (Hamlin, 2004; Pritchett and Pastron, 1983). Thuringian manufacturers enjoyed the advantages of flexible specialization, such as variety of products, responsiveness to consumer demands and low capital costs. Hamlin points out that, "Thuringian toy-makers, also thrived on the meager wages of the workforce, particularly for the numerous child laborers" (2004:34). Hamlin (2004) explains that although contemporary sociologists dispute the exact levels of Thuringian poverty, there is little doubt that incomes were well below the national average. Widespread use of unpaid child and family labor also served to keep production costs at a minimum. Ironically, child labor was commonplace and child laborers would not have been able to afford to purchase such dolls (Sherer, 1992). (Engmann 10)

Materials for dolls included carton, wax, and wood covered in gesso. Some of the so-called Queen Anne dolls of wood covered over in gesso with cloth joints are really Georgian dolls from the early 19th century. There were also dolls of cloth, and various native materials like leather and cornhusks. There were Native American dolls of many kinds, and these are well represented in works by Carl Fox (*The Doll*) and Max Von Boehn, (*Dolls and puppets*).

There were marionettes and puppets of many kinds from all over the world. Also, a reread of Laura Starr's *The Doll Book* would be instructive at this point. It is on Google books for free downloading.

Paper dolls in Europe became the rage in the late 18th century and the vogue continued with sets like *The History of Little Fanny* and *The History of Little Henry,* discussed earlier in our chapter on paper dolls.

Milliner's models with their elaborate coiffures and legends of being used as hat models or hat stands began to make their way into toy catalogs around 1820. One of these dolls was bought by Abraham Lincoln as a gift; it is displayed at Lincoln's New Salem.

There are many gesso-covered and ivory crèche figures and Santos from this time as well in Hispanic countries and colonies, and other countries in Europe and North and South America.

Still, not everyone could afford dolls and toys. Those still wretchedly poor worked constantly and they had no time for dolls. Even in the early 20th century, my grandmother in Europe had to work. She had no dolls as a child, only later as an adult, and these became the nucleus of my collection. My grandmothers worked, and went to school to be seamstresses so they could work even more. One of them lost her father as a little girl of six or seven; she had to wear black till she married twenty years later. She used to beg us not to wear black, even if someone died.

With the rise of the Middle Class, and more leisure time for children, there was more time for play, and for toys of all types.

In the course of the 19th century, doll production grew to be the main element in toy manufacture and in 1840 dolls made up 70 % of the entire sales in Sonneberg.

Wooden dolls were both plentiful and popular, particularly the Grodnertal wooden dolls favored by Queen Victoria. These sometimes had combs carved into their painted hair. The simpler examples came in many sizes, from around a ¼ inch to nearly two feet. These are often called "Dutch" dolls, a variation of Deutsch, or German dolls. These were featured in Florence K. Upton's book *The Adventures of Two Dutch Dolls and a Golliwog.*

Wood is a living substance, a very special material for making dolls. Tree are revered by all cultures, and Joyce Kilmer had a point in writing "I think that I shall never see a thing as lovely as a tree." Just think of the majestic redwoods, or the beautiful colors leaves assume in autumn. Trees provide wood for warmth, fruits and nuts to feed us, sap and bark for medicines, wood for furniture, art, and many other products. Dolls made of wood are particularly special, and examples date to Ancient Egypt and elsewhere.

Other wooden doll makers of note include Joel Ellis, Martin & Taylor, Albert Schoenhut, artists Helen Bullard, Robert Raikes, and others. Wooden dolls of note include Queen Anne and Georgian Dolls, Bebe Tout en Bois, Tottie of Godden's *The Dolls' House,* Miss Hitty, The Little Wooden Doll, Swiss carved dolls, Kachinas, Door of Hope Doll, and others. Ventriloquist dummies like Howdy Doody are also wood. Miss Hickory is a wooden doll that came full circle; at the end of the book when she has lost her hickory head, she grafts herself to the hickory tree where she came from in the first place.

In addition to the production of wooden dolls, more and more dolls made of papier-mâché. Then in 1830 porcelain was used. The porcelain doll from Sonneberg became a world-famous product made by porcelain manufacturers like Armand Marseille and Ernst Heubach.

Over the course of the doll-making industry, over 1 billion china heads and porcelain dolls were made. Their shards were found in droves all over old factory sties that were once in East Germany. I have a whole box of these that came from Germany. I bought them at Eleanor's Dolls, a former Pawn shop in Clinton, IA. The owner collected Mme. Alexander Cissies, and had custom out fits made for them, usually lingerie and black leather ensembles. His wife had a nice stock of antique and collectible dolls, and I bought several, including the heads dug up in Germany.

The Hertwig Company was discovered after The Berlin Wall came down; old stock was found and later sold buy Theriault's and other dealers. Some dolls were intact on their original cards. Opening East Germany made it possible for collectors to identify companies and marry their dolls to them. Many dolls, it turns out, were made by Hertwig, including some very distinctive china heads with prominent ears.

Rachel Engmann writes in "Ceramic Dolls and Figurines, Citizenship and Consumer Culture in Market Street Chinatown, San Jose." that porcelain dolls, heads, and figurines make up the largest group of items excavated from the 19th century. (Hume, 1969: 317, quoted in Engmann 1) I note that Japan Town in San Jose many shops selling Japanese and Asian products. I do not know of a San Jose China Town, though I have lived in San Joe, visited many times, and my mother's family has lived there since 1965. We were not there when China Town existed, from the 1860s, till arson destroyed it in 1887 (Engmann 5).

Engmann's thesis as outlined in her abstract as follows:

"I *suggest that analysis of the recovered doll and figurine fragments, rather than confined solely to Victorian ideologies associated with child's play, is also reflective of the tensions in the relationship between Overseas Chinese and White American society." (Engmann 1)*

Engmann's study focused on Frozen Charlottes and speculated on why these European doll and doll dishes were found in such numbers in San Francisco's China Town. Having been there many times, I can say that I have bought old store stock in China Town, including tiny porcelain dolls dressed as a Chinese couple. Dolls sold there are not always Asian. In fact, there used to be a Native American art gallery in the neighborhood that sold Kachinas.

Engmann acknowledges that doll play and the social development of girl go hand in hand. As she says, "Child play says a lot about the social lives of little girls" (Barthes, 1972; Burton, 1997; Calvert, 1992, cited in Engmann 3). She goes on to say that, "I quickly embarked from the position that beliefs and values are not necessarily directly accessible through archaeological data. In other words, I suggest that dolls/figurines do not necessarily reflect elite or middle class Victorian based ideologies" (3). Engmann feels that the presence of European dolls and figurines excavated from the 19th century San Jose Chinese neighborhood indicates pressure on Chinese immigrants to assimilate; hence they bought European Caucasian dolls for their children and as decorative bibelots.

In reality, the lives of 19th century Chinese women living in Chinese communities located in America were far more complicated.[2] Many were bought and sold into lives of prostitution or hard labor as servants. The lives of married women were hardly better; most were homebound and those of the scholar, gentry, merchant and landowner classes still bound their daughter's feet (Yung 19). According to Judy Yung in *Unbound Feet*, "Within the household women were expected to care for family…provide moral training for the children, observe customs and holidays[3], do the household chores of cleaning, washing, and cooking, and bring in extra income by handicraft work, such as spinning, weaving, and sewing." (19) This handicraft work also involved creating dolls. One remembers that Pearl Buck was familiar with the

---

[2] In China, women were sometimes sold into prostitution by their parents because the family was desperately poor. A prostitute could be saved by being married to a labourer, a practice that continued in the US (Yung 33). She might also run away, commit suicide, or she might go insane. In America, she might dare to go to the police for protection but might not necessarily get it.

[3] Included among the festivals was a Girls' Day Festival, cf. the Japanese Doll or Girls' Day Festival.

Door of Hope Mission in China, where young girls were rescued and taught skills, like making and dressing the dolls of pear [4]wood in costumes reflecting local culture. In the US, there were Presbyterian Missions that offered relief to Chinese women who wanted to escape the sordidness and virtual enslavement. These missions taught them western religion and values and clothed them in Western dress. (35) Remember, too, the Presbyterian rag dolls made about this time. Some proceeds from the dolls could well have gone to aiding Chinese women in need in America.

Actually, I think some of these Frozen Charlotte dolls were store stock, sold by Chinese merchants and others in the area. These dolls were plentiful at one time; 19th century Sears's catalogs advertise them for as little as pennies for a gross. Children like small toys they can fit into their pocket. In fact, Engmann admits that "Market Street Chinatown merchants also had access to non-Chinese goods, reflecting their privileged access to goods that the average resident did not possess." (Engmann 6)

Also, children have always had and loved toys from various cultures. Some were brought as souvenirs from around the world; others were dolls representing various ethnicities and lifestyles. People traveled, even in prehistoric times and the Ancient world. How else would the national costume of Mexico, the *China Poblana*, be based on the costume of an Indian princess who came to Ancient Mexico to marry a prince? For that matter, how else could a 3800 Caucasian woman's mummy be buried in a Chinese tomb in China? They brought back souvenirs, including figurines and dolls. Black and Native American dolls have always been made; children of different races played with dolls from ethnicities different than their own. Recently, the doll collection of Deborah Neff featuring black dolls and photographs of children, both black and white with dolls was on display at the Figge Museum, Davenport, IA. Black and white girl were photographed paying with black and white dolls, e.g., little black girls played with white dolls, and white girls had black dolls. My childhood play dolls reflected a multicultural mix; many French and German doll makers made dolls representing Native Americans, Africans, and Gypsies. Other dolls had black, café au lait, or brown skin.

After the recovery from World War II, toy factories began to produce again in 1945/46.

From 1948 on, craftsmen in the toy industry were forced to join cooperatives specifically established for purchase and distribution of goods,

---

[4] CF, *The Inn of the Sixth Happiness*, where the practice of foot binding was condemned, and the mission is similar to the Door of Hope. See, also, the Ingrid Bergman film.

following the expropriation and nationalization of the large-scale enterprises. By the end of the '50s, private companies were more or less compelled to accept state interference.

The foundation of combined collectives represented the next step of the economic centralization and the entire toy industry with its 27,000 employees, 10,000 of which working in Sonneberg, was coordinated from there. (http://sonneberg.de/stadtinf/vorgestellt/evorstel.htm)

The large-scale enterprises did not survive the fall of the Berlin Wall in 1989. Today about 1,000 employees are still working for small and medium size companies within the toy industry. Some of the local toy factories were able to make a name for themselves, so that Sonneberg nowadays is called Toy Town to display the international significance which it still has.

Chapter 25: Folk Dolls

As writings by writers of the late 19th and early 20th centuries show, collecting folk dolls and making them was a popular hobby for men and women. Some of these collectors also wrote about their doll adventures. These authors include G. Stanley Hall, 1897 *A Study of Dolls*, Laura Starr, *The Doll Book*, 1908, and Emily Jackson, *Toys of Other Days,* 1908. All can still be purchased, and they should be free on Google Books. These authors talk of dolls and doll making in countries that no longer exist on the world map. Loretta Holz's *How to Book of International Dolls* has great information about making folk dolls, but also about the history of international dolls around the world. Wendy Lavitt's American Folk Dolls is a great source, as are also *The Collector's Encyclopedia of Dolls,* Volumes I and II. Helen Young's *The Complete Book of Doll Collecting* and Mary Hillier's *Dolls and Doll Makers* have great chapters on folk and foreign dolls. My book, *A Bibliography of Dolls and Toys*, has many entries on them, too. You can still get this book from me, or from Amazon. My book on metal dolls, *With Love from Tin Lizzie,* addresses folk dolls made of metal. My friend, artist Jeanne O'Melia is well known for her dolls and figures made of found objects, both old and new. *Godey's* and other magazines of the era include ideas for paper dolls, paper dolls themselves, doll dress patterns, and doll patterns. Worsted or knitted dolls were popular at this time, and dolls made of shells for Brittany and elsewhere were popular souvenirs from about 1830 on. We have one in the museum from this era; it is of papier mâché, and is covered with tiny shells of brown and white. The doll has black, inset glass eyes that do not move and stands about nine inches. I also have a shell doll from Delphi, and many dolls from Florida and California, made of shells. Our doll house has a chaise lounge decorated in shells that was probably a Sailor's Valentine pin cushion. Sailor's Valentines are small objects often decorated with shells and bits of marine flora/fauna made on long voyages for loved ones. Scrimshaw is another example. Dried apple dolls date to the 19th century and early. Cornhusk and corncob dolls date from the 19th century and earlier and originated with Native American Culture.

The Little House Books feature Susan the corncob doll and discuss dolls of husks and tiny twigs made of acorns. Dolls from Africa and dry climates are often made of grasses or even banana leaves. Rushes, all kinds of paper, plants and dried flowers like holly hocks were made into dolls and still are. Pansies look like dolls all by themselves. Small clay dolls have been made around the world for centuries, including ancient terracotta and faience dolls of Egypt, Greece, Rome, and Latin America. They also existed in Ancient China and Japan. Laura Ingalls Wilder also writes about rag dolls, and paper dolls, all homemade. Lois Lenski wrote stories about a little girl who made dolls of gourds. Our local gourd festival boasts examples made as large, jointed dolls, all made of gourds. Old bowling pins show up at craft and doll shows, too. Louisa May Alcott, like the fictional Dickensian Jenny Wren, dressed dolls for a living at one point. Alcott collected chicken feathers to use in dolls hats. The Edinburgh Museum of Childhood boasts a doll made of an old shoe. Lobster and crab claw dolls have been made as souvenirs since the 19th century, too.

Our museum has hundreds of folk dolls made of Kleenex, plants and flowers, pine cones, seeds, found objects, old tins and cans, broken doll parts, wooden blocks, bricks, shells, leather/furs, dried fruit, rolled up newspapers, old magazines, old bottles, blocks of wood, paper towel holders, soap, wax, gourds, pumpkins, fake snowmen, wood, cloth, woven materials, mixed media, paper, clay and mud, elephant excrement made into paper, dried nuts, pasta, candy and sugar, salt dough, dried fish, paper clay, play dough, corncobs, cornhusk, rushes and grasses, raffia, canvas, old rags, animal bones and other fossilized materials, pecan resin, coal, metal, lobster claws, buttons, knitted material, crocheted material, tatting, and much more. Many are now over 100 years old. One of our favorites is a dried apple doll laid out in a coffin, created to explain death to a family of children born nearly a century ago.

American Black Dolls

Recently, I was privileged to attend a reception for a collection of unique black dolls, on loan from an exhibition of the Mingei Museum, San Diego. The current exhibit was at the Figge Museum, Davenport, Iowa. The dolls in the collection belong to Deborah Neff, who has been kind enough to allow the dolls to be transported and displayed at both museums. The black doll exhibit was part of an exhibit celebrating the art of the silhouette by Kara Walker, "The Emancipation Approximation."

The collector, Deborah Neff, was on hand for the reception celebrating the exhibit's opening at the Figge. She is a collector of dolls, quilts, and photographs of little girls with their dolls, especially black dolls. The dolls on display were made of cloth and mixed media and dated from around 1850 to 1930 or so. There were dolls by Leo Moss and Isabel Greathouse, the latter who used cocoanuts as heads for her dolls. Some were made by a contemporary artist, named Nellie Mae Roe (1900–1982). Many were cloth, but a few were wood or mixed media.

Neff states in *Black Dolls: from the Collection of Deborah Neff,* that she did not start collecting dolls by only seeking black ones. Her interests included handmade dolls and textiles, but as she sought for dolls to add to her collection, she realized the special artistry involved in making handmade black dolls that crossed "the boundary from craft to art in accomplished portrayals of ordinary souls." The doll clothes alone are worthy of study; many have beaded gowns, waistcoats and coats carefully lined jewelry, appropriately sized buttons, delicate collars, lace trim, and handmade shoes and stockings. Their hair is elaborately styled, in many cases similar to the hairstyles of the little girls portrayed in the photographs that Neff collected to accompany her dolls. Black dolls are important folk art and cultural objects that tell the story of humanity perhaps better than any other type of doll. Many have their roots in African folk art and doll-making. Undoubtedly, some of the dolls were made by slaves, while others were made as toys.

Some of the lady dolls wear mid-century outfits similar to those worn by china heads, Parians, and fashion dolls. The leather hands and feet on some of the dolls were probably repurposed from leather bodies originally created for porcelain and china heads.

Besides being toys and art objects, folk dolls have played a role as educational tools for centuries. Noted scholars including G. Stanley Hall, Laura Starr, and Janet Pagter Johl have written about the educational value of dolls for some time. Mary Hillier in *Dolls and Doll Makers* pictures two wooden dolls that were used to solve a murder, and Frances Glessner Lee, a forensic pathologist, created doll house shadow boxes to solve cold case murders. Dr. Kenneth Clark conducted experiments on children and their dolls. Dr. Clark and his wife Mamie asked black children if they liked black or white dolls better. The case of *Brown v. Board of Education* (1954) made Dr. Clark's experiment famous because it was mentioned in the opinion of the case. Dr. Clark's results helped win Brown for the plaintiffs, and thus the "separate but equal" case of *Plessey v. Ferguson* (1896) was reversed by the United States Supreme Court. Segregation in schools and elsewhere were now illegal in the United States. Dolls played a vital role in a case that was keys in The Civil Rights Movement.

According to Margo Jefferson, one of the contributors *to Black Dolls*, "Dolls have no rights a human is bound to respect. These black dolls present people with few rights a white person was bound to respect." Yet, to doll artists, doll collectors, and folk-art enthusiasts, these dolls are the epitome of all that is right with collecting. The dolls are expressions and portraits of the people who made them, and they speak eloquently for them.

In *The Art of the Calendar,* a mid-sixties calendar features a beautiful, nude, black woman holding a handmade black rag doll. By this time, dolls have found themselves placed in the American cultural conscience. Shindana, a company founded by Operation Bootstrap, began to make ethnic dolls, including black dolls like Afro Malika, and baby dolls that were meant represent black, Caucasian, Hispanic, and Asian babies.

There were a few black and brown composition dolls that appeared during the '30s, even a Black Patsy doll. Golliwogs had been made since the turn of the century. These were based on the illustrations of Florence K. Upton for her books, including, *A Tale of Two Dutch Dolls and a Golliwog.*

The first Black Barbie debuted in the early '70s along with Brad, her black boyfriend. Around the time of the Bicentennial, Black American family dolls using Mattel's Sunshine Family mold hit the toys helves. Black Chatty Cathys and Chrissy's were made, black and African dolls were created by Madame Alexander, Vogue, and Effanbee, by the '80s. These dolls were followed by Barbies of the world, including Nigerian Barbie, black Honey Hill Bunch dolls, and black My Child dolls. In Iowa City, I was able to buy large, black companion dolls at a local toy store. These dolls had authentic hairstyles and features.

Doll artists like Magge Head Kane, Floyd Bell, and Robert Bell were making portrait and character black children. Other artists for galleries like Franklin Mint, Ashton Drake, and The Hamilton Colleton began to make gorgeous black dolls of porcelain. Gambina of New Orleans created black characters that portrayed the people of New Orleans, including Mare LeVeau. The American Girls gave us Addie, whose books are written by Connie Porter. Connie briefly taught with me at Southern Illinois University, Carbondale, even though I did not know her.

When President Barak Obama was elected, there was a renewed interest in black dolls that represented him, First Lady, Michele Obama, and their daughters. Some of these were paper dolls produced by Dover, others were soft dolls, cookie dolls, or elaborate porcelain dolls. I had the pleasure of meeting the then future president when he was running for senator for Illinois. I wished him luck.

Ashanti and other black 11.5-inch fashion dolls wearing authentic Dashiki material populated the shelves of big box stores. A black Terri Lee was carried by K-Mart 'long with other remakes of Terri Lee.

Foreign Dolls: The most comprehensive account of a doll collection based on travels to foreign countries is Laura Starr's 1908 classic, *The Doll Book*, so popular, it is even available on Kindle and Google Books. Queen Marie of Rumania had a similar collection of dolls acquired as souvenirs. Many years later, another famous Romanian, Olympic gymnast, Nadia Comaneci, would also collect dolls from all over the world.

By about 1930, collecting foreign or souvenir dolls on travels was a popular pastime for young girls. Legendary collector Margaret Woodbury Strong began collecting on a yearlong trip around the word with her parents when Margaret was only a child. She was allowed to collect whatever fit into her pocket book, a rather large pocket book, and many small dolls found their way there and became a collection of over 30,000 at the time of her death.

The doll collection assembled for Shirley Temple consisted of dolls sent from all over the world from fans. The most usual doll was a five-foot Japanese doll that had to be shopped in a coffin. The doll is made like the traditional gofun Geisha Ningyo, but she is the size of a real woman. Temple writes in her autobiography, *Child Star*, that the dolls were an unwanted collection. For many years, they were displayed at Stanford's Children's Hospital in California. Then, in the early '90s or so, Temple took the dolls home with her. After her death, Theriault's sold them at auction, July 2014. I was able to buy one, a boy made of knitted pink yarn. Jane Withers, another child start who loved dolls, was able to revisit a Lenci doll she coveted as a child. The Lenci doll was a prop in a movie she did with Temple. Though Withers wanted her, Temple got the doll.

Chapter 26: Mechanical Dolls and Automata

Mechanical dolls are dolls and toys of which dreams are made. They are the magnificent dancing dolls of *The Nutcracker Suite,* and the dancing figures of Disneyland's "It's a Small World" attraction. Though they range from simple to complex, automata have origins that date back at least to Ancient Egypt. They were particularly popular in the Middle Ages. One of the earliest attempts at making an automaton was a Medieval Nuremburg crib built to contain live birds in its base. The birds' frantic attempts to escape made the figures move (Fraser 171). Also, among the earliest automated figures were those inside the Strassburg Cathedral clock tower. A mechanism allowed the figures of the Virgin and Three Wise Men to bow while a rooster moved its head and a crow flapped its wings.

Leonardo da Vinci is said to have created some marvelous mechanical figures while at the court of Lodovico Sforza, but we know of them only through his hints and through the sketches in his notebooks. The mechanical toys of Gustavus Adolphus of Sweden, however, still exist to give us a glimpse of early automated dolls. The dolls date to 1632 and dance. They are operated by a mechanism hidden under the lady's skirt. The lady has lost her head, but her male partner is still intact. The dolls are dressed in silk and gilt lace. Other early clockwork figures from this period were operated by steel springs and were called *Jacquemarts.* (Hillier Automata 111)

Mechanical figures were very popular by the eighteenth century and there was great competition among artisans who invented them. Some examples were not automatons; instead, they were French Court dolls made of wood with hollow heads, meant to be operated manually. The information below about these dolls comes from Jean Lotz's Internet *Antique Wood Doll Gallery.* These figures were clearly meant for adult entertainment and are often anatomically correct. There is a cavity in the head which opens. Former curator for the Museum of the City of New York and doll collector, John Noble, suggests that a cabbage could have been placed in the cavity as a joke. Lotz claims that the compartment could also contain miniature scenes, or tiny gifts and jewels. The author has read of examples in various books that were used as spy dolls, even as late as the American Civil War. Marie Antoinette and the Princess Lampballe supposedly had an example. Considering what happened to the heads of both of these ladies, the fact that their dolls heads opened and were empty is a little ironic.

One famous doll 18th century doll is the Dulcimer Player. Invented by Roentgen and Kintzing, it dates from 1780 and is supposed to have belonged to Marie Antoinette. The Dulcimer Player was so popular, that the composer Glück composed special music for her. In the author's opinion, she is the forerunner of modern computerized dolls such as Pamela, Julie, Cricket, Teddy Ruxpin, Computer Interactive Talk with Me Barbie, Baby Alive, and others.

Another famous figure is the clavichord player, circa 1774, by Jacquet-Droz. The clavichord player actually plays the keys of her instrument, and her chest rises and falls, as though she were breathing. Anyone familiar with the modern Mme. Tussaud breathing Sleeping Beauty will be amazed at the similar effect in the clavichord girl. The clavichord player was made by the now famous father and son team known primarily for being clock makers.

A doll called "The Artist" took two years to finish; the doll can draw a rabbit, dog, and child, with the doll's eyes following each stroke of the pencil, as if it were concentrating. This doll, too, is famous today. The doll has a wooden heard, torso and limbs. He wears a wig and has realistic eyes. He is approximately 27 inches high. According to Alfred Chapuis and Edmond Droz, the boy dips his quill in ink, shakes the quill twice, puts his hand at the top of the page and then stops. Further pressure on a lever makes the mechanism move, and the boy begins to write. The Jacquet-Droz dolls were part of an exhibit at the Smithsonian in 1961 (Fawcett 50). Accompanying them was Edmund Droz, descendant of their creator, and professor of mathematics (50).

If dolls can play instruments, draw, and breathe, then they can certainly perform everyday-functions like eating and walking. Chronologically speaking, walking dolls seem to be a fairly modern development. Yet, they appeared even earlier than talking models. One engraving dated 1743 shows a doll walking across a floor as a room full of delighted people watch (Hillier DDM 113).

One interesting variation on the walking doll is a rare example pushing a three-wheel carriage. One thing that makes this toy so unusual is that the maker himself provided a small doll occupant for the carriage. About eleven years ago, the author saw such a doll at a doll show in St. Charles, IL. The doll was eight inches long with a rubber head. The molded blonde hair was held back with a band in the style of *Alice in Wonderland*. The features were painted. A small necklace with a cross was painted around the neck. The arms were also rubber. The torso and legs were made of a series of metal links, chained together. The dress was tattered gauze that may once have been blue. In bad condition, and without the mechanism or carriage, this 1850s' doll costs $500.

John Noble shows variations of this type of figure in his book, *Dolls*. On August 25, 1868, W.F. Godwin of East New York took out a patent, No. 81, 491, for an "automatic toy." This doll had a papier mâché-head with metal hands and feet with swivel ankles. The hands were made to fit around the handle of a doll carriage that it either pulled or pushed. Originally, this doll may have belonged to the Amana Society, a religious sect that still makes its home in Amana, IA (Young 140).

Walking dolls either pushing carriages or carrying things continued to be popular through the end of the nineteenth century. Alexandre Nicholas Théroude made dolls in Paris between 1842–95 (Coleman I 614). He specialized in mechanical dolls. He advertised as early as 1843 that his dolls were sent even to the French provinces and abroad (614). In 1849, Théroude won a bronze medal at the Paris Exposition. By 1852, he was trying to make his dolls even more realistic, and received a French patent for an internal mechanism which would give his dolls sound and movement. He must have been successful, for in 1855, he won a silver medal for his efforts at the Paris Exposition (614). He also won prizes at the 1862 and 1867 London and Paris Expositions, respectively (614). All his success made him cocky, apparently, for in 1856, he began to brag he invented the "talking" doll, which is not really true. The heads of these dolls were composition, with pupil-less glass eyes, and upper and lower rows of bamboo teeth. Because of the teeth, they look as if they are baring their fangs at someone. The dolls walk by way of a mechanical device with wheels on which their feet rest. (Coleman I 615)

A French Christmas toy catalog from 1875–1876 shows a small doll representing a uniformed young man, mounted on a four-wheeled platform. He carries a balloon with the words "Louvre" written on it, thus advertising a famous department store of the time. His arms are full of toys, including a wrapped box, a Polichinelle clown, and a tiny toy dog. He is called in the catalog, *"Le Groom Des Grands Magazine Du Louvre"* (Theimer 11). In this example, the child pulled the wheeled figure on its platform to make it "walk," thereby providing the mechanism. This is probably not a true automaton, then, because no motor or mechanism allows the doll to move on its own power. One might think of the difference as one between a horse and buggy or trailer pulled by a car, and a motor vehicle of any kind which operates with its own mechanical force.

Other dolls from this period do, however, "walk" on their own. One fashion doll, complete with bustle, played music and walked. She held a lorgnette in one hand, raised to her eyes, and a hankie in the other (Theimer 73). The name of this doll was la *"Dame à l'Éventail"* (73). The French advertisement for the doll states that she is dressed completely in satin and that she has arm and head movements (73). She was considerably more expensive than the little groom on his platform, costing some 240 francs to his 6.5 francs (73). She was also for sale at the Louvre, during the 1877–78 season (73). Another couple, richly dressed in 18th century satin costumes, played music, but did not dance, and cost only 78 francs at the Louvre (73). Music had become an integral part of many of the 19th century automatons, and Antoine Favrer, another Swiss clock maker, supposedly invented the cylindrical music box movement for the figures, still used in some variation today (Knopf 341). Though the ads for these mechanical dolls in the Louvre catalogs do not say, the heads of these dolls were probably French bisque.

Others besides the French made walking dolls in the nineteenth century. Another famous walker is the Autoperipatetikos, designed by Enoch Rice Morrison, for the firm of Martin and Runyon, circa 1863. The doll has metal feet which walk. At least one writer has observed that "Duplicating human movement, rather than approximating the texture or appearance of the human body, was the chief aim for doll inventors" (41), including, apparently, Morrison. Most of Morrison's dolls represent women, though one original box label portrays a man dressed as a Zouave soldier (Hillier DDM 121). The mechanism has a strong spring, which, if not rusted, will still work. In 1862, A.V. Newton took out a patent for Autoperipatetikos in England. By trade, Newton was a mechanical draughtsman. According to Mary Hillier in *Dolls and Doll Makers*, manufacturers used different heads and clothing on the dolls. Most had china or bisque heads, while a few had wax or papier mâché heads. Some had French fashion heads of bisque. The doll's head was "mounted onto a stuffed bust with kid arms, and the skirt of the doll concealed a ball-shaped, hollow cylinder over a base" (121). Doll makers did not necessarily make entire mechanical dolls; according to Miriam Forman-Brunell in *Made to Play House: The Commercialization of American Girlhood 1830–1930,* individual makers "specialized in the mechanization of some aspect of the doll's anatomy" (41). She mentions a wax head which is "suspended in a wig-frame, swiveled on an axis revealing four faces..." Another doll head operated by means of a pulley (41). Still another mechanism allowed a doll's lower lip to move so that it would appear to be smiling. She also notes that some inventors even patented parts of doll bodies as though they were building machines, so enamored were they with their chief means of production (41).

The Autoperipatetikos ran on a clockwork mechanism similar to that in the automatons of Jacquet-Droz (Bartholomew 77). In dolls, however, the clockwork mechanism had to be made smaller, as it did not have to be in the often-life-sized automata. Bartholomew notes that, in earlier dolls, the mechanism is often bulky, so that long dresses were worn by the dolls to cover the machinery. The doll's full crinoline covered her mechanism. The fact that the Autoperipatetikos walked on two distinct feet made her unusual. As late as 1880, a walking doll by Steiner had no legs. She was driven by a single action steering wheel which determined the direction the doll walked. The 15 in (38.1 cm) high doll also had a talking mechanism which let her say "mama/papa." (Bartholomew 77).

Punch on a bicycle is a popular Victorian toy that walks with the help of a clockwork mechanism and cycles around with a central weight. The figure has a lead or metal head painted with enamel. One variation of this doll was made in around 1890 by William Britain. Even earlier examples exist in France. Catalogs for famous department stores like the Louvre show examples as part of their Christmas collection. The Louvre doll is mounted atop an elaborate drum that stands on its side. He gesticulates with his arms and moves his legs as though dancing (Theimer 11). The next year, the Louvre offered the figure of a mechanical Harlequin standing on a chair. This *Arlequin Gynasiarque sur chaise* cost 7.90 francs, a bargain for such an animated figure, and was offered in 1877. Also from the 1877 Louvre catalog is a female doll, elaborately dressed, that plays badminton when the wheeled platform on which she stands is pulled (77). Other dolls from these same catalogs were called Hercule and Pierrot and Polichinelle and were also mechanical dolls mounted on drums that stood sideways. A lever on the side of the doll activated it when wound (Theimer 93).

Another interesting toy from this period is a doll with a composition head and wooden body that skips when wires connected to her are fully extended and a wooden handle is turned. The doll is marked "Patent" under one foot and was made between 1885 and 1900. Several firms had the rights to make this doll which often wore a blue pinafore and cardboard hat. Between 1877 and 1889, dozens of variations of these small mechanical dolls appeared for sale. They include *Le Cuisinier*, a key wound Chef who held a pot in one hand, and drank from the cooking wine with the other; *Négre jouer de flûte*, playing a flute; The Smoking Monkey, dressed in colonial attire; *Poupée Papillon*, a mechanical doll holding a butterfly net aloft as she chases a butterfly that flies before her on a wire; more monkeys that are dressed as human beings and play harps or juggle; an artist; a mechanical doll with her own puppet show; a mechanical elephant with an exotic looking doll on its back; Mandolinata, a female doll that plays music; and *Amazone*, a female equestrian figure resting on a wheeled platform (Theimer 137).

The names of these dolls are in themselves poetry; their costumes are romantic and their occupations as varied as the people who admired and bought them. But dolls were not content to move and play music, they had several things to say, as well.

As far as talking dolls are concerned, Johannes Mäezel, not A. Théroude, is credited with having invented the first one. He was born in 1783 in Regensburg, Germany. He also invented the metronome, known to pianists everywhere. We do not know much about the Mäezel doll because the only doll he actually created no longer exists. In 1824, though, he took out a patent for a doll with a synthetic voice. At the 1923 Paris Exposition, he won an award, perhaps for this talking doll. Though his doll has not survived, its progeny have in the millions of "mama" dolls, Chatty Cathy's, and Baby Talks, that have been manufactured since Maëzel's time.

Charles Bartholomew notes in *Mechanical Toys* that in the nineteenth century, during the age of Parisian and fashion dolls, miniature accessories of all kinds were made for the dolls. Some of these were mechanical, and Bartholomew discusses a lavatory that actually flushed! (Bartholomew 76). In fact, the French were perhaps the greatest makers of automata. The famous workshops include those of Vichy, Leopold Lambert, Rouellet et Decamps, Phalbias, Renow, and the aforementioned Théroude. Roullet et Decamps were famous for animated animals and figures, like the photographer taking a dog's picture, which dates from the early 1900s'. In June 1986, this figure sold for $17,500 at Sotheby's. Another doll using heads by the firm of Jumeau is called *Magicienne* and stands over two feet tall. She plays a variation of the shell game using the heads in place of a pea. She is also by Decamps. As late as 1968, Decamps still made automata. The Movie *Scrooge*, with Albert Finney, uses a variety of automata and other antique toys and dolls as props. One of these appears to be the famous acrobat of Decamps. Another mechanical doll by Decamps is the swimming doll which performs a sort of breast stroke through the means of metal parts and mechanisms. A plastic version similar to this doll is still made. Decamps may have inspired the makers of other mechanical toys and dolls, including dolls made by American companies like the Poppy Doll Company of California. There dolls were made of California redwood, but a lever in the doll's back made it move.

Gustave Pierre Vichy made automata in the late 1860s and 1870s. He hid the mechanisms in the body or base of his dolls. The mechanisms were comprised of rods and cams that activated each move of the dolls. The stop; and start button shaped like an acorn was also Vichy's trademark. The heads were made of finely molded composition. The joints were covered with kidskin to ensure smooth movement. The "Magic Cupboard" by Vichy sold in 1986 for $23,000,00.00 at Sotheby's, so these are among the most desirable of all automata. In this example, a boy sits on a cupboard, turns, reaches toward the door; the door opens. A fly suddenly flies out. The boy cannot catch the fly, so he seizes a pot of his grandmother's gooseberry jam. The jar spins to reveal Grandmother's face. Her glasses rise and her jaw drops in alarm, and the boy leans back, gesturing with a biscuit in his left hand. Then, the child nods his head and sticks out his tongue. The door closes; a mouse runs up a block of cheese on the counter, and the performance ends. The action that takes place in this very "magic" cupboard remind one of a Rube Goldberg cartoon.

Some of the rarest automata include those representing cabaret stars of the late 1800s. Some of the performers were also famous subjects of Toulouse-Lautrec paintings. Black automata were particularly popular around 1885. One English distributor, Silver and Fleming, advertised three at one time. In the author's collection is a piece from a Black automaton dating from around 1940. The figure represents a man in a yellow suit and red shirt. It is made of hard plastic with metal joints. The man was once attached to a base and danced. The author believes he is meant to portray Bill "Bojangles" Robinson. Another rare and interesting toy is the Victorian "Hanging Mary" doll. The author has neither seen the doll nor its photo, but heard about it from a collector in Galena Illinois, about 45 years ago whose mother used to own "Lolly's Doll Museum." Supposedly, the doll hung from a noose on miniature gallows. When the key was wound, the body extended, the eyes bulged, and the tongue protruded. Background music included "God Save the Queen" and a funeral march. Hanging Mary was probably a representation of Mary Cotton, known as "dark angel" who died on the gallows after being convicted of poisoning several people. New evidence indicates she may not have been guilty.

Given the gruesome nature of some toys and books during the Victorian era, it is possible that Hanging Mary existed to teach children the value of obeying the law. Certainly, the Victorian age was as violent a time as any. It was an age fraught with war and with horrific crimes, including the Jack the Ripper murders. Executions were still public, and a popular Sunday excursion. It is entirely possible then, that toys, which often imitate and reflect contemporary real life, were made in imitation of the social events of the day, no matter how macabre. Even today, there are toy guillotines and electric chairs, and McFarlane toys has created a series of mass murderers and monsters from the movies, including Leatherface (*The Texas Chainsaw Massacre*) and Freddy Krueger (*Nightmare on Elm Street*). In the author's collection is a modern automation representing The Crypt Keeper from *Tales from the Crypt*. He sits in a miniature electric chair which vibrates when batteries are inserted and a small switch is activated.

Despite the Cult of True Womanhood that portrayed Victorian women as Angels of the House and helpmeets for their husbands, women entered the toy industry, and took part in making even the more gruesome toys of the era. In 1896, for example, Ellen Sheraton Fortrose Hodgson took out a patent for a clockwork swimming doll made of metal or rubber. Mrs. Hodgson was from Inverness, and was the wife of Major-General Hodgson, a retired officer of the Bengal Army (Hillier, Pollock's 104). Jules Nicholas Steiner also made a swimming doll. Steiner, according to Mary Hillier, was originally a clockmaker who patented a walking doll in 1858 (126). Bru, another famous French nineteenth century doll maker created dolls that walked, talked, even digested food; these are now rare and sought after, but when new, were unpopular. One Bru doll has a mechanism within its torso that allows its legs to swing out as if it were walking. One winds a key in the doll's left side, it says "Mamma" or "Papa." Paul Girard, who headed the Bru firm from 1891–99, took out the patent for this doll. In the author's collection is a beautiful French mechanical fashion doll of about 14 inches. Underneath her pink satin skirt is the wheeled mechanism that allows her to walk. When wound, she says "Mamma" and moves forward, also tilting her head to the side. Another lovely French example has an SFBJ bisque head, glass eyes, and blonde mohair wig. Her hands are bisque. Her body looks like a watering can with a handle on the back, but her metal feet are attached by wires. At one time, she walked by a combination mechanism and pushing action.

Besides these dolls, there are a variety of mechanical dolls that crawl, tumble, walk and sing. One, the TATA doll, has a cardboard body containing metal springs. Keys wound the springs so that the doll could move from side to side while raising its arm to its mouth. The doll stood nearly fifteen inches high, and had heads of composition, with bisque or wooden limbs. They were distributed by Abercrombie and Fitch, New York, circa 1939 and were called "Elfin." Some dolls are actually tin figures that are part of old tin toys. One of these is a toy upright piano with figures from the comic strip "Lil Abner" attached to it. When wound, Mammy Yokum would play, and Lil Abner would raise his arm. The author played with one of these when she was a toddler, and still remember detaching Abner and twirling him around her finger. A very expensive example, complete with original box, was recently featured on PBS's *The Antiques Roadshow.*

Enoch Paul Lehmann of Germany, made a variety of tin and clockwork toys in 1881. These had a heavily decorated surface. One typical example represents a frightened bride who jumps up and down in a trailer drawn by her husband's motorbike (King '58-'59).

Japan soon entered the tin toy market to compete with England and Germany. An unusual doll from Japan represents an elegant lady that moves on wheels similar to the Autoperipatetikos. Another Japanese example is a conjurer that makes a tin head appear and disappear in a box. These old tin toys seem to sell from $500 and up today if in good condition. The Chinese are also reproducing the older tin toys with great success. The author's galloping acrobat on a tin horse is one example. When wound, the horse "runs." German dancing dolls have a mechanism in their plastic bodies that makes them hop when it is wound with a metal key. They are about six inches high. Usually, these German dolls wear regional costumes, but some can represent animals. Russian mechanical dolls are also made. One five-inch doll is made of molded and painted tin and is dressed in a traditional costume. She is key-wound and moves on wheels. The dancing bear is another Russian toy. The bear is eleven inches high with a metal mechanism in his body. The arms are plus covered wire, and hold a musical instrument. When wound, the bear strums the instrument then jumps and turns as though dancing. The bear comes in a colorful box printed with a picture of the bear and slogan in Russian.

Karakuri are Japanese mechanical dolls that perform a variety of tasks. One family has been making these dolls in Japan for eight generations, beginning in the Edo Period (1603–1867). This era was one of the richest periods of Japanese history. There were significant changes in economic and cultural development in this time, and the Shogun rulers of the Edo Era brought 250 years of peace to Japan. Order was established, and culture flourished. Edo is the old name for Tokyo and this epoch is also known as Tokugawa Japan.

Bunraku puppets are also beautiful examples of articulated Japanese dolls, but these are operated in a way similar to marionettes. Puppet plays were written for them, and they are operated by master puppeteers by a means of sticks. It takes three men to operate these magnificent puppets that are two-thirds the size of the average human being. The puppeteers work blind; their heads are covered by black hoods (*Japanese History and Literature Guide* 117). One man operates the head (including eye and mouth movement) and the body, the second operates the left hand, and the third operates the right hand. So realistic are these figures that one forgets, they are not real people acting out a drama. The heads and limbs are made of *gofun*, or the oyster paste gesso paste, which covers the faces of many Japanese dolls.

Famous dramatists wrote for the puppet theater and for the live actors of the Kabuki stage. One of the most popular and well known was Chikamatsu Monzaemon (1653–1725), (*Japanese History and Literature Guide* 115) His first play was also one of the most important plays of the Japanese theater; it is titled the *Love Suicides at Sonezaki, or Sonezaki Shinju*, and it was written for the *Bunraku* puppets. According to Donald Keene of Columbia University, this might have been the first time that a play featured an ordinary citizen as a hero (115). The hero of the play is an employee in a shop that sells soy sauce. The heroine is an ordinary prostitute. The theme of their tragedy is that love sometimes involves self-sacrifice. Though Chikamatsu's play was wildly popular, the Japanese government soon censored him; too many young couples were inspired to commit suicide by the play (116). Still, Chikamatsu admired the puppet theater, and wrote several plays for it. His language is poetically beautiful and endures to this day:

"They cling to each other, weeping bitterly,

And wish, as many a lover has wished,
The night would last a little longer.
The heartless summer night is short as ever,
And soon the cock crows chase away their lives…"
(Keene, quoted in *Japanese History and Literature*
Guide 116).

As fascinating as the *Karakuri* and *Bunraku* figures of Japan are the mechanical figures of Disney attractions. Anyone who has ever been to Disneyland or Disneyworld is familiar with the fantastic automatons in the various exhibits such as "It's a Small World" and "Pirates of the Caribbean." These are a unique combination of doll and robot that are lifelike and detailed in every way. For example, in the "Hall of Presidents," the figures nod, lean forward, rock in chairs, and look at each other as if in agreement. Modern computerized dolls are quickly becoming the automata of the future. One, Julie, is perhaps the most sophisticated. "Julie" is the trademark of Worlds of Wonder, Inc. The doll uses radio frequency energy and is programmed to recognize her owner's voice and certain words. She comes with a book coated in a Velcro like material that allows her to read. She responds when moved, when the temperature changes, and when light changes to dark. For example, if a child takes Julie into a dark room, the doll asks "Can you see OK? It's kind of dark." Besides all her accomplishments, Julie is an attractive doll with blonde, rooted hair and large, blue eyes. She moves her lips and eyes as she talks and is two feet high. The computerized mechanism which operates her is hidden in a hard-plastic torso and runs on alkaline batteries. Similar dolls include Teddy Ruxpin, Mother Goose, and Mickey Mouse. More of these dolls are discussed in the last chapter about modern metal dolls.

Many of the favorite toys of all time have become high tech, along with the rest of the world. As a result, animated display dolls are becoming cheaper and more popular. In fact, one can purchase them for home use. Many have heads and bodies of vinyl, similar to Patti Playpal and other dolls of the fifties and sixties. Others have sculpted Styrofoam heads and plastic eyes. Most are large. Some are made with bisque heads, attached to a long metal rod, similar to that used on walking dolls in the 1950s. Inside the neck is a small metal plate with a hole in it to work the head rod must pass through this hole and touch one of the two round indentations on a box shaped metal device in the doll's body. When contact is made, the doll rotates its head and waves its arms. The arms are vinyl threaded with heavy wire.

In *A Cricket on the Hearth*, Charles Dickens describes a mechanical doll in terms of supposedly old, if not respectable men, as "insanity flying over horizontal pegs, inserted for the purpose, in their own street doors" (244). Caleb, the poor toy maker in the novel, makes a variety of dolls and doll houses for every station in life (242). In fact, he establishes a doll's hierarchy in his shop, with the wax doll and her "limbs of perfect symmetry," at the top. Next come dolls of leather and those of coarse linen. The dolls at the bottom of the pyramid are the wooden dolls which Dickens describes as "so many matches out of tinderboxes…established in their sphere (of life) at once, beyond the possibility of getting out" (243). Mechanical dolls, however, are in their own category, and for this reason, we must continue to explore their history in the next chapter.

Steiner made another doll, now in the Bethnal Green Museum of London, that did have distinct limbs and was key-wound. The bisque headed doll contained a clockwork mechanism that allowed it to move its head from side to side, as well as to swing its arms and walk. It also cried "maman" and "papa." (77).

Other walking dolls of the time were more complicated. Of these, Bartholomew writes, "levers pushed one leg in front of the other, the dolls balance ensured by her being shod in heavy metal, or like other toys, placed behind a cart which she pushed forward" (77).

Moreover, like the life-sized automata of the eighteenth century, many dolls of the next century were run by manipulation of an outside attachment, e.g., a tube attached to a hollow rubber ball. When the ball was squeezed, the mechanism was activated. This bellows mechanism originated in about 1765 (Bartholomew 78), but it is still used to day in simple toys.

Talking dolls were harder to make. Perhaps, Bartholomew says, because they required a more delicate mechanism which was expensive. In 1824, Mäezel patented a talking doll in Paris. Mäezel also invented the metronome, and succeeded von Kempeln as owner of the famous Turk automata (78). In 1853, Guillard patented a talking doll with a mechanism made of wood.

The Bru Firm of France, long known for beautiful bisque bébé or little girl dolls, also experimented with mechanical models. When Madame Bru succeeded her husband as head of the firm in 1872, she took out a patent for a singing doll. Ten years later, she faced German and American competitors who also developed singing dolls. These were respectively Webber 1882, Hölbe 1883, and Girard 1892. Girard's Bébé Marcheur could both walk and talk, and was the first doll to do so (Bartholomew 79). Note, this last Girard doll may still have been a Bru, merely represented by Girard. (79)

The 1897 Steiner kissing doll was, perhaps, the culmination of the French mechanical dolls. When a cord was pulled, it said "mama" and "papa" and would move its lips to kiss whoever was holding it. When put to bed, the doll could wail in protest. (Bartholomew 80)

Bartholomew notes that while interesting doll of wood, cloth, and corn were made in the U.S. in the nineteenth century, mechanical dolls were not popular until they were imported for Germany in the late part of the century (81). Perhaps this is because when Americans wanted luxury dolls, they imported them from Paris like everyone else (81).

Still, a few American dolls sewed, walked, or rocked cradles. The Robert J. Clay 1871 "creeping baby" was especially popular. Several firms including Ives produced this doll that wore a bonnet and dress in keeping with contemporary fashion. As it crawled across the floor, it would occasionally glance to the side. Variations of this doll are still made. Uneeda made hard plastic version in the late 1970s. Bartholomew makes an interesting social comparison between American and French mechanical dolls. He says that American doll reflected housework, or hard work in fields or shop (81). Perhaps these dolls reflect the American work ethic. French dolls, on the other hand, were more frivolous. They blew bubbles or scattered kisses and rose petals (81). Americans also preferred humorous caricatures of Uncle Sam, or the black preacher (81).

In 1969, Sotheby's provided an original version of Jean Roullet's Snake Dance (Bartholomew 84). This doll wore an elaborate costume. The example in Monaco is nude. Recently, another example of this doll sold for over a quarter of a million dollars.

The Webber doll, according to an advertisement, had a wax head and real hair, and was advertised as "French-made." (80) The more expensive version had closing eyes and wore a knitted chemise.

1880s German sleep-eye dolls were operated by eyelids that worked by lead counterweights so that the doll could open and close its eyes (Bartholomew 84). Earlier examples operated by a wire attached to the body. By 1906, Flirting eye dolls were invented.

The Edison doll first appeared at the 1890 Paris exhibition. The body as made of steel. The head was a Simon and Halbig model. The *Scientific American* magazine of 26 April 1890 discussed the doll. It had wax-like records placed on a phonograph like instrument. (85). A 1905 teddy bear of the Black Skirt company, and an "Electric Bright Eye Teddy Bear" could shake the right paw, and eyes lit up white or red (Bartholomew 88).

Today automata have made a comeback, and there are many examples for Halloween, Christmas and Easter. Particularly popular for Halloween are the characters licensed by Universal studios. These represent characters like The Bride of Frankenstein, Frankenstein's monster, Dracula, and the Mummy. They come in a 14-inch and 24-inch size (check sizes). The smaller doll's eyes light up red, and an eerie, mournful laugh emerges from them. There is also a raven sitting on a skull that flaps its wings and moves its beak. The skulls' eyes light up when it is activated. The bird acts like a tape recorder, so that when a button is pushed, it repeats everything said to it. It is especially effective if one recites Poe's "The Raven" to the bird. There are talking skulls, life-sized witches, and dangling skeletons that talk and/or move, as well as adorable toddlers that resemble animated cabbage patch kids. Also, animated dolls are once again appearing in horror movies like *The Tommyknockers*, *the Child's Play* films, and *Dolls*.

Christmas is a wonderful time to buy and collect animated dolls. Examples are made in both porcelain and plastic. The bodies of these dolls are often made of wire, and were once very popular Department Store decorations at Christmas. Anyone who grew up in Davenport, Iowa, will remember the fantastic window decorations comprised mostly of mechanical dolls that decorated the store fronts of Petersen Harned Von Maur's downtown store. The dolls with vinyl heads closely resemble Patti Playpal. There is a snoring Santa Claus, and one that climbs a ladder. Bob Cratchitt hoists Tiny Tim, Teddy Bears dance, and delicate Victorian dolls wave their arms. The author has a two-foot high snow angel that turns her head and waives alighted snow ball. She also owns a black version dressed in Green Velvet with high button shoes. The dolls are excellent quality and sell for under thirty dollars at chains like Walmart. A few companies are even reproducing the old French automatons. One figure of Snow White by Enesco stands on a beautifully painted box. The doll's body is made of wire and plastic, and she turns her head as the music plays. Gorham and Schmid also have made bisque headed dolls with music box mechanisms in their bodies.

There are angels of various sizes that flap their wings and hold lighted candles as well. A mechanical Santa's house plays fifteen Christmas carols and has moving figures. Enesco, Hallmark, and other companies make ornaments and music boxes of various sizes that contain often elaborate moveable figures. These also light up and play music. The author's favorite from Christmas 1993 is Hallmark's Salvation Army Band. The assembled band in miniature moves and plays music as a soft light glows from the ornament. The ornaments range from $30.00 to well over $200.00.

Toy robots of various kinds, from miniatures to three-foot-high models are also popular. The original *Lost in Space Robot* from the 1960s' T.V. program can command thousands. Modern, animated versions that repeat the famous phrase, "Danger, Will Robinson," can be had for under $30.00. Miniature key chain versions talk. Transformers and Shogun Warriors are other examples of modern robot dolls. The robot itself has been immortalized in Asimov's *I Robot* science fiction novels. The talking Barbie of the '60s even spoke Spanish. Talking Barbie has made another debut, and there was a controversy over her vocabulary a couple years ago because, among other things, she said "Math is hard." One "toy terrorist" group even sabotaged dolls in stores and switched voice boxes in

Talking G.I. Joe dolls and Talking Barbies. Of course, one could not mention animated dolls without mentioning Chatty Cathy and her progeny and relatives from the sixties. Chatty Cathy has been reissued by Mattel, but at a price. The new edition costs close to $100, many times more than the original doll. Original black Chatties are so rare, that some collectors buy white dolls and dye them. The summer 1998 movie *Small Soldiers* inspired toys and dolls. These are figures animated with microchips, supposedly from the Pentagon, that stage a small war in the film. Particularly amusing is group of Barbie clones that the small soldier dolls have turned into commandoes. The actual toys are not that deadly, but they do talk, and the thirty-inch versions are hard to find. Dolls that interact with Windows 95 and other computers are also popular. There is a Barbie of this type, but it did not prove to be a big seller. More popular are plush, computerized versions of characters like Arthur and Barney that interact with televisions and computers. Some even work like an alarm clock to wake young children in time for pre-school. These figures are simplified version of the animatronics pioneered by Disney for its theme parks.

Disney Studios recently produced a movie that used animated images of actual dolls. Tim Burton's *The Nightmare Before Christmas* used at least twenty dolls for each animated character. The effect was that the dolls looked like working automata. "Virtual" or cyber animated figures are the newest rage in animation. There are many CD Rom games of Barbie and other characters that appear three-dimensional on the screen. Perhaps the ultimate "baby" or doll-type toy in this medium is the Tamagotchi "virtual pet," that children carry on a keychain. Small timers go off when the pet needs feeding, changing, etc. Perhaps this is the most distilled, efficient version of the animated "doll" available, though it defies the definition of a doll most collectors adhere to.

Sky Dancer dolls, and various male counterparts continue to be popular choices. Mattel and Disney teamed together to make a series of five to seven-inch dolls of Belle, Snow White, Cinderella, and Princess Jasmine. These dolls either stand on a base that plays music, or come with special bubble pipes and liquid that allow them to blow bubbles. Various dolls with bisque heads play instruments, dance, sing, or talk. One company makes eight-inch plastic dolls that stand on a base. When a button is pressed, the dolls, which represent nursery rhyme characters or foreign countries, talk and say two or three phrases.

Chapter 27: Metal Heads

While the beautiful mechanical dolls often had heads made of delicate bisque, other dolls that did not move still had heads and/or bodies of metal. Dolls with metal heads have existed for a long time, but did not enjoy any popularity till the end of the nineteenth century. The three most famous trademarks were *Juno, Minerva,* and *Diana.* Karl Standfuss of Deuben bei Dresden made the Juno heads, which bear the crown mark. As early as 1880, German metal headed dolls may have appeared, though other collectors say that they were mass-produced in Germany by 1894 (Fawcett 213). Then, beginning in 1900, Standfuss made metal and celluloid dolls, heads and parts. One of the advantages of metal headed dolls was that one could push them back into shape if they were dented. Of course, doing so, left chipped paint and other imperfections. Metal used for heads in the 1890s included brass, zinc and tin plate. The heads were mainly mass-produced in Germany. Those made in 1894 often had sawdust-filled bodies, glass or painted eyes, and natural or molded hair. Some fancy hairstyle metal heads appeared when elaborate bisque heads, the so-called "Parian" dolls, were popular. Two of these dolls date from the 1870s and are made of pewter. They are from the late Gladys Hyls Hilsdorf collection and are considered quite rare. The heads have flowers molded into them and are set on wooden bodies.

Besides the Juno heads, there were many Minerva metal heads made at the end of the century. These heads, made by the firm of Buschow and Beck were made in Germany and sold in the United States through A. Vischer and Co., New York, NY. Several German heads, including some Minervas, were exhibited at the St. Louis Exhibition of 1904. Minerva dolls were advertised under different brand names, one of which was the "Wearwell Brand." This doll usually had a four-inch metal head with fixed, blue glass eyes. The head was marked "Minerva" across the front and "Germany/3" across the back. Sears Roebuck advertised these dolls in their toy catalog. AT one time, Minerva heads were so popular, that one Butler Brothers catalog equals the Minerva doll to the Kestner bisques, saying that "the Minerva doll enjoys a reputation equal to the Kestner brand of dolls." (Angione 167) Also during this time, Minerva heads were more expensive than bisque heads. For example, Minerva heads sold for $4.25 per dozen, while comparable bisque heads sold for $2.25 per dozen.

Furthermore, a 1903 Montgomery Ward's catalog advertised Minerva heads from $.25 for a head of 2 5/8 inches to $.75 for a four-inch head. A four-inch head was for sale for $45.00 at a doll show, held November 10, 1996 in Davenport, IA. The head had painted features and hair, and was in fair to good condition. Dolls with the added features of teeth and glass eyes sold for $.75 each to $1.75 for a head of 5 3/8 inches. Curly-haired doll heads cost $.50 to $.75 each. The same catalog advertised Minerva "Knockabout" dolls. These dolls were eleven inches long with Silesia bodies and came without wigs. Janet Johl, in one of her books, describes an unusual Minerva with a wig, glass eyes and four "china teeth." (Johl SMAD 114). Another collector told Johl of a doll "either Minerva or Juno" marked "Made in Germany/D.R. Patent and England Pat/D.R.G.M." (Johl 114). "D.R.G.M." means "patent applied for." This doll was 13 and one-half inches tall with molded/painted hair and a blue sateen dress which fit over a metal platform supported by four wheels. When activated, the doll turned around and around. A similar French doll that stands about 18 inches, with bisque head, glass eyes and teeth, and a long, metal skirt that covers a wheeled platform cost approximately $3000 at a doll show in Davenport, IA, November 10, 1996.

In 1912, Minerva advertised a doll that shed real tears. The author, however, has never seen one. Genevieve Angione shows and discusses in her book *All Dolls are Collectible,* a boy marked with the Minerva mark. The head is six and three-fourths inches in circumference with a number "three" embossed on the back. The eyes are painted blue and have white highlights and red dots at the corners and nostrils. The ears are molded and slightly detached. The hair is brown, the body stuffed with hair. The boy's hands are chubby and bisque.

Of course, other companies besides Minerva were making metal dolls at various times. One twenty-three-inch doll with a metal shoulder head has a wig, open mouth and sleeping eyes. The doll is marked "Germany 15." A similar doll with a closed mouth and no marks is thirteen-inches high (Schroeder 88). A metal headed boy has no marks and painted features. His body is cloth with bisque arms and leather legs. An R. H. Macy catalog of the early 1900s describes a "Diana" metal head as unbreakable with moving eyes and a wig. The head came in eight sizes and cost between $.44 and $1.39 (Simonelli 46). The Diana head is rare. According to Johl, a constant supply of metal heads for Europe was replacing fancy bisques and china heads (151).

American companies, too, made metal heads. The Metal Doll Company, which was run by Vincent Lake, made an all-metal jointed doll with interchangeable wigs. Lake was an inventor from Pleasantville, New Jersey. In 1899, he had patented a new typographic machine and had great hopes for his new invention. According to Miriam Forman-Brunell, in *Made to Play House: Dolls and the Commercialization of American Girlhood 1830–1930*, Lake's excitement was short-lived, the Linotype came along and rendered his brainchild obsolete (35). Apparently disappointed and jaded by what Forman-Brunell calls "the masculine world of printing," Lake invented the all steel doll, complete with steel springs. Forman-Brunell, whose book places a feminist slant on the doll manufacturing industry, calls the doll the "epitome of the American male world of business and production from which he came." (36) In fact, Forman-Brunell observes that by the turn of the century, "Men with origins as diverse as carriage manufacturers and typesetters would end up as doll manufacturer," placing their knowledge of making everything from pulley-belts and carriages to clocks and various machines to use in making dolls (36). In fact, many companies at this time were involved in the mass production of dolls and toys, and many of these were made of metal.

The Metal Stamping Company made walking metal figures of various kinds. An old soldier in the author's collection by Wolverine Toys is similar to these. He stands eleven-inches high and dates from the 1930s. The Drum Major, as he is known, is all metal. His arms are jointed, when key-wound, he plays a metal drum. Though badly rusted, the doll's painted features are still visible. A smaller example of the same doll stands seven-inches high. The Wolverine Toy Company originated in Pittsburgh, then moved to Arkansas. It operated from 1908–1984.

Metal Frozen Charlotte type dolls regularly appeared in Crackerjack boxes as prizes. One such doll in the author's collection is attached to a baby announcement card along with a metal stork. It dates from the 1880s. A very unusual, all metal baby doll was made by the Atlas Doll Co., between 1917–30. Heads from this company are generally unmarked. Atlas had its location in Baltimore, MD and produced about sixty-five types of dolls in 1921. The baby doll was modelled after the bent-legged bisque headed babies of the era. According to Lauren Jaeger in "Identifying Your Dolls," *Doll World*, Oct. 1993, Atlas and other American companies entered the doll marked during World War I to fill a need for dolls (12). Ms. Jaeger values an Atlas baby doll at $50.00 (12). Other unusual metal dolls represented young girls or baby. At the Lasalle-Peru doll show, held October 13, 1996, the author saw three interesting heads at the following prices. A girl's head, six-inches high, with blue sleep eyes and painted, "flapper" type black hair in fair condition was $45.00. Baby or toddler's head, no wig, with sleep eyes, fair condition, was also $45.00. A complete baby doll, about 18 inches high, with sleep eyes and old clothing, in good to fair condition cost $110.00.

The author has a metal girl in her collection that is about seventeen-inches high. The doll's body is cloth, her limbs composition. The hair is molded in a bob style with a molded loop for a ribbon. The original dress is of a taffeta, the print faded to a lavender color. The paint and features are in good shape, though the doll was a good price at $75.00. Dolls of this type were usually valued at $200.00 or more during the early '90s when she was bought.

Perhaps the most famous American metal head, however, is the Giebeler Falk doll by the Giebeler Falk Doll Company of New York. In 1919, the company took a patent, No. 18,550, for making dolls, outfits and parts. One of the marks on the dolls is "Gie-Fa" with the Star of David. The doll may also be marked with "G" inside a Star of David with "U.S. Pat." underneath. The doll came in sixteen, eighteen, twenty, twenty-two and twenty-five-inch sizes. These heads are made of heavy gauge aluminum and appeared during the latter years of World War I. They had sleeping eyes of metal attached to the head with five washers. A nut and bolt secured these to adjust the swing of the eye weight. The hands, feet and head were coated with baked-on enamel and the body was of lathe-turned wood and fully-jointed. In the author's opinion, these are among the loveliest of the metal heads and closely resemble the bisque heads of the era. The author is lucky enough to have a Giebeler-Falk head in her collection, though the wig, body and dress are replacements. In 1919, Giebeler also made a phonograph doll. The doll's crown was hinged and inside was the horn and turntable for the phonograph. The mechanism was in the doll's body and the crank was in the back.

A doll similar to the Giebeler-Falk head was made by the Unica Company of Belgium. This doll, however, is apparently all metal. It has a wig and sleeping eyes. Such a doll is extremely rare and is in the collection of Mrs. Betty McGuire of Buffalo, NY.

Janet Johl describes another metal head which dates from approximately 1900 and has a pink, kidolene body with carved hands. The doll came from the inventory of an old family store in Indiana (Johl 183). The Aluminum Head Doll Head Works of New York made dolls between 1919 and 1920. These dolls had aluminum heads and hands on ball-jointed composition bodies. Some also had stuffed baby bodies (Simonelli 46).

Ultimately, claims Miriam Forman-Brunell, these male doll makers produced indestructible dolls, but they did not do so out of a desire to save little girls the heartache of watching treasured, but fragile dolls of other materials break. Instead, men like Lake, Schoenhut, Joel "Cab" Ellis, Thomas Edison, and others made supposedly indestructible dolls "based on the machines they admired" (37). The dolls were supposed to be extensions of the male doll maker's machines. In fact, she argues that men were intent on entering what had traditionally been a woman's field, doll making, but that unlike women, the male manufacturers were more interested "in how a doll worked and looked" because men at the time were "still shaped by the dominant construction of manhood" (37). If one is to accept Forman-Brunell's theory completely, the names Juno and Minerva are significant; these dolls represent female soldiers, true war goddesses in the eyes of their male creators. Yet, the problem was that because men thought of the doll as an "autonomous object," they "strove to give the doll a semblance of a life of its own, but only succeeded in creating a 'thing' with little connection to girls who, as a result, rarely played with them" (37).

Unfortunately, Forman-Brunell writes, "The dolls were products of attempt to transform pulleys into profits" (37). She also writes that male doll inventors produced doll parts, but that a "network of business relationships" created an entire doll (37). Yet, a study of the doll making industry in Europe reveals that the famous firms often traded and interchanged parts and heads. Mothers often bought just the doll head and parts, preferring to make the rest of the doll at home. Rather than have a sinister, masculine conspiracy in mind, the manufacturers may have been deferring to consumer taste and preference. Also, many American metal heads are well-dented and chipped. They have homemade bodies and hand-sewn clothes. These facts indicate that little girls did, indeed, play with these dolls. They and their mothers would have found selling separate heads desirable, as doll makers still do today. Walk into any hobby or craft store, and you will see rows of doll heads and limbs made in various materials.

Among the heads considered desirable at different times were wax heads, either all-wax, or other base materials dipped in wax. Metal was used, as well as plaster and papier mâché. During the mid-1800s metal doll heads were dipped in wax. These dolls have sawdust-filled bodies with wooden limbs. Some had wooden squeakers and inset teeth (Fawcett 213). The drawback of these unbreakable dolls was that sometimes, the wax developed yellow spots. Perhaps these spots were a reaction of the wax touching metal. All in all, wax over metal dolls are unusual and appear to be a variation of was over papier mâché dolls.

French manufacturers were also experimenting with metal. One, René Poulin of Paris, invented a metal doll head in 1861. Another French metal head that turned was patented by M. Briens of Paris in 1862. A late 19th century French body from one private collection is all painted metal and contains a key-wound mechanism. Evidently, the doll was meant to walk and would have had a bisque head. The body is attributed to Steiner. Steiner, too, experimented with metal. His key wound bébé has an all metal body. A fine example is in the collection of Mrs. Vera Kramer, of St. Augustine, Florida. Many of these mid-nineteenth century dolls, whether made of metal or bisque, were inspired by the Empress Eugénie of France, the wife of Napoleon III (Billy Boy 154).

If women were excluded from the American doll making industry, they were not left out in France. In 1860, Mlle. Calixte Huret took out a patent for dolls with metal heads and hands. She began to make dolls in around 1850, when she took out the patent. Her dolls are among the rarest of the fashion dolls of this period, or of any dolls collected today, for that matter. Mlle. Huret is often given credit for inventing the swiveling doll head (Bennett 15). She regularly used pewter hands on her bisque headed dolls as well. Also, many French bisque dolls like those of Daniel and Cie had steel springs or metal parts. A few all metal French dolls were made during the 1860s by other firms including Huret's rival, Rohmer. Clara Hallard Fawcett in *Dolls, a New Guide for Collectors*, repeatedly mentions Huret dolls with jointed metal bodies and bisque heads. She claims that the bodies are marked "Huret." Similar models have wood incorporated into the makeup of their bodies (Fawcett 80). Huret dolls were expensive even when new. In fact, Rockwell and others write that the doll's elaborate costumes and diverse accessories were "as complex as women's fashions" (9), so that women and young girls who competed with each other over who had the most fashionable outfit extended the competition to their expensive dolls. Entire stores were devoted to accessories for these dolls, and in 1850, one French directory of commerce lists over 200 French doll shops and firms. Huret and others sold accessories in miniature boxes stamped with the firm name. Some of the shops even published magazines devoted to the dolls, comparable to those published today that are devoted to Beanie Babies or Barbie. In fact, the competition to have the best doll and accessories is similar to the competition during the '90s over who would have the most Beanies. Huret published a magazine about her dolls called *Gazette De La Poupée* in the 1860s. Another writer and human-sized fashion designer, who collects dolls, Billy Boy, writes that "The Huret-created fashions imitate the life-sized originals in absolutely perfect miniature" (156). This comment is particularly true about the hats Mlle. Huret created for her dolls. Perhaps it is the elaborate trousseau of a Huret doll Guy de Maupassant had in mind in writing his short story, "Mademoiselle."

Another French doll is an all metal marionette with gold tin armor. Some of the French dolls are really lovely; the Huret pewter head is an outstanding example. This doll has the dreamy, plump face of the typical Huret, but the brush strokes on the metal have all the delicacy of an impressionist painting. The doll has metal hands and a body made of gutta percha and metal. It is so unusual, that many veteran collectors have never heard of it. Two photos of the doll appear in Maureen Popp's and Marshall Martin's articles on Huret dolls and accessories that appeared in *Doll News* in the winter, spring and summer 1987 issues. The Huret and other French metal dolls are feminine and realistic; they seem transformed into a delicate work of art by the machines that made them. French interest in art, aesthetics and fashion may have favorably influenced the finished product where dolls are concerned.

The rest of Europe was not left behind in the race to produce metal heads, however. Unica, a Belgian company, has made a rare, all-metal doll. The doll, owned by Mrs. Betty McGuire, is believed to be the only one of its type. Since any doll by this company, even a vinyl one, is unusual, an all-metal example is super-rare.

On October 27, 1913, E.W. Hill and E.C. Cushing of London took out patent No. 21607 for metal dolls' heads and limbs. In Switzerland, Bucherer was making a fully articulated doll of metal constructed of hollow metal balls. This doll is marked "Made in Switzerland/Patent Applied for." According to one source, Bucherer dolls currently are worth around $200.00 or so. Comic characters like Mutt and Jeff are worth slightly more. Another Bucherer doll is the French comic strip character, Beccasine. The dolls have compositions heads, hands, and feet (Foulke 289). They were dolls meant for either gender, for adults, and for juveniles. Bucherer dolls are akin to modern action figures because of their emulation of popular comic characters and celebrities.

Besides the heads discussed previously, there are many other metal heads that are unmarked. Janet Johl describes several of these in her books. Furthermore, the author remembers seeing a brass head on a composition body, dressed as an African native in colorful feathers. The price in 1982 for this doll was $65.00. Johl also mentions a copper head doll with applied ears on a kid body. (Johl SMAD 219). Johl also talks of a "lard pail" boy who was left in a barn to rust. This doll had tin legs with knee joints rusted into a sitting position. His head and shoulder were in one piece. The doll was repainted because of the rust and wore overalls, a print shirt and black button loth topped shoes (219). Brass headed dolls are also made in Thailand, while Japan makes entire dolls of metal even today.

Early collectors like Johl often referred to all metal headed dolls as "tin heads." This title is, however, erroneous. Tin is a soft, bluish white and lustrous element with a low melting capacity. It is often used as a protective coating. Brass, on the other hand, was a common material for heads like the Minerva. Brass is an alloy of copper and zinc and is considerably stronger than tin. In any case, the variety of metal headed dolls makes collecting them fun and rewarding.

Despite their apparent indestructibility, however, Metal Headed dolls are not favored among collectors who prefer china and bisque antiques. Noted authority Helen Young called metal heads "secondaries" in the 1960s, and others did not collect them at all. That fact that they chip and dent easily contributes to their unpopularity. Yet, an example in mint condition is beautiful, and one collector treasured two Minerva twins dressed in light blue silk bustle dresses as her most valuable dolls in the late 1960s, even though she had many bisque and china headed dolls in her vast collection. Perhaps these dolls are "sleepers," or they are too much a product of the consequences of "The Industrial Revolution" to be thought of as nostalgic toys. Yet, in time, their day will "come," and they will also be treasured antiques.

Chapter 28: Miniature All Bisque

These miniature dolls go by many names including, Frozen Charlotte, penny dolls, teacup dolls, *Badekind*er, candy store dolls, All China dolls. Marilyn Monroe's favorite doll, featured on *Antiques Road Show*, was a tiny joined all bisque with blonde hair and blue glass eyes. Child actress Margaret O'Brien carried an all-bisque doll in her purse.

Curly was an all bisque sailor doll in Rumer Godden's classic tale of the dollhouse *Home is the Sailor.*

The now defunct Mott's Miniature Museum, housed in Knott's Berry Farm for decades, had thousands of small all bisque and china dolls populating the miniature shops and houses that comprised the collection. The doll shop had some that were almost microscopic.

The German firm of Hertel and Schwab made many of these dolls. Some old store stock was sold by Doll masters, the catalog division of Theriault's.

Genevieve Angione has written the definitive book about them called *All Bisque and Half Dolls.* Janet Pagter Johl has devoted whole chapters to them in her books.

When I was little myself, little dolls were my constant companion. Remember Stuckey's—Oh, that blue roof. There was one on the highway, not far from where I used to teach. When I was a toddler, they had a machine near the restroom that distributed for a quarter, two, tiny jointed hard plastic babies with clothes. The joy of my existence then was to get to Stuckey's at the end of a Sunday Drive, quarter in hand.

They were known for pecan candy, but I loved them for their eye candy. Many of my little dolls came from Stuckey's all over the country. Others came from a local restaurant called Town and Country, that had a toy cupboard or barrel where kids could pick out a toy. I always chose a doll, or a tiny baby with doll furniture. PeeWees by Uneeda and all kinds of knockoffs of these 3.5-inch dolls were around when I was in first grade. I had a whole case full of them, with tiny clothes to match. I still have them, and still find examples where I can.

Tiny dolls have long been the companions of artists and children; miniature idols and Ushabti managed to find their way to us from the Ancient World, silent time travels that witnessed worlds we can only dream of. The Nampa figurine of Idaho is tiny, measuring mere inches. Discovered in 1889 buried in strata that usually yielded artifacts 1 to three million years old, fossils really, its origins are unknown. It is delicate carefully preserved. You have to ask to see it. Many think the figure is a fake, but how could it have buried so far down if it were contrived. No one knows.

Doll house dolls as we know them have been around since the 17th century, but it is during the 19th century that tin dolls or pocket dolls came into their own. With them came all bisque, or even all china dolls called Frozen Charlottes or penny dolls. Charlottes took their name from a ballad sung by William Lorenzo Carter about a young girl so vain she wouldn't wear a coat on a long sleigh ride to a New Year's Eve Ball. Consequently, she froze to death. Other names were teacup dolls, Badekinder, even pillar dolls. King cake babies have their origins with these little dolls, as do the tin Milagros of Spain, Mexico, Greece, and South America.

Tiny porcelain dolls and half dolls found their way into pincushions, as bottle toppers, as brush toppers, on almost anything. Some graced boxes, while others were worn as jewelry. Fragmented dolls appeared on homemade jardinières. Carl Fox in *The Doll* has compared these fragments to the Venus of Willendorf figures. Today, artists use them to create jewelry or assembled sculpture. They are dug up from the ruins of old doll factories in former East Germany, and are considered buried treasure for those who buy and sell them.

Chapter 29: The Twentieth Century

Twentieth century dolls were once not that collectible, but most have now become antique or vintage. This means they are either over 100 years old, or over 75 years old. During the late '70s through the '90s, twentieth century dolls became wildly popular. Their popularity was due to a series of books by Patricia Smith called *Modern Collectors Dolls* and Johanna Gast Anderton's *Twentieth Century Dolls*, volumes I and II. I had the pleasure of meeting Anderton in San Francisco. I met Smith online on AOL's old Hobby Central, a site for collectors set up during the late '90s. Anderton was kind and helpful. Smith was, well, grouchy and critical. Still, these two authors were pioneers in the field of modern dolls. Twentieth century dolls were made of all kinds of materials including bisque, china, metal, wax, composition, cloth, plants, hard plastic, and vinyl. The last two proved to be the most popular and enduring materials.

Vinyl and Hard Plastic: Rubber is developed from the sap of the casein or rubber tree. Plastics and vinyl are made of various combinations of natural resins, and pecan resin is often used today to make figurines like those found in Dollar Stores or Seraphim angels. Coal and urea also figure in the manufacture of plastic, and many plastic or vinyl dolls are made by a hot, liquid substance being injected into rubber molds.

Hard Plastic is durable, and can gain realistic results as good quality Madame Alexander, Vogue, Terri Lee, Monica, Dollikin, even Kathe Kruse dolls show. It is, however, fragile, and will break if the dolls falls on hard floors like cement.

Vinyl is lifelike, and if good quality will last. I have a very rare doll from Unica, Belgium, in rubber, that has turned white over the years, and quite frankly, is smelly. She, and another rare rubber doll from Brazil with the same issue, are segregated and sit on their own shelves, away from the general doll population!

I have had luck gently cleaning the dolls with nail polish remover, but don't rub it in their eyes, which will often rust because their sleep eyes can contain metal, and the remover can take off eyebrows and face paint. This is probably why experts consider it a no-no. There are excellent films on YouTube about collecting these types of dolls. Pat Smith's books and Patsy Moyer's books are great sources of information on vinyl dolls. I also like to consult the books by mother/daughter team Pam and Polly Judd. I often thought if my mother had lived, she and I would be co-authoring books about dolls.

There are many famous companies that make great vinyl dolls, especially during the late fifties and early sixties. These include Madame Alexander, Ideal, Pedigree, Furga, El Greco, Kehagias, Royal Dolls, Regal, Kenner, Hasbro, Deluxe Topper, Mattel, Uneeda, Citti Toy, Nancy Ann, Effanbee, Vogue, Migliorati, Corolle, Sasha by Goetz, Engel, Cameo, Horsman, Lissi Baitz, Poupée Belle, Bild, World Dolls, and Marjorie Spangler.

Miss Revlon, Little Miss No Name, Chatty Cathy, PeeWee's Little Sophisticates, Saucy Walker, Kissee, Patty Play Pal, The Littlechaps, Tammy, Maddie Modd, Lili, Cissy, Dollikins, Giggles, Cheerful Tearful, Barbie, and many other famous dolls made in vinyl now live in museums and toy halls of fame all over the world. Barbie and Coleco's part vinyl Cabbage Patch kids are in The Smithsonian.

Chapter 30: Oddities

It is easy to be discouraged or overwhelmed by the overload of information about dolls these days. It is also upsetting to patiently bid, on line, or live, for a much-wanted doll, then see it go to someone else.

Frankly, my advice to anyone upset over losing or not finding a desired doll is, there will always be another doll. I've read some version of this advice in Eleanor St. George's books, in Helen Young's, and in Clara Hallard Fawcett's. A hobby is a retreat from the "slings and arrows of fortune," and a way to handle stress and pursue personal enrichment. I will quote my friend R. Lane Herron here, a legend in the collecting and doll book/doll artists world, "I don't know what I would do without the dolls ..." Lane and I have been regular correspondents since 1985 or 86, when I started writing *With Love from Tin Lizzie; A History of Metal Dolls*.

That there will always be another doll is even truer of the most expensive commodities; just read the ads in the major magazines, or go to Ruby Lane or eBay, as well as other wonderful sites. There will always be a Tete Jumeau, or even a Jumeau Triste, and even Huret dolls are to be found for those with the funds and knowledge of where to look. The rare AT is found at major auctions by Theriault's, Frashers, and others.

I take issue with terms like "serious" collector and "high end." They dismiss many out there who write about dolls and doll history, and are not mad enough, or can't afford to spend, upward of $1000 on one doll, or more likely, upward of $10,000. We at the museum will not deny we have our share of high end or "serious" collectibles, but we also find that though we love them, they are not the examples that make visitors smile. Again, note, all dolls are collectible, to paraphrase another legend, Genevieve Angione. My issue with some major clubs and organizations is that, as one major dealer I know puts it, they have become cliquish. I was horrified when I offered to donate a copy of my *Bibliography of Dolls and Toys* to the most venerated and oldest doll club of all to receive a letter stating that if I wanted to sell my book, I could take out an ad.

I wasn't trying to sell anything; it was a donation to their museum, and all I would have wanted, at most, was someone to review it honestly, as the lovely family of *Doll Castle News* did.

Of course, it is crucial to encourage and inspire other collectors. Dolls are a luxury, but there are many wonderful dolls to be found and many fits within any budget. I don't like being copied, either, but I take imitation as a form of flattery in general. I started with foreign/international dolls and then antiques, slowly incorporating my childhood dolls, characters and celebrities and others. My collecting model was influenced by Helen Young, Janet Johl, and others like them who collected good, and varied dolls for their general collections. I admire those who specialize in only one type of doll, but I also get bored with that kind of collection after a while. That's just me.

I have come to prefer going to doll shows alone; whoever I am with suddenly becomes a collector, or wheedles me into giving him/her something I found and bought first, or I have to deal with other folks' schedules and time issues.

Do your own thing, and keep your ideas to yourself. Or, you will find everyone is suddenly into foreign dolls and metal dolls, and soon, they will try to publish your ideas. Not good.

In any case, stay collectors; remember why you began. Kudos to dealers who also collect and are knowledgeable. It is great to make a living off what you love, but let's not do the grade school competition and the elitist behavior. If dolls do tell the story of all humanity, let's be the bards of a harmonious choir, not a cacophonous chorus of noise pollution.

Manikin Pis: I would like to write about Manikin Pis of Brussels, or the "famous manikin of Brussels, Belgium" as Laura Starr calls him in her excellent *The Doll Book* (1908). He is a statue turned into a doll, and treated as one. Manikin Pis exemplifies the doll motif beautifully.

Starr writes that the manikin was created by a sculptor named Duquesnoy to honor the victory of Ransbeck. When star was writing the little statute was nearly 300 years old, and even then, he had a wardrobe. As happens with other statues and talismans, the manikin has been carried off and has traveled. Gnomes have nothing over him. The English took him to Britain after the Battle of Fontenoy, according to Starr, but the people of Belgium took him back. The French also stole him, but they, too brought him back. There is a story from 1817 associated with him as well. A convict took him and Brussels went into mourning for their most famous and cherished citizen. It was found and recovered, however, and the thief had to go to the pillory. According to Starr, an iron railing has been placed around the little boy ever since. Starr delicately neglects to tell us that the statue of the little boy is, of course, relieving himself, hence his name.

Many honors have been conferred on him as well, including one by Archduke Maximilian whom Starr writes actually gave him expensive clothing and a servant! Starr goes on to say that "Louis XV made him a knight of his order, and, later on, Joseph II, of Austria, conferred on him the same honor. In 1908, Manikin Pis was dressed in the robes of the Louis XV order, and similar outfits exist today."

Rick Steves featured the statute on one of his TV shows, as well as the museum that houses his many outfits. The little boy is a cultural icon the world over, and he is reproduced in miniature as key chains, chocolate pops, lawn ornaments, jewelry, etc. My father-in-law has a fountain of him, and I have a tiny metal corkscrew, one of my more unusual portrait "dolls" done in metal, this time bronze.

Chapter 31: Teddy Bears

After I read *The Grizzly Maze*, my attitudes toward bears, live or stuffed, changed dramatically. I moved all of them from my room. The thought of anyone being eaten by a grizzly bear was horrifying and nauseating, even if it was a Timothy Treadwell, self-styled naturalist, who knew nothing about bears, yet chose to live among them in the wilds of Alaska. He and his girlfriend were killed and eaten, while his tape recorder rolled, one hour or so before a helicopter as to pick them up and take them home for the winter.

My family had two encounters with bears in the wild; we weren't even related to Teddy Roosevelt. When my mother was still single, she, her sister, three brothers and parents took a trip to Yellowstone. They saw a mother and two bear cubs, and got close enough, and were foolhardy enough, to get a snapshot of the trio.

When my family and I visited, a whole group of cars stopped for a bear in the road. The bear walked up to our stopped car, and put its paw on the window sill, on my mother's side. Thankfully, the window was rolled up. It looked her right in the eye. Long before Jean Auel's *The Clan of the Cave Bear,* the bear and my mother must have recognized an ancient ancestral totem they shared. Dad said it was professional courtesy, and called Mom "Griz" for a long time. She didn't like it. I have to say the bear up close was nearsighted and stupid, with bugs crawling all over its nose.

There was a stuffed polar bear on display for many years at the Moline Holiday Inn. It was mounted rearing up on its hind legs. He fascinated me, and I mourned him when the Holiday Inn was torn down and he was moved. Today, he resides in the private home of another admirer in Coal Valley, IL. Our former Jumer's Castle Lodge, also torn down, was full of all kinds of taxidermy, with some animals carrying other animals in their mouths. I saw a mounted taxidermy bear at the Great River Road Flea Market years ago, and mused how fun it would be to have him in our teddy bear gallery at the museum. I saw a very tiny mounted cub in an antique shop in Galesburg and felt very sad that its life was cut so short, like the cub in the Roosevelt legend. He didn't shoot it, but the poor orphan was dispatched with a knife by one of

Roosevelt's servants. "Now you know the rest of the story," and I'll bet you wish you didn't.

Though my interest in all bears, taxidermy and toy, waned after *The Grizzly Maze* and the accompanying documentary, *The Grizzly Man,* I loved Dan Haggerty as *Grizzly Adams*, and have the doll. I loved how the bear would eat at the Table with Adams and Mad Jack. I also loved *Gentle Ben*. No more.

Still, I managed to amass a large bear collection, with several Steiff examples, many vintage and antique. From my dear friend, the late D.A. Horton, I bought a large antique bear wearing a cut down World War I uniform. I was able to purchase large collector bears in mohair from my friends at Summer Kitchen Antiques, Durant. Tiny bear families populate my doll house. I've managed to get over my terror, and love all the bears in my life once again.

Chapter 32: Artist Dolls

I was only 10, and had been wandering Knott's Berry Farm with my dad. My mom was in the gift shops out front, including Virginia's Gift Shop and the Toy Shop. It had been a long night, and I had made many trips to the bathroom due to something that really did not agree with my ten-year-old stomach. Wish I could remember what it was, but it doesn't matter.

It was the first time I'd seen Mott's Miniatures, the creation of Mrs. Lucretia Mott, her husband, and two daughters. Mott's contained every type of doll house, doll shop, miniature scene, attraction, attic, ball room, etc. There was a doll shop full of mini dolls of all kinds. It was my dream room for sure, and I made up my own when I went home. There were micro minis, like the Lord's Prayer inscribed on the head of a pin, the world's smallest book that could sit on the head of a pin, a working two-inch TV, and more.

It was heaven for me. I wandered and wondered, and my poor dad waited and talked to Mr. Mott, now a widower, about the doll house he had built me.

Lucretia Mott remembered traveling on a covered wagon as a child, and she had a tiny doll in her possession that she found in a wagon trail. Mott collected antique dolls of all sizes, then sold them to feed her miniature habit. Her two daughters claimed they gave up dates to stay home and make doll houses and the miniatures in them, including a house of their own.

It wouldn't be the first time a mini obsession took over the need for a conventional social life. Peter the Great loved doll houses and miniatures, and Queen Mary was finally built a fantastic doll house by her subjects because of her acquisitive nature. If she went visiting and saw a tiny treasure she loved in her host's house, it had to be given to her. Queen Mary, once Princess May of Teck, was also connected to Jack the Ripper histories; she was engaged once to Prince Eddy, Duke of Clarence and heir to the throne, who some believe was Jack the Ripper. His tutor, James Stephen, was an uncle of Virginia Woolf. Stephen starved to death in a mental hospital where the royal family put him away; some authorities claim he actually wrote the Ripper letters. Maybe that's why Woolf refused to create a mini volume for the royal doll house library, even though her friend T.S. Eliot did.

Back to Mott's. Dad bought me a doll that had been theirs, a five-inch composition lady dressed in housecoat and cap, painted in a yellowy shade. She has lived in my red doll house, carpet sweeper resting against her, for many years.

On the way out, my mom found all kinds of Shackman bisque doll replicas, including a baby, and my favorite jointed wooden doll with a porcelain head, and modeled long curls and flowers in her hair. I named her Mary Ingalls.

My mother told us about a beautiful little girl dolls, so rare, only three were made, and the artist broke the mold. The artist was Susanne Gibson of Capitola, a ballerina turned doll maker. There were glorious BJD porcelain ladies and little girls with glass eyes, creamy porcelain skin and long lashes. They had long, dark or strawberry blonde curls tied with ribbons. They started at $45, with tax, $47.25. I know, because Dad bought me the strawberry blonde with the white eyelet dress. I was floored! He said for years that his hand hurt him for paying for that doll, which now, would be like paying $500 for it. The doll is worth over $1000. Years later, Gibson and I became pen-pals and remained so till she died in 2010. She sent me an autographed copy of her book about the Kalico Kids dolls, and I kept her up to date on what her dolls sold for.

She later mass-produced dolls in vinyl for Reeves International, and I was lucky enough to find several. She also sent me a photo of one of the other little girl dolls. She was a talented woman, who loved pets and campaigned against puppy mills, danced, and sculpted. She belonged to NIADA, and was my first glimpse into the world of artists' dolls.

Chapter 33: German Doll Makers and the Future of Dolls

In an allusion to the legendary statue of Memnon and the theory that Ancient Egyptian statues had souls, Rilke has written that dolls were fed and made alive through children's imagination like the "Ka" of the Egyptians is fed on imaginary food.

Some doll makers, however, were not content with inanimate dolls that only lived through the power of a child's imagination. They strove to make dolls so lifelike that they could actually imitate human movement and sound. Forman-Brunell and Kuznets would have us believe that there were serious gender differences among doll makers, and that male toy makers saw the dolls they made as extensions of both themselves and the machines that they created. Thus, even female dolls had male anatomy and characteristics, and like their creators, they were made of hard, efficient substances. These tiny human impostors were not meant so much for love, as durability.

In any case, the doll, as cultural artifact, is our "double," the other which both repels and attracts us. It perplexes us that something so "dead," can also be so alive, and that something the modern world has relegated to the toy box can have such a rich and complicated history.

Dolls will continue to be made as long as there are human beings to conceive of new designs for them. They will continue to reign predominantly in the children's realm, though individual adults and museums will still collect them as tangible artifacts of human history, miniature representations of humanity for their respective ages.

Metal dolls, while still not prized in most important collections, may have the richest history of all. From the golden idols of the Inca and Aztecs, to the toy soldiers of lead and silver and the Minerva and Juno heads of the last century, metal dolls could form a fascinating collection in themselves. It is hoped that this book will inspire others to take up the "iron" gauntlet and add to the dialog that I hope this research has created. Until then, to all who are interested in doll history and doll collecting.

Kestner and Germany: Kestner's name is a synonym for "king," and king he was in the doll world. He also was perhaps the first doll maker of the modern world for the way he ran his factory and diversified his inventory. A Kestner recently appeared on the season finale of the new *Roseanne.* I grew up collecting and believing Kestners were among the finest of dolls, and then I began to hear grumblings about them in the dolls' Peanut Gallery. The first time was nearly twenty years ago when AOL still had Hobby Central, sites where collectors met in groups and instant messaged about their hobby. It was fun; I made good friends there and bought a couple very nice dolls.

On the Antique Doll Folder of Hobby Central, someone posted a commented that Barbara Streisand received a doll from Rosie O'Donnell on Rosie's talk show that was a "tacky" Kestner, and the ever-gracious Babs tried very hard to be grateful. Streisand is also a doll collector and talks about some of her dolls in her book *A Passion for Design.*

I'm not sure where this doll snobbery came from. I'm fortunate to own several versions of Baby Hilda and one or two other dolls by this firm. Historically, I can't write enough about the firm's importance.

Johannes Daniel Kestner was born during the 18th century. He made dolls and other related novelties of papier mâché, china, wood, later porcelain, in a factory where he employed his whole family. He was also somewhat of a rarity for his time. He was divorced and remarried. What made him even rarer was his sense of duty. He employed his first wife and second in making dolls. His first wife lived upstairs in the factory. Many of his children worked there, too.

His firm went on for over 100 years. Most of these firms disappeared in the '30s, many c. 1938. They were run by Jews, and I suspect taken over by the state when the NAZIs overran Germany.

Armand Marseille: For many of us, the first antique doll we add to our collection is an Armand Marseilles. Mine is small, about 8 inches, and is named "Melinda" and she joined the doll family when I was 11. She was dressed as a Dutch boy in Vollendam attire, with a short, puffy brown mohair wig with a center part, almost black glass, stationary eyes, and an open mouth with tiny teeth. One ankle needed repairing. She is a painted bisque doll, which means the paint was applied to the bisque after it was fired, not fire into the bisque as most antique bisque dolls are made.

I nearly died for love of her.

My mother went back to the Antique Show where we first saw Melinda, and brought her home. We undressed her, and discovered her five piece, "stick" papier mâché body. Mom glued her foot, and repaired the paint job with calamine lotion! She still bears that paint job! A little spot on her chin Mom touched up with her own make up.

Since that day, Melinda has been dressed as a little girl. She wears tiny ballet flats on her feet, and a lace, pale blue dress and white straw hat. I wouldn't trade her for anything.

Because of Melinda, A & M dolls have become personal favorites. Alma, Floradora, Rosebud, the beautiful 1894, a large, rare sized Dream Baby, Mabel, a Gypsy, several Native American dolls and a Scots girl have joined us.

One very large 370 came to me from my friend Jim R. She is mint, and has never been played with. She has sleeping blue eyes, wears an antique green velvet dress, and her original, blond mohair wig. When she arrived at my office at school, the young girl up front brought in the huge box, then, as a joke, dropped it on the floor! I nearly fainted, but the doll was none the worse for wear.

Another mint 390 head is as perfect as a Meissen figurine. It has never been attached to a body, and may have been used as a salesman's demo.

When I teach classes in diversity and culture, I mention Armand Marseille.

As many of us know, Armand Marseille, founder of the firm, was born in the mid-19th c in St. Petersburg, Russia, the child of French Huguenot parents. According to Dollreference.com, he left Russia with his family. They moved to Germany after 1860.

In 1884, Marseille bought a toy factory in Sonneberg, Germany, that of Mathias Lambert. In 1885, he bought the Liebermann & Wegescher porcelain factory in Koppelsdorf.

Perhaps the most prolific of doll makers for that time, he is said to have made over 1000 bisque heads a day. Indeed, the 370 marked doll heads on kid bodies and 390 marked doll heads on jointed composition bodies are the most common of the "dolly faced" dolls, still made into the '20s and early '30s, still treasured by original owners now in their '90s and up.

He made dolls for other companies, including Columbia for CM Bergman. Other trademarked name heads or models besides those above were Bessie, Darling doll, Duchess, Lilly, Lissy, Miss Millionaire, My Companion, My Dearie, my Lovely Doll, My Playmate, Our Anne (label reads P.D.G. Co.), Daisy Dimple, Sunshine, Dainty Dorothy, and Real Kid Doll. Some of these were distributed by Sears.

Many of the heads found in old dumps, or buried with bottles, were Marseilles heads. I still love to rescue these heads and make them into new dolls, restored to their former glory.

Rare Googlies and characters can bring thousands of dollars. The recent Cotillion Auction included several Armand Marseille's dolls, and lovely dolls in mint, factory direct outfits also come up for auction. Enjoy these wonderful dolls, and happy hunting!

China Heads: These glazed porcelain heads first showed themselves in about 1830–40, with some bald examples called Biedermeir dolls. Some of these heads boast a black spot for a wig. John Noble's *Dolls* and *A Treasury of Beautiful Dolls* have excellent examples. There were glazed figurines even before this, with busts dating to the 17 century, and Della Robbia porcelains dating to the Renaissance. Glazed pottery was also found in Ancient Rome and Egypt. Meissen and Staffordshire figurines are older, but it is true that you often see these types of heads on dolls, and doll heads share the same hairdos. The same is true of stone bisque or Parian dolls and bonnet heads; their hairdos and faces early on figurines as well as dolls. Royal Copenhagen makes lovely brown-haired dolls, featured in Nobles' books and in books by Eleanor St. George, and at least one "portrait" head of Jenny Lind in a dark wig is attributed to RC. I know the make figurines, and they started making dolls in the 1980s. Royal Doulton joined with Peggy Nisbet of England about this time to create a series of dolls, including one of the infant Prince William and a series of about out 9 in little girls showcasing Days of the Week.

The Chinese and later Japanese brought china production to a fine art, and these examples, Ming, Satsuma (from which figurine dolls are made today) and other figures are very collectible and priceless. China dishes seem to come into use in the 18th century, with the ubiquitous Blue Willow pattern still being used today. I also collect Blue Willow and look for examples in old TV shows like *Daniel Boone* and *Dark Shadows*. You can find a set on display at Hearst Castle in Sam Simeon, too. China comes from white kaolin clay, and this type of clay can be found today. I've made small toys and figurines from it, sometimes glazed, in art classes. Bone china, which I collected in the forms of mini animals and teacups, actually is fired with ground bone and ash. Wedgwood, Noritake, and Royal Doulton still make fine bone china dishes. Havilland china is another company that created wonderful glazed dishes for use in homes. For me, these china heads are the quintessential antique dolls. I saw my first ones when I was in kindergarten, and received my first when I was eight, not counting the Frozen Charlotte Mom and I bought at the Women's Club Antique Show when I was seven. My first was Japanese, with the molded bobbed hairdo young girls wore in the fifties. She was a head for a Holt Howard Christmas angel, with a cone cardboard body covered with red feathers, wire chenille covered arms, and a gilt songbook. Her features were painted and her hair was white. I still have her, but she is on a regular doll body with china limbs. She wears a red velvet medieval Barbie-sized dress Mom sewed, and a black lace flower hat to conceal damage and cracks. My Aunt

Rose gave her to me, and she also made in ceramics the second china head in my collection. This was a 24-inch low brow, black glazed hair for Xmas 1968. The doll has china limbs, with high heeled painted black boots and garters. She is dressed in white silk damask with a white lace overskirt, and red ribbon trim. She wears a black velvet choker, as I did at the time, only where mine had a cameo, hers has a tear shaped agate. My mother knitted her a red shawl, and sewed a wardrobe of bright materials from Aunt Rose and my grandma. There is an antique flannel nightgown, underwear, dotted Swiss in red, red and blue polka dots, brown print and blue print with daisies and vintage flowers, a bright yellow daisy print, and a few hats and bonnets. All lived in a vinyl Barbie case. The next dolls, also 1968, were a replica, that would fool an expert. She wears a red ring leg o' mutton dress and lingerie. Her shoes are white, high heeled, button down shoes. She is from The Tinkerbell Toy Shop in Disneyland. I have her receipt still. She cost $20.00in 1968, a huge sum for dolls. She is a little thinner than Aunt Rose's Doll, but can wear her clothes. I added for her a flannel jacket in green with removable felt symbols for each season The China Sisters, Rose and Rosalie had many adventures, and are honored members of The Museum. Rosalie, from The Magic Kingdom, was meant to be another Christmas gift. When Mom saw Aunt Rose's doll, lying in its beautiful tissue-lined box, she waited until Valentine's Day 1969 to give the Disney china head to me. I was ecstatic. She was a big sister to the dollhouse dolls, and could use their attic as a bed, where she could lie flat comfortably, if a little claustrophobically.

My first antique "low brow" doll was five inches high, all cloth, with cloth arms and legs. My first large low brow with black hair was a name head, "Helen," and I got her at 15. Whole and fragmented "low brows" joined the collection, many doll-house sized, some replicas I made from kits created for doll houses by my friend Violet Page. Aunt Rose made me a replica with red hair, a ribbon, and flat boots. She wore a green dress similar to Rose's white one Mrs. Brandmeyer of the 18th Avenue Doll Hospital assembled and dressed both dolls. Another small doll in the style of highland Mary never was glazed! I got impatient, and Mom and I made her a body and dress.

Later, I found a Marie Antoinette Sherman Smith doll, and two other Smith dolls on wooden bodies, more Christmas Angels, including choirboys, in sizes from 3 inches to 9 inches. There were more and more half dolls to explore, including some with medieval headdress Eleanor St. George considered china heads though they were pincushion or half dolls. Another grey-haired doll from the '40s is now vintage; her glazed hair is braided and gray. This style is also called "Marie Antoinette," though we don't know how many actually resented real women. Others in Noble's works are called Pavlova, Adelina Patti, Jenny

Lind, and Highland Mary. Some old heads have braids worn on their heads as a coronet. My largest ceramic head is about 12 inches high with such a style, she is an artist head by my friend Violet, and she "nodded" forward in the kiln due to her weight. She makes a doll nearly four feet high. Many years later, a woman in the audience at one of my doll talks gave me the whole doll, all four feet of her. I was astounded there are also Spanish china heads with wigs and painted features from Balos, and some from Capo di Monti and Marin, Italy and Spain.

I learned of Rohmer dolls, with zinc bodies, and Huret dolls, with glass eyes and wigs. Anne Marie Porot sent me a photo of one of the zinc bodied dolls for my book on metal heads. I added a Patty Jene artist doll of a china head with a wig. She was assembled with old limbs and clothes, and has re-1860 colored flat boots. Both Huret and Rohmer intrigued me because of a lawsuit these two women got involved in at a time when women hardly ran their own businesses. Huret won, and many dolls were destroyed, those that survived are priceless. It reminds me of the Haley suit Toys R Us lost when they copied Mel Odom's Gene. It was the beginning of their end

In September 2017, I was able to add a pink luster, or pink tinted, 29-inch French china head with wig and glass eyes to the museum. She belonged to Gigi, the mother part of the mother/daughter doll team, Gigi' Dolls and Sherry's Teddy Bears, and was in Gigi's original collection.

Every year, my doll club and I ride The Zephyr train to visit Gigi's and Sherry's. They open just for us, and we have a nice lunch beforehand. We always have goody bags, and a selection of freebies to take home, and special offers. I always go home happy. This time, I went with a bad case of non-contagious, asthma related bronchitis. The cough alone early killed me. I was afraid to go because Dad was getting weaker, and was homebound. We had round the clock caregivers, lovely women who were devoted to us. After a long consultation, they sent me off. My husband was working in the same town where I had to catch the train, about an hour away, but this year, he couldn't take me. He was working all night, and I had to leave at 5 am. A bout of bad road construction almost cost me the trip. It's true that we have only two seasons in the Midwest; winter and road construction. I had to call one of our club, a good friend called Beth, who guided me into the station.

In California during this trip, my uncle was in rehab, and we were working on getting him out. Of course, it rained, and I kept coughing and my phone kept ringing. The whole trip. On the way back, a conductor who looked like a female Howdy Doody puppet from hell bitched me for being on the phone. Really! You can use the phone on the train. I ignored her, but it was too much. I was so sick, by this time. I had to drive home after 11 pm in the rain, but I got my doll. I got to my parents' house to check on Dad. Even Dad admired the Rohmer, and she sits today safe and sound in her locked case with a Bebe Gigoteur, a Jumeau Bebe Reclame, several china heads and antique Korean and Japanese dolls.

I have a few other rare dolls like the Rohmer. My rarest china head is a man's head, with black hair, painted eyes, goatee and moustache. I think he may represent Napoleon III, husband of Eugenie, and I have an old head representing Eugenie herself.

There is a Victoria doll from Shackman, and several Jenny Linds, one by Emma Clear, on an antique. One small doll has a waterfall hairdo in a net. Some have molded ribbons. There are swivel necked chinas, and I have one in bisque from Japan with the curly lowbrow hairdo. I think these dolls are meant to have a Gibson girl type hair do with the rest of their hair pinned up in back. They are the most common and plentiful, and cost pennies. Many were made by Hertel and Schwab, and some were found intact after the Iron Curtain came down, in their original East German Factories. Shards of these and other bisque dolls that were thrown out are still buried in the soil and turn up. I have a box of them, sent from Germany, with the dirt in which they were buried still clinging to them The box still has its German label.

Tours allow visitors to the factory sites to scoop up as many shards as they can carry, or at least they did. There is a brisk trade in Etsy, eBay, and other online sites for these doll heads and shards. Artists use them for art dolls, found art, shadow boxes, and jewelry. I make pins from them, and I bought several Christmas ornaments form the Cincinnati Art Museum and other galleries. I also make barrettes.

I have some doll heads that were buried, some in ancient privies. Sanitized these many years later, my mother and I made dolls from them. Blondes are more unusual, and we have several in different sizes. The smallest china head is about two inches high, a blonde Alice-in-Wonderland type artist doll, in a real blue dress and pinafore. She has a cloth body and china limbs and is microscopic. I have heads that size made by artist Pat Wolford.

We have another French type man with a side art, and a black china head, which is rare. Standard Doll Company made many historical heads, including Harriet Tubman

My flat top and curly boy antiques are nearly three feet long, and came from my friend Violet. This flat top is sometimes called a Mary Todd Lincoln head, but a documentary showing Mrs. Lincoln's girlhood home showed her doll from childhood, and it was a flat top, so the style dates even older than that. The Mrs. Tom Thumb doll, made about the same height as the tiny lady herself bears this fact out.

Ruth Gibbs made china head dolls with china limbs wearing outfits under the Godey's Ladies Dolls trademark. I have several of the small six-inch versions, and one large 12-inch version with painted jewelry. Gibbs was most active during the 1940s.

Glass eyed dolls, men, dolls with teeth and sleeping eyes, a super rare example owned by a friend with sleep eyes, china bonnet heads, and all china Frozen Charlottes, dolls with fruit and flowers molded in their hair; these are the rarities of China heads. Limbach made many like this in bisque and china, including the bisque Irish Queen.

Emma Clear, of the legendary Humpty Dumpty Doll Hospital is credited with making the first "modern" china heads, now over 70 years old themselves. These are excellent dolls, and we have several, including the mold for her grape lady. We purchased the pink scarf doll from the Marry Merritt Museum auction and treasure her; she was an absentee bid, and the hammer came down online for us to our great pleasure. God Bless Noel Barrett auctions. I love Emma Clear's story; she had some kind of law degree, and tried to raise chickens before she turned her hand to doll making.

I have a china bonnet head, about six inches long, with brown eyes that I bought from noted authority Helen Draves. I also have a half doll with gray hear and brown eyes mom bought in about 1983 at a local doll show while I was still in law school. Later, I added a 25-inch brown eyed china doll in original clothing of dark blue print. There are china dolls from Tibet, in traditional costume, of blue and white china that looks delft. There are Japanese heads, very early, that look to some like the famous Nymphenburg, so called 18th century china head which may now be an early twentieth century doll.

Lowbrow dolls are featured in Disney's' film, *Child of Glass*, and Grace Ingalls allegedly had one, as did the mean Nellie Olesen. One of my Chinese heads has a molded tri-corner hat; he represents a British soldier with blonde hair, but Asian features. He came from a store called "Z Best things in Life," San Jose in the '80s. More on him in *With Love from Tin Lizzie*. Many rare dolls are in the Coleman's books, too. The Merritt Museum's *All Color Book of Dolls* features more. Mona Borger and Jan Foulke have written books on china heads with rare examples

Older examples had wooden bodies, and some, with the long Lydia sausage curls resemble Milliners' models and other early earlier mâché heads. Metal heads, my area of expertise, were meant to imitate china heads, and Effanbee and other companies made them in vinyl. I thought they would catch on, but they did not. One head in my book on metal dolls I really made of china—the Minerva metal head was reproduced as a china doll! I have an all china

Motschmann reproduction and a Schoenhut reproduction made in china and bisque, as well as a penny Wooden; my friend Violet made these in the '70s. I have one modern "china" done in shiny hard plastic.

Early doll books state that about 1 billion china heads were made in Germany alone in the early 19th centuries. Not many are reproduced today; glazing them at least three times and the china under glaze painting makes them expensive dolls to make. They also require skill, more than other dolls.

I made others from salt clay, and glazed them with nail polish, and I made paper dolls of sketches and photographs of others. They live in the Museum dollhouses, and some double as Xmas ornaments. I have seen them featured in Golden Glow of Christmas exhibits and in museums. There was a flat head or doll on display for many years at Ft. Cody in Ogallala, NE, and I have a picture of her. The doll is no longer there.

One head as a printed body in patriotic material. Other dolls have ABC material. Mark Farmer Co, of El Cerrito, CA reproduced many china heads, including the beloved Jennie June, which featured the low brow. One of my low brows survived the 1906 SF earthquake and came from the legendary Indiana Antiques in San Jose many years ago.

Finally, how do you tell an antique china head from a vintage or new head? Ruth Gibbs dolls are very distinctive, and have red hair and other non-antique shades. Their clothes and boxes are labeled. Old china heads have a grayish caste to the china; they have worn marks on their hair, and little specks of kiln dirt that look like beauty marks. New dolls are stark white or creamy colored. Old pink luster heads like a couple of mine have a pinkish caste to them, created by adding gold power or dust to the glaze. I have it on good authority from Luel's China Studio and other sources that this is how the glaze is made.

When I bought my 29 or so inch Rohmer pink luster with glass eyes from a major store in Chicago, they called the glaze pink luster. Many now call it pink tinted. I once had a zealot dealer attack me and stalk me on line because I quoted Luel's and called it pink luster. She demanded I quit "printing this rubbish." Meanwhile, she hasn't published anything, except the interview I edited for her. I later deleted it from my blog. She did not 'know I was working for an antique doll magazine and About.com. She attacked me personally on those sites and elsewhere, until I talked to the magazine's editor. I will live by my threat that if she ever stalks or attacks me or my work again, I will sue her, win her stupid little dolls in the suit, and break them in front of her one by one. When the magazine got a new editor that knew nothing about dolls, I had to leave. She and the owner, also a non-doll person, stole my intellectual property and locked me out of my own social media page. This is called larceny by trick. Unfortunately, the antique and doll worlds are full of these pitfalls.

Doll nastiness not withstanding, covered wagon dolls are very interesting, too. They often have the sausage curls or "covered wagon" look. One in my collection came from Dixon, IL, not far from the boyhood home of President Ronald Reagan. Older dolls, at least large ones, have a red line over their eyes to simulate eyelids. The rouge on their cheeks is almost orangey, very pale. Black dolls are coal black; modern are usually chocolate brown glazed like Harriet Tubman. If chipped, older dolls have a grayish bisque underneath

Some very old examples are pressed into molds and you can see the Kling dolls are marked with a bell in a K. Some, dressed and sold in France, may have labels on their clothes. Some dolls come with original wardrobes and are stuffed with sawdust. A few have kid bodies. If they are original and the body and clothes are old and came with the doll, it could well be old.

Motschmann dolls are mid-19th century; they have a bisque or china pelvis as well as limbs and heads in the style of antique Japanese Ningyo dolls, see Lea Baten. Some dolls have a cup and saucer joint. Goldsmith dolls are on bodies with cloth boots and altitude corsets. Look for dolls with synthetic clothes; they aren't old. Also, dolls wearing Velcro or snaps may not be antique. If you get a rarity like a glass-eyed doll for a song, be careful. I have a Parian with molded hair, flowers, and glass eyes, but she has a tiny hairline flaw, hence I didn't pay book value. If it's too pristine, like some "rare" half dolls on the market a few years ago, I'd worry. I did, however, find very detailed Parian head for under $4 at a local thrift shop.

Kestner and some of the famous German companies allegedly made china head dolls, or assembled china heads. As with all dolls and antiques, read, look at price guides, online sites and doll shows and sales. Check with museums, bottle collectors, join a group that digs for old china, but get permission from landowners so you don't trespass. If you can handle old dolls, or visit collectors with newer and antique china heads, do so. Even the common dolls are antiques, and there is a finite number of them. I don't turn my nose up at them, and neither should you. Rare examples are really fine china. Earlier Toby jugs and majolica figures are the ancestors of these dolls and belong in a good collection. Earthenware dolls with china doll hairdos are nice, too. I have one in highland Mary style made from native Iowa Clay. Some are on the bodies of mechanical dolls, like Autoperipatetikos featured in *With Love from Tin Lizzie*, and some are dressed as foreign dolls, Scottish highlanders and Breton fisher folk. More books with information on these dolls are in my *A Bibliography of Toy and Doll Sources*. One is tempted to make the request the little girl in the famous doll children's story makes, "Mommy, buy me a china doll; Do, Mommy, Do!!! There are also china heads made in Sweden and other countries."

Be careful how you use the term; I once got comments for a sex site on my blog about china dolls. Seriously!

In fact, dolls dresses could be as complicated as a real woman's, so that women and young girls who competed with each other over who had the most fashionable outfit extended the competition to their expensive dolls. Entire stores were devoted to accessories for these dolls, and in 1850, one French directory of commerce lists over 200 French doll shops and firms. Huret and others sold accessories in miniature boxes stamped with the firm's name. Some of the shops even published magazines devoted to the dolls, comparable to those published today that are devoted to Beanie Babies or Barbie. In fact, the competition to have the best doll and accessories is similar to the competition today over who will have the most Beanies. Huret published a magazine about her dolls called *Gazette De La Poupée* in the 1860s. As Rockwell writes, these dolls "were a reflection of life as well as a desired "Sunday" toy" (9). Another writer and human-sized fashion designer who collects dolls, Billy Boy, writes that "The Huret-created fashions imitate the life-sized originals in absolutely perfect miniature" (156). This comment is particularly true about the hats Mlle. Huret created for her dolls. Perhaps it is the elaborate trousseau of a Huret doll Guy de Maupassant had in mind in writing his short story, "Mademoiselle."

Chapter 34: Celebrity and Storybook Dolls

I always thought the first celebrity dolls were the Venus of Willendorf figures, some which date back over 4,00,000 years. They represent some deity, perhaps the ancient version of Mother Nature. Some speculate they were meant to be toys because they are so tiny, but they appear on cave paintings too, which indicate they were important in society, not just toys.

Santos representing saints and deities, ancestor figures, funeral effigies like those in Westminster Abbey, wax funerary figures, all these are celebrity dolls in their own right.

A few years ago, *Atlas Obscura* interviewed me for an article they did on celebrity dolls, and we explored just what the definition meant. Today, they are almost ubiquitous, perhaps made so by the wild success of Shirley Temple dolls. They are all over the place, and the countless action figures and WWF figures stretch the numbers.

Chapter 35: Bratz

With the coming of Barbie, and with the authorship of book like Betty Friedan's *The Feminine Mystique* and Germain Greer's *The Female Eunuch*, feminist scholars began to write about dolls and the agenda behind their creation. Margaret Jacob writes in *Playing with Dolls*, that as one scholar puts it, many "feminist scholars have interpreted dolls as agents of a hegemonic patriarchal culture in which girls were passive consumers." The Barbie doll and its mass marketing in the post-WW II era has particularly caught the attention of feminist researchers (and activists.) (15).

Bratz dolls were controversial almost from their inception. Right before they came on the market, I was teaching English at a local community college. I had a young lady in class who frosted her hair, wore unusual shades of lipstick that she outlined with a lip pencil, wore heavy leather belts, tight jeans and boots. She looked just like a Bratz doll.

Made by MGM, Bratz found themselves in **a** law suit with Mattel, who claimed Bratz dolls infringed on their My Scene Barbie line. For a time, Bratz dolls could not be produced. Then, MGM won the lawsuit, and My Scene Barbie and friends disappeared.

Bratz have been accused of sexualizing little girls, but then the girls themselves were asked, and it was discovered that the multiethnic doll encouraged diversity and boosted self-image among the girls who played with them. (Jacobs, 2008, 1)

Recently, MGM Entertainment announced it would try to buy failing Toys R Us and continue the brand while keeping the stores open. (Fickenscher 2018)

Chapter 36: Composition

Much of this chapter is indebted to Helen Young's excellent book *Here is your Hobby, Doll Collecting,* GP Putnam's, 1964. Many collectors are also familiar with Ms. Young's *The Complete Book of Doll Collecting* and with dolls she made for Kimport Dolls. I have found her to be extremely knowledgeable and well-documented about dolls. She also shares ideas for display, repair, and doll making. I share her philosophy that a good doll collection should contain as many different types of dolls as possible, or at least one type of each available doll as possible. She gives directions for making wax dolls, cloth dolls, and wooden dolls to round out good general collections. Young discusses composition dolls in her chapter "Heads of Paste and paper," Chapter 5. She first gives the history and recipe for papier mâché, and the English translation for the French, literally, "chewed paper." Young also gives us the exact language of the first doll patent, that of Ludwig Greiner, March 30, 1858 (57). She credits Lazarus Reichmann of New York City with inventing a composition of sawdust and glue, but without using paper (59). Therein lies the difference between the two materials. As late as 1964 when Young wrote, composition was being improved with resins and other strengthening ingredients (59). It is interesting that she writes as late as 1964, there were still compo dolls in the store, something I don't remember at all. According to her Patsy and Shirley Temple are compo dolls "well worth looking for," and she states good compo dolls are nearly as "time proof" as plastic or vinyl dolls. For years, Pat Shoemaker has been the expert on compo dolls for *Doll Reader* magazine, and she has authored many articles on the subject. Books by her, Johanna Gast Anderton, Patsy Moyer, Pat Smith, R. Lane Herron, Jan Foulke, and many other authors have excellent sections on composition dolls. These were among the first vintage or old dolls I collected. My first was Arranbee's Little Angel baby doll, bought in 1967 for $2 from The San Jose Flea Market. I was very little myself. My next was bought the next year in Old Spanish Town, Albuquerque. She is jointed with red boots, painted, a brown mohair wig of braids winding her head, painted features, about 9 in. She wore a severely dirty and faded China Poblana outfit, the woman's national costume of Mexico, based on a story of a Chinese princess brought to marry a native prince. She was so homesick, she created a dress with the colors and embroidery of her native land, which became known as The China Poblana, still worn today.

My doll now wears a dress my grandmother sewed for her. It is a pink blend Calico trimmed in gold sequins. Her name is Mrs. Birdie Plantagenet, of Godden's The Dolls House fame, and she lives in my own Plantagenet house with the rest of the family. I had a floor to ceiling wooden cabinet at my parents' home for all the large composition dolls, some of which date to the Greiner. I have some very large examples, and some small Frozen Charlottes made of compo. Several Shirley's Patsies, and Jane Withers make up part of my collection. Coleman's walking doll has a composition head, as do three dolls that came as old store stock from a dept. store that closed in Herrin, IL in 1932. Over the years, my dolls have stopped crazing, though some were in pitiable shape. My mother used to love to dress them, and one Shirley look alike was her favorite because it was like the doll she had to leave behind in Europe during the war. She had her drying on the bushes after a bath, and my little girl friends and I never noticed. There are many fine miniature doll house dolls made of composition, and even some Steiff hedgehog dolls. They are still plentiful, and while prices went sky high in the late '70s, they seem to be coming down now. I have at least a couple examples over 80 years old that are in mint shape with their original tags. Since many of these dolls are over 75 years old, they are often considered antique, not vintage. Dolls from the '20s and earlier seem to withstand the weather and crazing very well. I am told it is a myth that cold cream, will preserve them, but I used it on my dolls once a year, just a thin film, and few of them ever continued to flake or craze.

Chapter 37: Vinyl and Hard Plastic

Typical Carlson Doll, Representing A Cowgirl Dino Milani

Vintage dolls are defined as those made before 1960, and include antique dolls. Antique dolls are those that are between 75 and 100 years ago. Since, dolls made in 1960 are now over fifty years old, the term Vintage is liberally and practically applied by most dealers to dolls made roughly thirty years ago or earlier.

For example, many early reproductions, like those by Emma Clear, are hitting age 75, or close to it. By some definitions, these are now antique dolls, much as the Caryatid maiden Lord Elgin supplied The Parthenon with over 200 years ago is now an antique, even if it is fake. He took the original home to England with the other so-called Elgin Marbles.

To others, though, these 75+ year old reproductions are merely vintage dolls. Also, many hard plastic and composition dolls have hit age 75, same argument applies to them.

My childhood dolls fall into the vintage category. To some, they are Antiques. The first time I bought a 1960s' eight-inch vinyl Girl Scout doll in a thrift store, the young clerk wanted to know if I collected "antique" dolls.

I was flabbergasted! I hardly think of myself as an antique, and this was a doll from my early childhood.

I would have loved to have more of my mother's and aunt's dolls, but alas, they took a trip to Europe in 1938 that cost them eight years of their lives. My mother only had a few dolls, and two were the dolls like Duchess and Carlson dolls used, 7.5-inch hard plastic dolls. She dressed them in Greek national costumes.

The interest in Vintage dolls is increasing. Now that the Baby Boomers are becoming seniors, many have discovered an interest in the dolls and toys of their childhood. Books like *I had that Doll!* have become best sellers in the collectibles world, and many books have popped up that are devoted to these dolls. Johanna Gast Anderson, Pat Smith, A. Glenn Mandeville, Judith Izen and Patricia Schoonmaker are just a few of the authors who have written books featuring Vintage dolls.

One company whose dolls may be considered vintage is Carlson Dolls. Carlson Dolls were founded in Minnesota in 1946 by Ray and Ann Carlson. Apparently, they were the manufacturers of the "Skookums" dolls designed by Mary McAboy. They began to create the costumed dolls for which they are famous in the 1950s. I saw Carlson dolls in museum shops as late as the early 2000s, but have not seen any new dolls since. One source says the company went out of business in 1997 despite the efforts of sons Lowell and David. Once again foreign imports, this time, from China, affected production, this time forcing the company to close.

Besides Skookums, Carlson produced Minnetonka Moccasins for the Arrowhead Company and novelty salt and pepper shakers. They made plush toys and ski boots at one time, too. By the 1960s, allegedly due to competition from Japanese manufacturers, Carlson devoted itself to dolls.

In its heyday, Carlson made 500 different dolls, created by 100 employees in three factories. The dolls were sold in tourist parks and National Landmark sites. I bought Carlson dolls in Fort Cody, NE, Disneyland, The Buffalo Bill Museum, LeClaire, IA, Springfield, IL, and other tourist shops. Wisconsin Dells shops were good sources, and the largest selection was at the Wyoming report, Little America.

Chapter 38: The 21st Century

I see a trend which indicates reproduction dolls are making a comeback, at least in value. Pat. Loveless dolls trend between $200 to $300+. Other artist Halopeau repros can bring over $1000 on eBay. Commercial reproduction porcelain dolls average about $50+. Perhaps this trend is due to rising prices of a few super rare dolls, like the K&R 108 or the Jumeau 225.

Dolls have also appeared on stamps, and Shirley Temple has also been honored this way. From the USPS, Below:

Shirley Temple Black
One of the most beloved child stars in film history, Shirley Temple Black (1928–2014) went from Hollywood actor to distinguished diplomat in a life filled with adventure, fame, and service to her country. As a pint-sized star, she cheered Americans during the last years of the Depression. A talented performer, she was the number one box office draw for four years in a row and was awarded the first-ever juvenile Oscar.

The stamp shows a very attractive portrait of the young Shirley, the dimpled little girl so many have grown to love. I was fortunate enough to win one of her dolls at the Theriault's auction last year; I was also fortunate to have seen them when they were first displayed at Stanford Children's Hospital, Palo Alto, CA. They were there nearly 20 years. I have photos of them from when I was 11, and later, when I was 30. I also was able to meet her at a book signing of her autobiography, *Child Star*.

In my own collection, there are numerous Shirley dolls, paper dolls, mugs, pins, teddy bears, and pictures. I have the "Photo Play" article that featured the installation of her doll display at Stanford, and I have her films and many memories. My mother and aunt loved her, and were interested in her career for some time.

She was everyone's sweetheart, and like this stamp, she is "forever."

Brides

Brides and wedding dolls are special to collectors. Some collectors specialize in brides and wedding dolls from various countries. I have looked for a Norwegian bride doll for years, but haven't come up with one yet. A childhood friend of mine had one, and I've wanted one ever since!

Still, I do have brides of all types, from all over the world. They decorated the tables at my wedding reception. My fiancé, now husband, drew the line though, when I wanted to include Corpse Bride dolls and the head of Dracula's bride. "Spoil sports," I say! I also have cake toppers, some humorous, with brides chasing down grooms, and others vintage and sentimental, like the hugging wedding Kewpies that topped my babysitter's wedding cake over 70 years ago. She gave them to me, to use for my wedding.

Special wedding dolls in my collection include those dressed in material from my mother's and grandmother's wedding dresses. Wedding dolls are special, and international bride dolls are intricate and unusual. They commemorate a happy time in a couples' life, and are as beautiful and varied as the people and dolls that wear them.

Chapter 39: Music and Dolls

Dolls have been associated with music for many centuries. Maezel, who invented the metronome, also invented he mamma doll. Many automata and mechanical dolls play music, and some dolls are part of music boxes. All kinds of doll have sat on top of music boxes, including cloth Bradley dolls, Japanese ningyo, Greek costume dolls, bisque figurines of all kinds, Josef Original figures, and many more.

Marie Antoinette's' surviving automaton plays a harpsichord, and another very early android plays the lute. Automata monkey bands were popular, and Zula the Snake charmer dances. Another automaton, a near life-sized Dulcimer player, even breathes as she plays. The many specially constructed automata at The House on the Rock play all sorts of instruments. The best part of Disney's Haunted Mansion are the dancing host couples waltzing We've mentioned It's a Small World, but many other Disney attractions sing, including Pirates of the Caribbean and The Country Bear Jamboree.

Songs have been written about dolls, like Natalie Merchant's "Frozen Charlotte" from her Ophelia album. Then, there is the actual Ballad of Frozen Charlotte made famous by folk artist William Lorenzo Carter. There is a song about paper dolls, "I'm gonna have a paper doll that I can call my own…" and a '60s number called, "Mamma, when my Dollies have Babies." I used to beg for a dime at The Pizza Hut for the jukebox that would play the song for me. Skeeter Davis, herself a singer, has a doll collection.

Shari Lewis's puppets, especially Lambchop, sing ("The Song that Never Ends") The Muppets sing and even do musicals.

Jem and the Holograms had their own groups, and there were countless '90s dolls made of Josie and the Pussycats, The Spice Girls, Boys to Men, New Kids on the Block, N'Sync, Cindi Lauper Barbie, and many, many more. There are dolls made in honor "High School Musical," "My Fair Lady," "Grease," and "Wicked." Others are made after "Annie," Jon bon Jovi. "The King and I," etc. The Beatles have been made into dolls and figurines, and so has Shirley Temple, wearing many costumes from her song and dance numbers with celebrities like Arthur Treacher, Bill Bojangles Robinson, and Buddy Ebsen. One Rare Shirley plays a pipe organ.

Barbie has had her musical numbers with '70s dolls that had their own rock group and later during the '80s, Barbie and the Rockers. There is also a Martina McBride Barbie. Remco's Mimi sang "I'd Like to Teach the World to Sing" in several languages that required records, and Harmony played the guitar. Grace Slick of Jefferson Starship is a doll collector, and she owns a Harmony doll. M.C. Hammer and Michael Jackson have been dolls, as have KISS. Dolls and vintage puppets were made of The Monkees and The Mammas and the Pappas during the '60s, and there are singing dolls of James Brown, Frank Sinatra and Dean Martin. Dolls of Fred Astaire and Ginger Rogers, Sinatra, and dolls inspired by Duke Ellington's music were made in limited editions for collectors. Singer Lena Horne herself admired dolls.

Miniature pianos by Bliss and Schoenhut as well as other musical instruments, phonographs and records players are popular with collectors.

Music has been written for Raggedy Ann and other dolls, and of course, dolls figure in *The Nutcracker Suite.* Debussy wrote The Children's Suite, including *The Golliwog's Cakewalk,* for his daughter. There is a recital piece called *The Japanese Doll* for piano, and another suite called *From a 19th Century Toy Box* by Craig A. Penfield that includes a piece called *The Jumeau Doll.* According to Simbel.com:

Craig A. Penfield was born in Hartford, Connecticut on August 29, 1948. There were many musicians on both sides of his family, and at a very early age Penfield began composing music and performing as a violinist, pianist, and organist. His primary studies began with Gordon W. Stearns, Sr. of West Hartford and eventually culminated with post-graduate study at Trinity College with Clarence E. Watters. (Watters himself had been the first American student of Marcel Dupré.) As a composer, Penfield has published hundreds of compositions, including many works for organ, as well as works for other solo instruments, orchestra, and chorus. For many years, Penfield was active as an organist/ choir director and concert recitalist in New England as well as on the West Coast. His works have been performed throughout the world, most frequently in Germany, France, the Netherlands, the United Kingdom, and the USA. http://www.zimbel.com/penfield.html

There is a *March of the Tin Soldiers*, and *Babes in Toyland*, and many more pieces devoted to children, toys, and dolls.

Chapter 40: Toy Soldiers and Robots

Millions of children throughout the centuries have enjoyed fighting mock battles with toy soldiers. Little boys and girls have long saved their pennies and pocket money to buy small figures of lead and tin with which to people their dreams of heroism and glory. In fact, the Brontë children's earliest literary endeavors were stories that they wrote about a set of toy soldiers that belonged to Branwell Brontë. Much has been written about the dangers of war toys, including soldiers. Yet, all the criticism does not seem to quell interest in them. One wonders, why this is so; recent films including *Apocalypse Now, The Killing Fields, Platoon,* and *Saving Private Ryan* have accurately, perhaps too accurately, portrayed the horrors and senselessness of war. In the same light, many novels like Stephen Crane's *The Red Badge of Courage* and Wilfred Owen's poem "Dulce et Decorum" have also done much to debunk the romanticism of a soldier's life. Yet, children still adore toy soldiers. Some may claim that playing with war toys is cathartic because such play allows children to act out their aggressions in harmless settings, while others may seek to foster courage and patriotism through soldier play. One need only think of Lovelace's famous poem, "To Lucasta on Going to War" and its famous line, "I could not love thee so, dear, loved I not honor more."

War games, and even violent play, are an innate part of childhood. Even if one takes away all toy guns from a little boy, he will chew a peanut butter sandwich into a gun, point it, and shout, "Bang! Bang!" Whatever the reason for their existence, however toy soldiers, particularly of metal, are here to stay and are more popular than ever.

The earliest model soldiers were probably made of wood. They represented Prince Ensah's guard and date to the twelfth Egyptian Dynasty, 2000 B.C. Like other dolls, the early toy soldiers were not meant to be toys. Rather, they accompanied their deceased owners to the underworld. One historian has said that model soldiers were not really popular in the Ancient world, (Alberini 5), but he then cites a Roman legionary made of tin from the Imperial Epoch (6). Also, a 15-inch bronze model of an equestrian survives from ancient Greece. Flat lead soldiers existed in Rome in the third century A.D. The most famous model soldiers of recent times are probably the life-sized army which once adorned a Chinese emperor's tomb. These are currently reproduced as clay miniatures and may be purchased in many import and specialty stores.

As toys, model soldiers first appeared in the Middle Ages (Fawcett 215). Of these, Leslie Gordon has said that "(e)xcept for the ancient 'magic' doll, it is possible that the toy soldier, who made his first appearance in Europe in Medieval times, was the first doll to be made of metal" (43). Some of these soldiers may have had model accessories and buildings. For example, there is a four-inch wooden model of the Bloody Tower of the Tower of London which may have belonged to the Little Princes who were murdered there. One author speculates that this model had little figures, perhaps made of metal, to go with it (Garrat 12). Such a concept is not hard to envision; even ancient dolls had tiny dishes and other accessories with them, and companies like Playskool and Lego, manufacturers of educational playthings, make toy castles complete with knights and guards.

Interest in toys that teach is not unique to our century. In the 15th century, historical model soldiers first appeared. Marie d' Medici is supposed to have had silver toy soldiers made for her son, Louis XIII (Alberini). As an adult, Louis supposedly melted them down to fund his wars (6). Bronze-cast tournament toys existed as early as 1490 and the Kunst Historiches Museum in Vienna has several examples. Also, a toy museum in Salzburg has a large collection of toy soldiers and model figures. One group represents five members of the ski patrol. They are complete to their clubs, rifles and ski poles.

Another group from the Salzburg Museum represents an open carriage with two, well-dressed passengers. The driver and his groom wear plumed helmets and the horses are white. The entire piece is well-painted and appears to be beautifully preserved. Still another interesting arrangement represents a group of jockeys. Part of the display includes dice, coins, and other paraphernalia of gambling. In the background is a flier explaining the steeple chase.

Some of these early soldiers and models were breathtaking in detail. One incredibly intricate lead musketeer is French and dates from about the time of Henry IV. It stands three inches (Garrat 13). At Cluny are two medieval knights made of tin. Some of the Cluny soldiers were worked in gold and silver decorated with enameled bronze (Harris 8). A similar ship with soldiers in the Victoria and Albert Museum is German in origin. One of these ships represents Charles V and his court moving on deck (8).

By the early sixteenth century, some model and toy soldiers were on rollers and held miniature lances. The eighteenth-century discovery of alloys facilitated the manufacture of toy soldiers (Alberini 7). Now, other metals could be mixed with the inexpensive tin to make a variety of goods. Standardized uniforms also came into use. As a result, the figures could be mass produced. Early boxed sets were sold unpainted by military unit in wooden boxes. They came in weights of 1 lb., 1/2 lb. and 1/8 lb. Each kit contained from twenty to 150 soldiers (7). It is difficult to determine which manufacturer made these early soldiers because they were made before registration laws existed. Some manufacturers, however, marked their figures with initials (White 58).

Apparently, Frederick the Great inspired the creation of model soldiers in England (Hillier APOT 70). One early version was a "flat soldier," 30 mm in height (70). This height became standard for one maker, Henrichsen of Nuremburg, and was gradually adopted by others (70). Heinrichsen's sets included well-written histories to educate children (70).

In France, Ronde-Bosse created solid, three-dimensional soldiers in the eighteenth century (Alberini 7). Lucotte produced lead soldiers in 1789. Other sets came in elaborate boxes with the trademark CBG for Cuberly, Blondel and Gerbveau. This trademark is still used today. The Napoleonic sets wrapped in cellophane are popular.

Interesting and amusing stories about toy soldiers abound. the most famous is, perhaps, Hans Christian Andersen's "The Brave Tin Solder." Webster's play, *The Duchess of Malfi,* mentions toy soldiers as does Ben Jonson's *The Devil is an Ass.* Furthermore, in her memoirs, Catherine the Great discusses how the Czar Peter played with his model soldiers when he was Grand Duke (Harris 12). Some of these were lead (12). Supposedly, Napoleon used toy soldiers to plan battle strategies (Wenham Museum Collection 81). Some of his soldiers have been exhibited at the Coopers Union in New York. Also, a goldsmith named J.B. Odfiot is said to have made toy soldiers for Napoleon's son in 1812 (811).

Because of their popularity in the nineteenth century, old sets of soldiers were often forged. There is one anecdote of a dishonest shopkeeper who threw new soldiers made in the medieval style in the Seine, then fished them out to sell as antique (Alberini 6).

The historical archives of Barcelona, Spain, have a variety of metal figures and soldiers made from nineteenth century molds. These include dancers and figures in costumed, religious figures, etc. They are platy, painted in bright colors (Galter 498). The Salzburg Toy Museum has a large collection of unpainted, flat figures.

In 1820, William Britain devised hollow metal soldiers. This development was quite an innovation because now, more and cheaper soldiers could be produced, and more could afford them (Alberini 8). The United States contributed to the popularity of hollow soldiers by beginning to sell kits with molds and ready-to-paint soldiers (Wenham Museum Collection 81). American poet Robert Lowell describes an amusing childhood incident where he convinced a friend with a fantastic collection of model lead soldiers to trade whole battalions of them for his own crude, papier mâché models.

A variety of metal soldiers are still made. Several years ago, the television show "Falcon Crest" even had a character with a whole collection of them. A 1965 Hauser catalog shows of variety of soldiers, animals and fairy tale figures done in the style of the older, three-dimensional models. All, however, are plastic. The cover of the catalog shows a smith hammering with a red-hot iron on an anvil. The latest movie to star Robert DeNiro, *Ronin*, features an enviable collection of Japanese samurai lead soldiers.

Furthermore, Helmet Kranks of Salzburg has created an incredibly detailed model of an armored general, circa 1580, in papier mâché, wood, leather and metal. Every feather in his helmet is in place and his real sword rests properly in its tiny scabbard (Garrat2). My favorite model soldiers are those of English artist Russel Gammage. His Gauls, Celts and Barbarians are complete with long hair awash in lime, long moustaches, breeches and colorful tunics. The Gauls lean against their long shields, arms crossed in defiance. They look as if they are awaiting further orders. These life-like figures are interesting to compare with the original Celtic bronze idols made centuries before. Gammage is a trained artist who used to design figures for the firm of Graham Farish (89). These lead models have influenced current action figures like the Spawn series by Todd McFarlane. Many of these are also created in cold cast resin, but are painted in the colors and traditions of the old metal soldier. McFarlane Toys also insists on paying great attention to detail, so that figures like Cosmic Angela are near-perfect miniatures with life-like dimensions. These "soldiers," however, recreate in three dimensions characters from old comic strips based on Celtic and Medieval Epics. Hence, the Spawn figures, and other dolls like them, allude to the Celtic Warrior Queens like Cartimandua and Boadicea.

If warrior queens and women soldier figures are popular as collectibles, one has to observe that many of the artists who design and create them are also women. Women also collect toy soldiers. Two are Kathleen Ball Nathaniel and Mme. Fernande Metayel, Paris. Mme. Metayel is an outstanding artist who took up painting models after the deaths of her husband and father. She has won many honors for her work (Garrat 77). Margaret Cruikshank, who started the Mystery Doll Club, a mail order club where girls received a kit for dressing dolls from foreign countries, collects dolls in military dress. I, too, enjoyed toy soldiers when young and played nurse to the fallen plastic models of a childhood friend. He relegated me to this position because "I was a girl." A noted collector and doll author, Mary Hillier, has similar memories. Another time, I rescued and reclaimed a number of tiny, red plastic revolutionary patriots from the gravel of a friend's drive way where they had been abandoned.

Aramis men's cologne offered lead British guards as a Christmas promotion in 1988. Other figures in lead were made by the same companies, but they represented other people besides soldiers. I have figures dating from the forties which once belonged to my uncle. One is of a tiny farm woman. In her molded left arm, she holds a basket, but her right arm is separately jointed and swings back and forth. I also have older figures representing comedian Charlie Chaplin and Abraham Lincoln. These remain unpainted. Many painted models from the forties and fifties of this century, represent Native Americans of various tribes in different poses, horses, Civil War soldiers, and Arabs and their Steeds, the latter, perhaps, in tribute to Lawrence of Arabia. All these are marked "England" in embossed letters underneath their stands. For a while, British companies painted the skin tones of their soldiers according in various shades of brown and tan, so that African soldiers were dark brown, but Greek and Turkish soldiers were light brown.

Toy soldiers, then, were among the earliest toys. They are a colorful source of history for everyone and continue to be created to the delight of children everywhere.

Since the days they were made in metal, they have been recreated in many materials. One unusual doll comes from Hong King. He is a china head doll with china limbs, dressed as a British soldier. What makes him interesting is that, while his dress and painted blonde hair and blue eyes are European, his sculpted features are Asian. To the people of Hong Kong who created him, he is their portrait of the British who colonized them. Also, besides the famous G.I. Joe, there are companies making historical soldiers of plastic representing Napoleon, Civil War Generals Lee and Grant, George Washington, and others. There is even a set raising the flag at Iwo Jima. G. I. Joe by Hasbro has several series of soldiers, including one representing Generals Patton, Colin Powell, and MacArthur. Another doll fittingly represents Bob Hope, who entertained American Troops so many years overseas. Women are not ignored, either. Israel produces female army soldiers, and the G.I. Joe Nurse is among the most desirable Hasbro figures. Recently, the company created a special edition G.I. Jane, after Demi Moore's movie. (Ms. Moore, it will be remembered, is also an avid doll collector.)

That dolls often echo social and political trends is apparent in the history of G.I. Joe. Betty O. Bennett writes that G.I. Joe's sales suffered during the height of the Vietnam War because of the outcry against war toys (78). Before that time, G.I. Joe and his buddies were bringing Hasbro thirty-five to forty million dollars in revenue.

Chapter 41: When We
Are No Longer Here

Many authors have addressed what will happen to our dolls after we are gone. A grim topic, but one I've dealt with recently. You may, as a collector, be asked to advise, appraise, or comment on an estate. I do not appraise, but I will help with organizing and inventorying a collection. Recently, I helped with the collection of a self-made business woman. I was able to purchase several of the dolls, and there were over 700, as well as numerous miniatures houses, movie collectibles, Native American collectibles, books, doll furniture, and holiday ornaments. I asked the family what they wanted to do, and also provided them with a list of auction houses, estate sale dealers, antique stores, and museums that would be interested.

I called the museums and put together proposals and partial inventories. We discussed donating some of the dolls in their loved one's memory, perhaps to some local historical societies. The dolls were mostly modern, a few hard plastic, 1980s Effanbees, World GWTHW, 1970–90s Alexanders, Danbury Mint, tourist, Cabbage Patch, played with vinyl, a few artist antique reproduction and composition. I was quite taken with them, but it was hard to explain prices and values. Non doll collectors think that because a doll has its box, it should demand top dollar. A careful eBay search revealed that prices were everywhere, and in our area, Danbury and modern porcelain dolls only command a few dollars, as low as 3.00 or less in some cases. Our thrift stores are full of lovely dolls of this type, many with boxes and certificates, MIP or NRFB. Some cost over $100.00. In Canada, when I visited 20 years ago, they would have been near that in antique stores, but the market here is not good, The same is true for vinyl dolls, even vintage, which suffered after online auctions made them plentiful Different regions command different prices; in California 22 years ago, I could find antique Japanese dolls, some Hinamatsuri festival dolls and 80-year-old Ningyo dolls for as low as $5.00. In the Midwest, the same dolls cost considerably more, with the Hina dolls over $75.00 each. The Japanese dolls were more plentiful in California. Yet, the Native American dolls, even tourist examples I used to find out west, cost much more in California. Back to my Estate family, we had many talks about realistic expectations, storage, the time it takes to set up an estate sale or yard sale, how auctions work, how thrift stores work. The museums were a good bet, but they would take at least one month to decide. It could take more than a year for this estate to settle. The dolls are in good shape for the most part, and I enjoyed looking them over. My husband took some photos. This was a good learning experience, and one I recommend.

Chapter 42: Doll-Making

Sooner or later, every collector tries her hand at making dolls. While there are doll artists who don't collect or keep dolls other than those they make, most collectors get involved in doll creation, if only to understand the artistic process behind it. Of doll making, Miriam Forman-Brunell discusses the following:

"Handmade Identities: Girls, Dolls and DIY" examines the study of dolls, girls' identities, and the contemporary DIY (do-it-yourself) craft movement, areas of inquiry that until now have remained separate.

Departing from the more typical scholarly focus on mass-produced dolls and their impact on feminine socialization, April Mandrona uses memory-work analysis in order to examine the doll-making activities of girls. She argues that young doll makers' creative productions are active negotiations of cultural meanings that make possible girls' participation in the construction of their girlhood identities. (11)[5]

I dedicate this section of my book to Miss Stickler, my 6th grade art and music teacher who taught us to make puppets and scarecrows from papier mâché and Styrofoam balls. I still have all of my puppets, and I couldn't tell you how many I made, or how many plays I wrote for them. I couldn't wait for art class, and would get so absorbed in what I was doing that I didn't always remember where I was. I also learned in Miss Stickler's class to make dioramas out of bits of wrapping paper and folded construction paper. I used this technique to build tiny stages for paper and cloth shadow puppets I made for Mrs. Foss's 6th grade language arts class. These puppets were no more than three or four inches high. The top half was a figure cut from a magazine, and

---

[5] Liboriussen writes in "The Freedom of Avatars, "As Roland Barthes (2009) puts it, toys that are created rather than merely owned "act by themselves," they "roll" and "walk" (40). Drawing on *Pinocchio* and other examples from cinema and literature, Lois Kuznets (1994) notes how "toy making [exemplifies] art, with the toy maker as consummate artist, who experiences great joy when toys take on life" (180, my emphasis). The avatar-crafter has something in common with the toymaker; both enjoy that their creations take on a certain life of their own.

the bottom half was a bit of cloth, ribbon, or lace. I used seed beads for buttons, and would enhance the dolls with paint, if needed. I liked making backgrounds for them out of sturdy department store boxes like the one's Marshall Field's used to give. I painted skies with watercolor, and for Christmas scenes, used salt sprinkled over things to make snow.

Honorable mention would have to go to my high school art teacher, Mrs. Glassner, who taught us to make cornhusk dolls as a class project. I did large scenes based on antique paper dolls with their own landscapes. I did a forest for Red Riding Hood and her wolf made from overturned Styrofoam cones covered with fallen leaves. I painted basic mountain scenes as a paper doll backdrop, and then cut out houses and people in various sizes. It was a study in perspective, because Mrs. Glassner taught us to arrange them by putting the larger houses at the bottom, and the smaller houses up the top of the mountain.

Dolls as school projects are traditional but also teach valuable lessons. In a study done in Latvia, to scholars studied dolls from all over the world that represented teachers. They have the following to say on handmade dolls, "One of such groups of toys that has existed already since the origins of the humankind is making dolls and using them in games that over time have been improved and reaching huge scopes bear the idea about important and popular images for the mankind that people want to use also in their everyday life—in developing and educating their children." (Kalke and Rudzlte 541)

I made dolls at home too, though, sometimes too many for my parents' liking! I made all kinds of dolls and furniture form Plasticene clay, which doesn't dry. I made an entire set of Ancient Egyptian furniture and accessories out of it for a bronze figure of ISIS my mother bought me at The Rosicrucian Museum in San Jose. I figured out how to preserve the clay by coating it with several coats of nail polish. I can't sing the praises of using nail polish as varnish enough. I saved many Mello Crème Kewpie dolls and licorice Scotty dogs this way. With clear polish, I coated doll heads made of eggs.

One Sunday, Diana, my favorite baby sitter who was only 16, taught me at age seven and my friend Brook, age six, to cut paper dolls of all types out of the funny papers. These comics' dolls filled a grocery bag for each of us. We cut them holding hands in linear and circular style, of all shapes and sizes. I made other paper dolls with clothing using crepe paper, fake hair, and wrapping paper. Some of these were very tiny, and lived in my doll house. A few were inspired by Rosemary Clooney's "Susie Snowflake" song. After reading books by Flora Gill Jacobs, I made my first paper doll houses using magazines, and alas, dust covers from books on dolls! I have had to sit through many boring meetings that weren't entirely wasted because I used to sketch entire families of paper dolls that I later took home, painted, and arranged in doll houses or albums.

Later, after visiting miniature shows and doll shows, I used homemade clay or Play Dough to make mini fruits and vegetables. I also made miniature doll heads and dolls. I used it later to make repairs on dolls.

When I was 8, I started to take ceramics. I painted all kinds of small figures and dolls, and went to ceramics studios with Aunt Rose, my baby sitter who also made me dolls. I kept painting even into the early '90s, and still pick up plaster ware or unpainted bisque when I get the chance. My good friend Violet Ellen Page was a doll maker in all media. I learned to make dolls, to paint them, and to sew doll bodies and make repairs. In high school, I began to work with clay, though I could never throw well on the potter's wheel. (See John Denver's song). I did mold by hand and made even more dolls and figures, come dressed in antique fabrics with real wigs and handmade jewelry.

My big Home Ec. project was to sew the life-sized Betsy McCall doll. I got an A+. We also made bean bag frogs. Later, I made Pippi Longstockng and Hollie Hobbie from popular patterns. I wove a doll on a cardboard loom after reading a book one summer. I learned how to drape material over dolls and to adapt simple patterns, and soon, I was making wardrobes for dolls of all shapes and sizes. Learning to use the sewing machine revolutionized my methods.

My favorite way to make dolls is one I've never heard anyone else use. I used to Xerox black and white photos of dolls and doll heads I loved. Sometimes, I had to beg my parents to give me a dime and to take me to the library where the Xerox machine was. I'd cut out the dolls I wanted, mount them on cardboard, and use clay or papier mâché to build up the dolls' features, sort of in Bas Relief. Sometimes, I used enamel paints, like the ones model builders preferred. I made wigs out of Dr. Scholl's mohair, yarn, or fake Halloween hair. For some, I used beads or cats' eye shells for eyes. For one, I made a body out of cardboard tubes and strung it like an antique doll. With my mom's help, I made fancy dresses of brocade and lace. This was how I satisfied early longing for antique French and Bisque dolls. Later, some of the authors of those books I used would become my pen pals.

Artists have long been fascinated with dolls and with collecting in general. Picasso, Rembrandt, Renoir, Degas, Picasso, Hans Bellmer, Alexander Calder, Jeff Koontz, David Levinthal, Jarvis Rockwell, Tasha Tudor, Albert Marque, and many, many others were influenced by dolls and doll related objects in their work. Others turned to making dolls themselves. Folk artists have long made dolls their own means of expression, using everything from clay, wood, dried apples and pears, nuts, leather, cornhusk, grass, bone, shell, peanuts, rags, and much more to express themselves through the dolls they made.

During the '70s and '80s, there were lots of dolls at craft shows, and lots of doll making supplies at Woolworth's and big box stores. Hobby shops always carried plastic doll heads, arms, legs, hats, and later, bodies. When angels became popular, bisque and plastic doll heads that looked like antique dolls appeared, along with dolls of Mr. and Mrs. Santa Claus. I used these for all kinds of projects, but saved some just as dolls. I loved the plastic and celluloid doll faces that cost under a quarter at the dime store. I used one to make in elaborate Joan of Arc doll for a school project. She still wears her aluminum foil armor.

Hallmark made a series of doll cards based on hand made dolls they commissioned artists to create. One of these was made into a doll, but I never found it for sale anywhere. When I tried to order it, I was told it was never actually produced by Hallmark, even if it showed up in a catalog.

Many porcelain reproductions flooded the market; some were made by real artists and were stunning. Then, mass-produced porcelain dolls began to appear. Some are called Waldas by collectors who love them, which aren't many. All the modern porcelain dolls began to disappear, but they are slowly climbing in value on Internet auctions and there are Facebook pages and social media devoted to them. A good place to look for information on Waldas, modern porcelain dolls and craft dolls is the site *ThriftyFun.com.*

There is an interest again in making dolls, usually with found objects and broken antique heads. Artist Karla Byl makes some wonderful examples. There are several organizations for doll artists, especially NIADA, or National Institute of American Doll Artists that has been around for over 50 years. Founded in 1962, NIADA was created to sponsor creative doll making (Young 188).

According to Helen Young in *The Complete Book of Doll Collecting,* the designer of the Bye-lo baby, once predicted that "someday the most distinguished artists would design and make dolls that were true works of art…" (quoted in Young, 188)

Doll artists come from all over the world and have many reasons for making dolls. Egli Figuerens, 1964, are Swiss dolls created to tell Bible stories. (Wikipedia)

Sherman Smith: On September 22, 1907, an amazing woodcarver/ doll artist named Sherman Smith was born. For many years, his work was unknown. Now, there is a thriving interest on eBay in his creations. Collectors are specializing in his wooden dolls, and wooden dolls with bisque heads, some antiques, and some artist's reproductions by Phyllis Park and Jean Johnson.

My first encounter with a Smith doll took place in 1975 when we visited the now defunct Dolly Dear Clinic, one of our local doll hospitals. (The demise of the doll hospital will be another topic). The owner sold a few dolls and parts now and then, but while she was a lovely lady with a first-rate collection (Bru, Jumeau, complete Schoenhut families, rare china, wax, and Parian, all mint!); she was a terrible doll snob. Since I was a teenager, she had hopes for me, but she sneered at my small lowbrow china head that needed parts. She sold me the Smith doll, about eight inches, with porcelain "Marie Antoinette" head for about 12.00. My mom shelled it out, even though she thought the price was high. A similar doll was selling on eBay this week for 225.00. I have seen it as high as 350.00.

Mr. Smith began making dolls and carving after a heart attack in 1955. Allegedly, he was on bed rest for three years. His first projects were heart shaped pins and interlocking chains, good exercises for a man who had been a whittler since age eight. Soon, he was winning prizes, and inspired to carve a doll featured in a craft magazine. A meticulous craftsman, Smith spent a year perfecting his doll making skills. His first dolls were up to 24 inches high; these are rare and can command over $1000.00. He soon decided to carve dolls between ½ inch and seven inches. Smith dolls were never dressed, and early dolls were not signed. Later Examples made in the '60s were signed. He carved Hitty, Miss Unity, Mary Poppins and other characters. He did tuck comb dolls, and tiny brooches with wooden dolls on them. The brooches were numbered. He began making the bodies with bisque heads. Some had his initials, some not. These bisque headed dolls resemble 1850 china heads with wooden bodies featured in John Noble's books. He carved a souvenir doll for the UFDC in 1963 called Miss Angelita, and Patty Reed's Doll for the Sacramento Doll Club. This doll represented the doll belonging to one of the hapless children of The Donner Party. Miss Angelita sold for 179.00 in eBay in 2012. There is a Sherman Smith Doll Club, and I have a Raggedy Ann they made, with their logo of a wooden doll and his name embroidered into the doll's body.

Smith died in 1977, just two years after I bought my first Smith doll. Shortly after, a five-inch, unsigned Penny Wooden joined my Marie Antoinette. Two four inches bisque-headed twins joined them last year. Prices have spiked on eBay; I see ranges from 95.00 for small dolls with bisque heads, to 400.00 for characters with bisque heads like Lincoln. Now, there are books, newsletters and articles about his work. An Internet search will provide many good sources to learn about this talented doll maker.

Chapter 43: Doll Hospitals

Making dolls and doll repair go hand in hand. The oldest recorded doll hospital was established in 1830 in Lisbon, Portugal. We know they existed in Dickens' England because of his portrait of Jenny Wren, the doll maker of *Our Mutual Friend.* Another old doll hospital existed in Melbourne, Australia, 1888. (Wikipedia) Louisa May Alcott supplemented her family's income by making doll hats at one point. Beth of *Little Women* runs a sort of private doll hospital of her own because she takes in and cares for the castoff dolls of her sisters.

Ordinary people learned to assemble their own dolls and to repair broken heads and fragile limbs. Frances Hodgson Burnett retells in an article about her own doll collection how she had to have a head replaced on her favorite doll. Last fall, I bought several bodies for antique china heads that were old store stock from a shop that operated in the 1910s. They owner of the estate was a woman who lived to be 99, and who practiced law up until a few days of her death. The bodies were there, along with doll heads of different sizes, because of the need for home doll repair.

We had two doll hospitals in my area that operated while I was in grade school. There was another one open around 15 years ago. I loved visiting doll hospitals here, and in California where my grandparents lived. The doll heads and doll parts were full of possibilities for me. I thought of all the dolls I could make from them; I was only limited by my small allowance and the fact that many of the parts were not for sale. They were there to be used on patients. I could have spent hours matching bodies to heads, selecting fabric for clothes, and combing out wigs. They inspired at least one author, too. Shirley Holub has written the *Doll Hospital* series by Scholastic books that tell the story of two sisters and their grandmother who restore dolls from various historical eras.

Madame Alexander got her start working in her father's doll hospital, dressing dolls. Later, she created magnificent doll fashions.

Chapter 44: The State of the Doll House

Trousseaux Steal the Show along with the Confessions of a Collector who's had many adventures, Well, maybe I've had more musings than confessions. I'm proud of my hobby, and of my collection. I note again, that early collectors were teachers, artists, historians and psychologists. They identified dolls of peoples that no longer exist on the earth. Their cultures are gone or assimilated, and we only have their dolls to see how they lived and dressed. In fact, many older dolls and related artifacts are displayed in their contemporary, ethnic settings in The Milwaukee Public Museum for this reason.

Again, I plead for the release of the "Talega 11" Dolls in San Clemente. I'm considering a campaign to raise bail for them; American Doll and Toy Museum is willing to pay it. Dolls shouldn't be universally considered creepy. Doll play is important, and dolls are portraits of their makers. They should be children's muses for all kinds of imaginative projects, not objects of fear and revulsion.

Some of us still get it. Kudos to Laurie McGill, former editor, and the staff at *Doll News,* for intelligent, informative, and gorgeous issues. I love their article on nautical dolls, especially the German bisque bathers and the "old salt" figures. I am very fond of both, and have a favorite old salt in a red slicker, holding a green bag for Christmas gifts. I dearly love my mermaids, lobster claw dolls, and shell dolls too. In fact, as a result of *Doll News*, there are now two mermaids sitting in the bathtub of my spare boudoir!

Once again, I applaud Theriault's for helping in fundraising efforts for the UFDC museum, and for the kindness and friendship they offer to doll lovers everywhere.

Such wonderful social media sites inspire me, and encourage me to look around. A recent visit to Goodwill revealed six or seven lovely modern porcelain dolls from the '90s, dubbed "creepy" by the press and San Clement PD, for only $5.38 each. There was a lovely Alexander vinyl doll for only $2.38 that joined my collection, and an Applause Raggedy Ann I found for only $.88. At our local Cancer Society Discovery Shop, I found a Nancy Ann Storybook, the hard plastic, thin model with swivel head, in a wonderful flouncy dress and elegant felt bonnet for $25.00, and a mint, hard plastic, very old Red Riding Hood, in mint shape. There are good dolls everywhere; on only has to look.

Below is one of Theriault's press releases, which they have graciously allowed me to reproduce. It is about the auction, "As in a Looking Glass," which "drew collectors from around the globe to San Antonio." Words in italics are Theriault's.

It isn't very difficult to see why the trousseau were so desirable, a brief survey of the stunning and intricate costumes and accessories was nearly enough to leave one satiated, particularly when they were as lavish and extensive as the trunk and trousseau featured alongside the French bisque wooden bodied poupée in lot #56. The doll, circa 1867, was presented from an original chateau estate in La Bourboule in the Auvergne region of central France. Her extensive original couturier trousseau included fourteen extraordinary gowns, ten bonnets, various blouses and jackets, coat, extensive undergarments, long train petticoats, small accessories, and her original trunk which bears the shipping label from to Nantes La Bourboule on its side. Of special note was the "Album de la Poupee" with 12 early sepia miniature tipped-in photographs of poupées in fashionable costumes (the earliest known commercial photographs of dolls) that was included in the trousseau. Selling for $36,000, the doll and trousseau exceeded the presale estimate and left a lasting impression on collectors fortunate enough to see the beautiful dolls and costumes in person.

Later on in the auction arrived an exceptional porcelain lady, circa 1850, who was accompanied by an elaborate trunk and trousseau containing and original hand-stitched couturiere costumes, bonnets, and accessories all in superb condition. The doll may be considered a precursor to the classic French bisque poupée, and with the original trunk boasting its original paper label fetched an impressive $16,500. Additionally, not to be overlooked was a German papeir mâché *doll, circa 1860, named "Hattie" that had been owned by the young Harriet Simonds of Franklinville, New York, who died in 1863 at the age of sixteen. To pass the time during her invalid years, she sewed for her doll, creating an extensive wardrobe of costumes and accessories. The doll was sold from the collection of Jean Strong along with provenance documents for $8, 750, more than five times the high end of its presale estimate of $1,100/$1,500.*

Other dolls with trousseaux featured in the auction included an exceptionally beautiful French bisque bébé by Schmitt et Fils, circa 1882, welling onsite for $11,000, and a petite French bisque block-letter bébé by

Gautier, circa 1884, which sold for $6,500 far exceeding its presale estimate in all, the auction was an exciting and fruitful mid-week event to remember, providing collectors the opportunity to see outstanding trousseaux, rare and wonderful delightful automata, and a wide assortment of accessories and miniatures.

I couldn't have said it better myself. Nothing "creepy," anywhere, just fellowship and friendship revolving around professional, historical, and nostalgic interest in dolls.

Chapter 45: Where Dolls Will Go

There are two kinds of people who like dolls; dealers, and those who aren't. The world of doll collecting has changed considerably. There isn't enough time to go into the many changes that have taken place. I will note that when the first established collectors began to emerge, like Queen Marie of Rumania, the dolls were international, and often were sent by admirers from all over the world. The same is true of the collections of writers Frances Hodgson Burnett and Eugene Field. Before that, one could note that the first collectors might have been the adults who collected miniatures for cabinets of curiosities and baby houses, especially in the Netherlands, as discussed in the novel, *The Miniaturist*. Or, perhaps, the women who cherished and sent each other fashion dolls, some as big as real women, to showcase the latest trends in couture.

As we've seen, there were collectors in the ancient world; though some would quibble they collected small pieces of art or idols. Think of Emperor Montezuma who allegedly had his own dolls, or the little girls of the Ancient world who dedicated their dolls to goddesses and who were sometimes buried with them. The great Plato, and other writers, have made mention of dolls' furniture, toys and dolls in their works. In the Bible, there are idols, and the story of Genesis where God formed man from clay, a story which later became part of the Golem and Frankenstein legends.

Early collectors, as chronicled in the excellent books of Susan Pearce, (*The Collector's Voice* (, were fierce in completing their collections, in expanding them, displaying them, and appreciating them. Collectors of all kinds of things appear later in novels by Dickens, Henry James, George Eliot, even Jane Austen.

By the time Alice Trimpey wrote about her dolls in *Becky, my First Love,* c. 1938, doll collectors were getting organized. The UFDC came along in 1947, and Kimport Dolls went into business about that time, supplying collectors' needs through handmade dolls and dolls from all over the world, as well as antiques.

Many collectors were dealers, but they were more like stamp and coin collectors. They traded up and sold to build their own collections and to make friends. Profit was not at the heart of their collecting. Marks were important to identify dolls, but good general collections were eclectic, and were meant indeed to tell the story of mankind through dolls, as the UFDC's mission is today.

Then, something happened. Antiques began to climb in price. Reproductions became popular so collectors could have examples of bisque dolls and old dolls in their collections. Then, the replicas and reproductions became a craze and an art in themselves. Old dolls became scarce. Collector dolls or limited editions just for collections began to be made.

Madame Alexander dolls went through the roof; only a few made it to a few department stores, and the list was longer than the ones out there for the Hermes Birkin Bag (something else, I'd like, by the way).

The slogan at doll shows became, "You can't buy a good doll for under $500." Then it was, "under $1000." I had a very big collection by the time I was 15, and my parents referred to the dolls as "the bodies." It was disconcerting to their friends, sometimes, who had to think a minute about what the bodies really were. Some of their friends were on board big time; they brought me dolls from trips, made them, and even gave me their childhood dolls.

One of my brownie troop leaders took us to her friend, who had an amazing doll collection. I got special treatment because they told our hostess I was collector, too. She treated me like an equal, pointing out her best dolls, and her favorites were two perfect Minerva tin heads dressed in twin-blue bustle dresses. The other brownie leader was my best friend's mother. She was good to us, but would never buy me a doll, or let my little friend give me hers when they moved. Her dolls went to another family across the street, famous for destroying dolls and toys, including mine. My friends' mother, we'll call her Bette, told my mom she just "couldn't do it to her" by giving me another doll. My mom was shocked. She answered with, "You don't have to give Ellen another doll, Bette, but they're a family hobby my own mother started. We like the dolls very much, and we like to bring them home from trips." Bette never did give me a doll, though we gave several to her daughter and to the destructive little girls across the street.

By the time I was in college, doll collecting was in full swing and declared to be the number one US hobby. Porcelain dolls became mass produced in Asia, some by famous companies, some sold in Kmart and Dollar or dime stores. Some had no brand names, like the little doll called Walda sold mail order. In Canada, these dolls were expensive in the late '80s, and a few appeared in doll museums. They seem to be the weeds of doll collecting, and even the limited-edition dolls that were expensive are pooh-poohed, but one has to ask why they existed in the first place.

191

Many were even used as movie props. They were affordable, very pretty, and mostly Victorian. Not everyone could spend 100s or 1000s or 10,000s on dolls of porcelain or antiques. Not everyone could make them, and making porcelain dolls was very pricey. Seeley and Duncan molds for the dolls alone could cost a lot of money. The kilns cost over $1000, along with paints, patterns, clothing, and time to make them. There was a danger of getting asbestos related diseases as well from kiln dust.

The modern porcelain dolls are beautiful; perfect for young collectors. They inspired the study of Victorian history, literature, doll making, and costume, they displayed well, and they didn't cost a fortune.

Around 1972, Patricia Smith wrote and compiled her series of *Modern Collectors' Dolls* books. It made dolls that were once secondary collectibles. When I was young, vintage Barbies, vinyls, hard plastics, weren't a "thing." I loved all dolls, so I included them in my collections, but I bought a No.3 Barbie with case and some clothes for only $3 when I was a teenager from an established collector who had lots of old bisque and china dolls. Composition dolls were old, but not that collectible unless they were Shirley Temple or a Dionne Quint. I bought Arranbee's Little Angel for $2 when I was only 7 at the San Jose Flea Market. There were tables full of compo babies, and other dolls, including a Bonnie Babe by Averill. I used to see French dolls then for around $75, even Bru. That was a ton of money for a little kid; $20 was a big deal. When my dad bought me an original bisque Susanne Gibson Little girl doll for $47.25 with tax, he said his hand hurt for weeks after writing the check. I used to get irritated, even as a young girl, by the old lady doll snobs who declared their dolls were too expensive for me, and who would try to find something "cheap" to sell me. They lost an opportunity to teach an eager young kid about dolls and their history. No wonder young people aren't interested in dolls or collecting these days.

By the '70s, collectors specialized. Composition dolls became very expensive, even if cracked, and hard plastic dolls like Miss Revlon and Toni cost 100s of dollars. Vintage Madame Alexanders went through the roof, sometimes commanding thousands of dollars. Supply and demand became everything; collectors now began to specialize. Some only collected eight-inch Ginny by Vogue, others Alexander. A few only Raggedy Ann, then the Barbie collectors, modern and vintage, began to emerge. Antique collectors separated themselves from everyone.

Foreign and folk dolls were disgraced as souvenir or tourist dolls. Bachmann would disagree here, as would most teachers. These little souvenirs broke down barriers among people, and taught appreciation and tolerance for all cultures. Early collectors cherished them; I still do. The line is blurry for many dolls. Fine antiques were often dressed in regional and national costumes, or even as Native American dolls. One wonders why so many counties preferred using a certain type of doll to wear so many costumes. There was universality about the whole thing of dressing these dolls that brought the world together. Case in point is the collection of The King of Dolls, Shankar's International Doll Museum, and Shirley Temple's former doll collection.

As people specialized, collecting became boring. Too much of one thing was what Helen Young called an accumulation, not a collection. I think this happened with the CPK fad. I know of one multimillion-dollar collection where nothing apparently cost under $10,000. The trouble is; all the dolls look alike to me. They smack of money, true, but not good taste. They are not imaginative, and are an accumulation of wealth. That's the only story they tell.

Hence, the doll snob or doll diva is born. We know them; the people who constantly quibble with history. They sniff at everything with disdain; they don't like anything. It has to be minty mint, but they don't want to pay money for it. They correct everything anyone else says. They reared their ugly little heads recently at the Myla Perkins Auction, Tears for Mina. There was a Facebook attack on the dolls of Leo Moss. The divas claimed this black, itinerant folk artist who made such beautiful dolls never existed. They came to this conclusion because they couldn't find records of his birth on the Internet. He was born, of course, over 100 years ago. Some claimed that the late Ralph Griffith of Ralphs Antique Dolls concocted the dolls and their stories, yet, there is documentation that Moss and his dolls did indeed exist.

I've learned that there are doll racists, just as there are people racists. At a local country auction, I was able to buy the black and ethnic dolls because no one in this little one-horse town bid on them. More than I care to admit, I've heard collectors say they "don't care for black of colored dolls." What!!! When the CPK craze was at its height, my mother walked into a Kmart and found two rows of black CPKs just sitting there. One clerk told the other that they were "ugly" and no one wanted them. My mother promptly bought one for me. That was the beginning of my CPK sub-collection. The Leo Moss dolls brought over $60,000 on the March 16–17 Auction weekend. Good for them.

Chapter 46: Dolls and Therapy

For many years, dolls have been used to help abused and criminalized children to cope with their trauma. Some dolls have acted like the Chinese doctor ladies; children would point on the dolls where they had been physically hurt. Other dolls and doll houses were the tools by which children told what had happened to them. Some of the dolls used were traditionally anatomically correct, but recently, these types of doll have come into question. (Kendall-Tacket 1992). Many organizations give out dolls and teddy bears as ways to comfort children who have been the victims of crimes and natural disasters.

Currently, dolls are use in therapy with dementia and Alzheimer's patients (Schaefer 2003). Many collectors enjoy donating dolls to nursing homes because they give the residents so much pleasure. Reborn baby dolls or realistic baby dolls seem to be more effective in helping dementia patients deal with agitation and depression. Still, some therapists frown upon the practice because they feel the patient's dignity is assaulted.

Other therapists disagree with doll therapy because they find doll play to be regressive, childish behavior.

Yet, robots and dolls have been effective therapies for autistic children. (Wada, et all 2008)

Dolls are used in the medical field as anatomical models to teach health care professionals. Martha Chase made life-sized dolls for hospitals so that nursing students could practice on them. Some nursing students called these dolls "Mary Ann Chase."

Drama therapy involves using dolls, puppets and masks to create a narrative of the client's trauma. It sounds a lot like the dolls of the Chinese Opera, or Bunraku puppets, or the puppet theater in general. (RJ Landy – The Arts in Psychotherapy, 1983)

Doll making is used as therapy in grief recovery. Doll maker Elinor Peace Bailey notes in one film on doll making that victims of abuse often reveal their struggles to her during her doll making classes. For them, the dolls they make are part or their healing process.

I know that for me, dolls have kept me sane in difficult times and have been my saving grace. I often say that when the going gets tough, the tough print paper dolls. I've lived it many times, and my mantra is sometimes a little tongue in cheek but true, "I look to the dolls, whence cometh my help." One might say the same about any pastime or hobby. Recreation and play are crucial to well-being; they help us to play out stressful scenarios, but also to create and to invent. Many inventors note the importance of play to their work, also scientists. Ata recent exhibit of space models and the work the University of Iowa played in NASA, toys of the some of the scientists were displayed with their models. Their toys were the seeds of the inventions and space modules they would later create. It is no accident that the geniuses of *The Big Bang Theory* love toys, games, comic books and action figures. Nor is it an accident that the ate Stephen Hawking had a keen sense of humor and allowed himself to be portrayed as a doll patterned after his Simpson's character.

Chapter 47: Auction Adventures

As a child, I developed a healthy fear/anxiety over auctions. It came from watching the *Dick van Dyke Show*. It's an old skit; Rob, Laura and friends attend an auction where Laura has her heart set on a large, crystal Victorian gewgaw. She wins, and Rob leaves to get the car. He motions to Laura to come, and his gesture is taken for a bid, and a very expensive one at that. Rob and Laura end up going home with a lot more than they bargained for.

Through the years, I gained a little auction experience. At my grade school frolic, I won a floral wall plaque for my mother for $0.50. It hung on my parent's wall for years till Dad knocked it down with a sweeper attachment and it shattered. Many of our household bric-a-brac met with a similar demise through death by sweeper attachment. If the casualties were not fatal, the pieces to be reassembled would magically appeared on my desk. It must have been the vacuum fairy.

My next adventure got me two faux jade Chinese wax candle dolls, severed at the waist like the Black Dahlia murder victim, but unlike her, held together by their wicks. I also won a chipped Victorian moustache cup for the same price as the candles. $.50 must have been my forte. This auction was held on the premises of an old clapboard house, about to be demolished for a hair salon called, ironically, "Visible Changes." There were a few other things I bid on, but a man who looked like a snake oil salesman from a penny dreadful always bid against me. He always won. Each time, he flashed his gold toothed grin at me, even as the afternoon sun glanced off of his oily hair.

My next experience came when I was starting graduate school at SIUC. It was my last weekend home. Our neighbors up the street were selling their house and having an auction. They were consummate collectors, too. A couple of years before, they had a killer yard sale after 45 years of collecting. While I was at the yard sale, another neighbor's mother, an antique dealer, grabbed a bag right out of my hands. This is not atypical behavior for some. Read Jonathan Gash's Lovejoy novels.

At the auction, before I left for SIUC, I ran into the mother of a classmate, areal Mrs. Von Munchausen if ever there was one. She promoted her oldest, mediocrely gifted oldest daughter shamelessly for years, a regular Nellie

Olesen type. Mrs. B, wife of a not-too-successful accountant, rarely spoke to me. I was always scapegoated for her daughter's failures. At birthday parties she made me feel like a second-class citizen

She cornered me at the auction to tell me her esteemed daughter was now a graduate student going to London on an internship. The game rules were set; it was her point, now in my court.

I told her I'd been to summer school in Spain a few years before and was busy, too, I'd finished a law degree and masters concurrently, and was on my way to start a Ph.D. On school breaks, I would be working at my law firm. As soon as I got my story out, B excused herself quickly. Dad was standing there; she'd know him for over 35 years, and my parents had taken her daughter places, fed her, bought her gifts, but Mrs. B said not a word to him.

I sent condolences when her husband died, but she never responded. The few times I ran into her, she made a snide remark or two in my hearing. That's all.

Back to the auction, I had an argument over a $10 button tin. I misheard a bid. A bid can be withdrawn, but they refused to do it. Dad was furious; the old woman taking money was just rude. It was awful, and the auction personnel just ignored me. That is not good customer service.

The next time I was at an auction was 1997. I attended a couple of doll auctions; the auction houses are now defunct. The first was in the country, Fulton, IL. I managed to get a couple rare Hallmark ornaments in a box lot; that's all. For $5, I got ornaments worth $60 each. The auctioneer was focusing on two or three bidders only; everyone else was ignored. Most were pros, and prices were high. I wasn't impressed at all

A month or so later, I went to an all doll auction. I watched people fight over plastic dolls, break a couple of dolls, etc. I couldn't hear very well, and lost out on a couple nice dolls. I did get the lovely Lawrence Welk Champagne Lady, a doll head with a wig, several small dolls, including a Lissi Baitz colonial woman. I should have tried to get the man. The dolls were "first serve." After someone won a lot, she could choose if she wanted all or some of the lot. The rejected lots went to whomever spoke up first and then to the next bidder in successive order. I didn't enjoy it. I watched women I know couldn't afford it pay hundreds of dollars for common dolls. A few couldn't make up their minds, and were openly shaking and sweating. One woman scowled at anyone who bid on what she wanted. I won a Dutch Day doll, dolls dressed for the Fulton Dutch Days festival then. I won it. The nasty, wiry little woman with a bull dog face put her hands on her scrawny little hips and glared at me.

Barring a couple women, this group never appeared at any of the doll shows, flea markets, or antique shows I knew. They were, however, aggressive and nasty. The crowds at Lohmann's and Filene's Basement have nothing over them.

I was successful at a doll auction in 2009 when I went with my husband. We got many wonderful dolls there. At one point, my husband said, "Sit on your hands, Dear," and took away my paddle. I was able to get many ethnic dolls, including the black Chase dolls and the Sioux doll made for the doll postage stamps. We were in a tiny, Illinois town, and my husband told me I would do well with ethnic dolls; the predominantly white population of the little down didn't want dolls of color. That's so sad. The same little town allegedly escorted any person of color out of town if he/she dared to show up at the local café.

Since 2009, I've done well at online auctions by Frasher's, Tom Harris Auction, Theriault's, and Noel Barrett. Mr. Barret and Andy Ourant were very good about answering questions ahead of time. Several great dolls became mine through absentee bids. I'm not sure if it was because the auctioneers were experienced or organized, or if there were items no one else appreciated, but they were much better auction experiences for me. I watched the 2014 Shirley Temple auction, and won a doll that belonged to her. I also wrote about it in my blogs and for About.com. I won a cute knitted doll, which was important. I had seen Temple's dolls several times, and there were pictures of me with them. They had been on display at the Stanford Children's Hospital for many years.

Chapter 48: Rinker's Rule: Collectors and the Entrepreneurial Spirit

In "Entrepreneurial Spirit Index Wanes," noted antiques and collecting expert Harry Rinker states that "Collecting is an entrepreneurial enterprise. Collectors assemble, study, ad preserve a specific group of objects" (2).

He goes on to say that in the process of collecting and curating objects, collectors may "fill a void that exists within the collecting field." He calls the collector's approach business like, and states that the collector may understand his collection or "inventory" better than most businesses. (2)

Thank you!

Rinker has just distinguished the collector from the hoarder. People who collect nothing do not understand this. Yet, the Uniform Commercial Code, brain child of Karl Llewellyn, does understand. Merchants for the purposes of the UCC are experts in their fields, and experts include collectors who know their "stuff" and its history. Those who publish, appraise, and deal in collectibles are definitely experts.

Rinker sees collectors, dealers, auctioneers, estate sale and managers and others in the antique/collectibles industry as entrepreneurs who must often be good strategists and competitors to achieve their collecting goals. He continues to compare antique folk to business people who have left the "paycheck" community to work for themselves, and he is correct. Doll collecting is no different; it takes networking skill, detective skills, management and organizational skills, financial prowess, intelligence, and perseverance. Many small businesses in my area are antique stores, vintage stores, privately owned thrift shops, and locally owned galleries and antique malls. Add to these, small doll shops, like those in my old neighborhoods in California, and you have Rinker's business model.

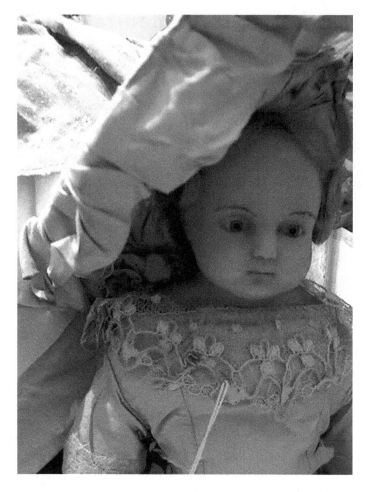

Poured wax doll, English, 19th century with original silk clothing and glass eyes. Author's Collection.

Assortment of 19th-century china heads. Center doll in knitted dress is American, by Irwin. Boy in brown suit has a German celluloid head. Boy dressed by author, knitted dress by author's mother. Author's Collection.

Contemporary doll house inspired by Disney film "Frozen". Dolls by Playmobil. Author's Collection.

Dolls representing the ancient world, including the Lion Man figure, a reproduction of a 10,000-year-old carving. Author's Collection.

International dolls from the author's collection in cases built by her father, 1979.

Royal Copenhagen's reissue of their 1840s brown-haired china head. Author's Collection.

1980s doll house assembled from a kit by Greenleaf. Author's Collection.

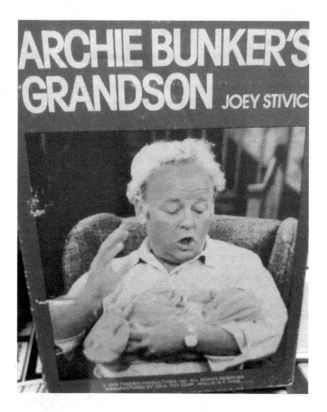

Joey Stivic doll, anatomically correct vinyl baby. Author's Collection.

Four-foot nutcracker. Author's Collection.

L: Papier Mache 19th-century roly poly doll in Greek or Armenian dress. R: Early Kathe Kruse boy doll, early 20th century. Kruse was a sculptor who first used a potato as a model for the realistic doll heads she would create with paint and cloth. She was influenced by the Bauhaus art movement. Author's Collection.

Beth, a 21st-century life sized mannikin from former Younker's department store. Author's Collection.

21-inch portrait doll, vinyl with sleep eyes by Madame Alexander, 1960s. Author's collection.

Two Marionettes from the Sound of Music, created by Bil Baird. Currently in The MacNider Museum, Mason City, IA. Photo by the author. Baird, with his mentor Tony Sarg, developed the giant balloons displayed at Macy's annual Thanksgiving parade.

Assorted masks, including a plaster Arab by Bosson's, England, flanked by two Mardis Gras masks. The wreathe is made of antique buttons. The plastic figure, lower left, dolls made of Vermont maple sugar. Author's Collection.

Viny Cabbage Patch Kid, by Coleco, Author's Collection.

Dolls can be made of anything. This emergent figure is made from a broom, old clothes, and assorted hardware. Author's Collection.

Two five-inch, vintage dolls from Mexico, made of wax. Author's Collection.

19th century untinted bisque or Parian doll, because she resembles Parian marble. 1870s, Germany. Author's Collection.

Artist's version of Rachel Field's Hitty posing before a postcard of The House of Seven Gables, where wooden dolls have been traditionally made and sold. Hitty was a gift to the author from her dear friend and noted paper doll artist, the late Stephanie Hammonds. Author's Collection.

King Tut's personal mannikin, used for tailoring his clothes. Photo by the author, travelling King Tut exhibit, April 2017.

The author's so-called Good Year rubber doll, 1860, purchased from the late Pat Vaillancourt. Author's Collection.

Early Barbies with contemporary doll furniture made for their Dream House. Courtesy, Theriault's.

The doll in its most primitive form, a corn dollie from England. These fertility figures are made from braided wheat and have been created for centuries. They even inspired a work by Joyce Carol Oates. Author's Collection.

German Frozen Charlottes of porcelain, 19th century, pose with a 20th-century Voodoo doll of yarn. Author's Collection.

Appendix

Appendix Dolls and Artifacts displayed in Hearts and Hinges for GAHC, January through Feb 2014.

1. 20" + tin baby, VG cond.
2. 1 sheet robot paper
3. Dolls Nations book
4. 1 metal head, brown wig, blue eyes, peach dress, tag
5. 1 Shadow Dancer metal rabbit
6. 1 6" teddy bear mold
7. 1 Japanese doll, white kimono/floral blanket
8. 1 squeaky metal baby, about 9"
9. 1 roly poly tin Santa
10. 7" cast iron mermaid, hobby lobby
11. 4094 cloth/metal ballerina with Tag 17.50, Klumpe type
12. 1 Minerva/ Diana head with body and dress, 40-
13. Minerva head, 5.00 tag
14. Keystone mfg. international card with U. Sam
15. Bucherer Man
16. Bucherer Woman from Noel Barrett
17. Naughty 1920s jumping jack
18. Hobby lobby silver pilgrim
19. Juno, cloth body, flannel blanket with pink
20. Automaton on base, green dress with cat
21. Red mechanical tin Santa, body and head
22. Jungfrau cup
23. Metal angel/guilt
24. Rosalie/Whyel doll, German costume with pink blanket
25. Tin Lizzie car
26. Oscar Statue
27. 1/2 metal skeleton
28. 7" mechanical man
29. Knights head

30. Clock figure reading
31. 4" silver candle girl
32. Bull fighter
33. Pumpkin robot, head separate
34. Blue corkscrew doll
35. Brass
36. Q Eliz II head
37. English bell La Reine Anne
38. Indian Bell
39. Pewter balance beam mini
40. Doll head with quilt
41. 1992 dist. Award
42. Copper Africa
43. Pewter model 4"
44. Metal pump
45. 1" Amish girl
46. 7" tin soldier
47. Pig
48. McD tin man
49. Burkina Fasso girl
50. Small white robot
51. Door knocker
52. Spiderman dog
53. Vulture toothpick mechanical
54. Karakuri with box
55. Angel
56. Metal Wiseman
57. Robot chicken
58. Scot soldier tin
59. Greek peasant
60. Mech. Frog
61. Roman soldiers
62. Sasha, red hair and white dress
63. Metal chair
64. Annalee wire/felt rabbit girl
65. English hard plastic walking doll
66. Large, glass eyed Minerva, yellow dress
67. Steiff afghan hound
68. Heartbeat doll
69. Digital Barbie

70. Angel candelabra
71. Edison's Eve, book
72. 18" enamel metal head, purple check dress, pink check bonnet
73. Hula Girl
74. Hawkins studio, little girl with doll
75. One metal black cat
76. Porcelain doll with wire arms, pink and blue print dress
77. All brass baby with crocheted dress and afghan
78. Czech rod puppet
79. Brass head of Homer
80. Compo head and metal neck parts
81. Buck Rogers toy
82. Musical Japanese Doll
83. Book, Dolls in Color
84. Paris bébé torso
85. Musical Charlie Brown Beanie
86. Soccer Lion Key Chain, Germany
87. 6" Minerva head eye painted
88. Glycerin Venus of Willendorf
89. Silvery Jungfrau, gold inlay
90. 3" Rug Rats walking Chucky
91. Giebeler Falk doll
92. 16" Juno doll with beige plaid dress
93. Baby head, pat pen
94. Grey accordion folder with research
95. Cano f Doll Lain Drape as prop, local doll Shoppe at one time
96. Coleman Cage doll
97. Chatty Cathy
98. Creaming witch
99. Black talking alien, 11"
100. Ellen Marie's Blue Minerva sister
101. HP walking doll
102. Mummy
103. Repainted baby
104. Cast iron Geisha
105. White mesh cage doll
106. Minerva, purple dress
107. 1st metal baby with my dress
108. Rocking chair
109. Merlin Jack in the Box

110. Large Diana, white dress
111. Shirley type, polka dot red dress
112. Green and white metal doll with wig
113. Pat Loveless Bru
114. Boy, large Silvestri android
115. Lindbergh portrait doll, with wire armature, collector of automatons
116. Vintage toy airplane box
117. Metal head baby, VG white crocheted vest
118. Vintage Schoenhut Advert.
119. Schoenhut piano
120. Marie Osmond doll, wire frame
121. Chinese cloisonné doll and box
122. Wooden doll chair
123. The Robot Kit, Lost in Space
124. Fem Sapien robot
125. ILL. Digest book 10A.
126. Tea tin
127. Cast iron doll pot
128. Tin doll tea pot
129. Assorted photos in frames

Author Background

The author began collecting dolls and studying them when she was three years old. Her collection began with 3 Greek dolls, her first, that were purchased for her in Athens or that were purchased years before as part of her grandmother's collection. Dr. Tsagaris' family has traveled, lived, and worked on every continent except Antarctica, but a very close family friend traveled there, so even that territory is covered and represented by the items in her collection, which encompasses over 15,000 dolls, a library of books on dolls and related subjects that numbers in the thousands and is the subject of its own book-length bibliography, some 50 doll houses and shadow boxes, thousands of miniatures, hundreds of vintage toys, and thousands of doll related ephemera, antiques, children's items, paper dolls, and doll clothes.

These items have been displayed in local museums, libraries, and schools, including The German American Heritage Center in Davenport, IA, The Bettendorf Public Library, and Kaplan University, Davenport, IA. They are now displayed in American Doll & Toy Museum.

She has published hundreds of articles on dolls and their history in publications that include *National Doll World, Doll Reader, Doll News, International Doll World, Doll Designs, Hope and Glory: The Midwest Journal of Victorian Studies, and The Western Doll Collector*. She has published two books about dolls, *A Bibliography of Doll and Toy Sources,* favorably reviewed by the editors of *Doll Castle News*, and *With Love from Tin Lizzie: A History of Metal Dolls and Automatons*. She has also presented papers about dolls and about children's books that feature dolls at the annual Convention of the Midwest Modern Language Association. These titles include "They want to Play with You; Dolls in Horror Movies," and "A Literary Shelter for Misfit Dolls," "Sara Crewe's Emotional Debts in A Little Princess" and "Rumer Godden's debt to Children's Literature." She has written a book review for the *American Journal of Play,* published by the Strong National Museum of play and corresponds with many well-known doll makers, authors, collectors and dealers. She is affiliated with The Warren County/West Central Illinois Doll Club, is a friend of the Fennimore Doll and Toy Museum of Fennimore, WI, a Friend of the Eugene Field House and Toy

Museum, and has been a member of the United Federation of Doll Clubs. She has taught classes on the historical and literary significance of dolls, including The Doll as Other, for Comm University, a series of weekend courses mentored by St. Ambrose University and other institutions of higher learning. She has lectured on various literary and historical subjects, including dolls for The American Association of University Women, The German American Heritage Center, various Churches, The Quad City Literary Guild, and The Putnam Museum.

Dr. Tsagaris writes several blogs, and most are devoted exclusively to dolls and doll collectors. These are *American Doll & Toy Museum*, a historical web museum of the history of dolls, *The International Doll Museum Blog,* and *Dr. E's Doll Museum.* She also writes blogs on green living, which often features folk dolls, *Dr. E's Greening Tips for the Common Person*, blogs on memoir, *Writing Your Life Story*, a blog on the works of Barbara Pym and Charlotte Bronte, *Miss Barbara Pym meets Miss Charlotte Bronte* and *An Apologia for Erzebet Bathory*. These blogs often include stories and information about dolls. Over 4 million people around the world have visited, read, and occasionally commented, on these blogs. She maintains several Pinterest boards including one called "Doll Collection," and has her own Facebook Page for dolls, "Dr. E's Doll Museum." Her hash tag on Twitter is Dr. E's Doll Museum. You can find her on LinkedIn, Twitter, Instagram, Tumblr, Flickr, and other social media, promoting dolls and collecting.

She also writes guest blogs for Virtual Doll Convention, Ruby Lane and the renowned doll artist, R. John Wright.

Education: Dr. Tsagaris holds a law degree (Juris Doctor) and a Masters and Ph.D. in English. Her Bachelor's degree is a double major in English and Spanish. She has published widely in many fields, including a chapbook on poetry, *Sappho, I Should have Listened*, and she is the editor and a contributor for an anthology of ghost stories, *The Legend of Tugfest*, 918 Studio 2012. She published a book of literary criticism, The Subversion of Romance in the Novels of Barbara Pym, The Popular Press, 1998, and has published in anthologies of fiction and poetry. She published college study guides in Legal Writing and Administrative Law and is currently working on a book about the death penalty, two novels, and two books about vintage jewelry. She chaired departments in Criminal Justice Legal Studies and Humanities for a major University. She currently is a free-lance writer and Executive Director of The American Doll and Toy Museum.

Bibliography

"The Aechulean Goddess." *JBL Statue*.2013 http://jblstatue.com/acheulian.html

Alberini, Massimo. *Color Treasury of Model Soldiers*. New York: Crown Publishers, 1972.

Alcott, Louisa May. *Little Women*. Boston: Roberts Brothers, 1868.

Amudi, Betsey. "Dolls in Saudi Arabia." *A Different Doll* (blog) 2003.https://adifferentdoll.wordpress.com/dolls-in-Saudi-arabia/https://adifferentdoll.wordpress.com/dolls-In-saudi-arabia/

Andrew. Alex. "The Ethics of using Dolls and Soft Toys in Dementia Care." *Nursing and Residential Care*, 2006 – magonlinelibrary.com

Angione, Genevieve and Judith Wharton. *All Dolls are Collectible*. New York: Crown Publishers, 1977.

Argyriades, Maria. *Dolls in Greek Life and Art from Antiquity To the Present Day*. Lucy Braggioti Publications, 1991.

Bachmann, Manfred. *Dolls The Wide World Over*. New York: Crown Publishers, 1973.

Baten, Lea. *Japanese Dolls: The Image and the Motif*. Tuttle, 1986.

Bennett, Betty O. *Collectible Dolls: Facts and Trivia*. Vol. I. Nashville, Hipp-Daniel Publishing, 1994.

Billy Boy. "Enrich Thyself." *Dolls*. August/September 1991. 154.

Brasier, Debra. "30 Years Later, Tom Gets His Polar Bear." *Quad City Times*. 2013. http://qctimes.com/news/opinion/editorial/columnists/bill-wundram/years-later-tom-gets-his-polar-bear/article_f55ae5ae-d276-5538-bd5a-798fbb560b9f.html

"ChacoIndians." 2019.htps://www.google.com/search?q=chatco+indians&rlz=1C1AWUA_en US739US740&source=lnms&tbm=isch&sa=X&ved=0ahUKEwixu4GTrZ3b AhVEs1kKHdV8CKIQ_AUICygC&biw=1366&bih=662

Chudacoff, Howard P. *Children at Play; an American History*. New York: NYU Press, 2007.

Coleman, Dorothy, Evelyn Jane and Elizabeth Ann. *The Collector's Encyclopedia of Dolls*. Vol. 1. New York: Crown Publishers, 1968.

The Collector's Encyclopedia of Dolls. Vol. 2. New York: Crown Publishers, 1986,

The Collector's Encyclopedia of Doll Clothes. New York: Crown Publishers, 1975.

"Collecting." *Wikipedia.*2020. https://en.wikipedia.org/wiki/Collecting

Conrad, Joseph. *Heart of Darkness.* New York: Dover, 2014,

"CornDollies." 2019. Delcampe.net. https://www.delcampe.net/en_GB/collectables/postcards/argentina/argentina-native-nude-chaco-indians-indias-chamacoco-girls-1907-440877184.html

deCuba, Johannes. *Hortus Sanitatis.(*orig. 1491).*Wikipedia.* 2020, https://en.wikipedia.org/wiki/Hortus_Sanitatis

"Doll." 2020. *Wikipedia. https://en.wikipedia.org/wiki/Doll*

"Dr. Es Doll Museum." *Facebook.* 2010.

Dombrowski, Jennifer. February 4, 2013. "History of the Venice Carnival Masks." *Luxe Adventure Traveler.*
https://luxeadventuretraveler.com/history-venice-carnival-mask/

Dorr, Marguerite. "Fashion History Through the Story of Dolls." *The Iowa Homemaker.* 1939. vol.19, no.7.

Dumas, Alexandre. *The Man in the Iron Mask.* New York: Penguin Classics, 2005.

Engmann, Rachel. "Ceramic Dolls and Figurines, Citizenship and Consumer Culture in Market Street Chinatown, San Jose." Unpublished paper (2007)

Etquest1, *Flickr.* 2018. https://www.flickr.com/photos/86675146@N03

Fawcett, Clara Hallard. *Dolls: A New Guide for Collectors.* Charles T. Branford, 1981.

Finkenscher, Lisa. "Toys R Us is in Talks to Keep its Brand and Some Stores Alive" *The New York Post.* 2018. https://nypost.com/2018/03/14/toys-r-us-is-in-talks-to-keep-its-brand-and-some-stores-alive/

"Fontaine's Offering Estate Furniture, Smalls Nov. 20." *Antique Week.* November 7, 2016. Vol. 48. Issue No. 2462. no page.

Forman Brunell, Miriam. "Interrogating the Meanings of Dolls New Directions in Doll Studies" *Semantic Scholar.* 2012, DOI:10.3167/GHS.2012.050102.
https://www.semanticscholar.org/paper/Interrogating-the-Meanings-of-Dolls%3A-New-Directions-Forman-Brunell/3b3ea69c51ee53c328a64e28720df7c1d751250b

Made to Play House. New Haven: Yale University Press, 1993.

Foulke, Jan. *The 16th Blue Book; Doll & Values.* Grantsville, MD: The Hobby House Press, 2003.

Fox, Carl. *The Doll.* New York: Abrams, 1970.

"Fulla." 2020. *Wikipedia.* https://en.wikipedia.org/wiki/Fulla_ (doll)

Gaiman, Neil. *The Sand Man. Dream Country*, Vol. III. New York: D.C. Comics, 2010.

Garratt, John G. *Model Soldiers: An Illustrated History.* New York: New York Graphic Society, 1972.

Gross, Kenneth. *On Dolls.* Notting Hill Editions, 2018

Puppets. Chicago: University of Chicago Press, 2011.

Grizzly Man. Dir. Werner Herzog. 2005,

Halloween Costume History. https://fashion-history.lovetoknow.com/clothing-types-styles/halloween-costume-history

Hargrove, Sandy. *Makaleka Hawaiian Souvenir Dolls; Reflections of Historical Hawaiian Dress Design.* Berthound, CO: Sandy Hargrove. 2017.

Hatch Collection of Black Cloth Dolls. www.blackclothdolls.com. 2020.

Herron, R. Lane. *Much Ado about Dolls.* Des Moines: Wallace-Homestead, 1979.

Higdon, Michael J. "It's A Small World: Using the Classic Disney Ride to Teach Document Coherence." *Perspectives: Teaching Legal Research And Writing.* Vol. 17 No. 1 Fall 2011. 111–114.

Hillier, Mary. *Dolls and Doll Makers.* New York: Crown, 1969,

"History of Dolls". HistoryofDolls.com, 2020.

The History of the Halloween Mask. https://www.superpages.com/em/halloween-mask/

History of Masks. http://www.historyofmasks.net/

"History of Puppetry and Puppet Theater." (blog), June 11, 2020. *The Theater Seat Store.* https://www.theaterseatstore.com/blog/history-of-puppetry,

Holman. Martha and Lamar Gailey. "Sharing the Arts of the Blue Ridge Mountains, Corn Shuck Dolls." *Authoring Institution: Pioneer Cooperative Educational Service Agency*, Cleveland, GA.

Holz, Loretta. *The How To Book of International Dolls.* New York: Random House Value Publishing, 1988.

Hume, Ivor Noël. *A Guide to Artifacts of Colonial America.* Pennsylvania: University of Pennsylvania (1969)

Irving D. Chais, 2020. *Wikipedia.* https://en.wikipedia.org/wiki/Irving_D._Chais

Jacobs, Margaret. "Playing with Dolls." *The Journal of the History of Childhood and Youth* Volume 1, Number 3, Fall 2008 pp. 321–328.

Jaeger, Lauren. "Identify your Dolls." *Doll World.* October, 1993. 12.

Jans, Nick. *The Grizzly Maze.* New York: E.P. Dutton 2005.

Johl, Janet Pagter. *The Fascinating Story of Dolls.* New York: H.L. Lindquist Publications, 1946.

More about Dolls. New York: H.L. Lindquist Publications, 1946.

Still More about Dolls. New York: H.L. Lindquist Publications, 1950.

Your Dolls and Mine. A Collector's Handbook. New York: H.L. Lindquist Publications, 1952.

Johl-Weissmann, Jan. Phone call. Autumn 2014

Kalke, Baiba and Meldra Rudzite. "History of the Childhood: The Reflection Of the Teacher's Image in Dolls." *Proceeding of the International Scientific Conference May 23rd–24th, 2014* Volume I 541.

Keller, Helen. The *Story of My Life*. New York: Signet Classics, 2010.

Kendall-Tackett, K.A. "Beyond Anatomical Dolls: Professionals' Use of other Play Therapy Techniques." *Child Abuse & Neglect,* 16(1), 139–142. https://doi.org/10.1016/0145-2134(92)90014

King, Stephen. "The Children of the Corn." *Night Shift.* (1976). New York: Anchor, 2011.

Kurtz, Karen. "Collecting Black Dolls: A Walk through History." *Antique Week.*19 Feb. 2018. Vol. 50. Issue No. 2527. pp.1+.

Landy, R. J. "The Use of Distancing in Drama Therapy."
The Arts in Psychotherapy, 1983 – psycnet.apa.org

Lavitt, Wendy. *American Folk Dolls*. New York; Knopf, 1982

Liboriussen, Bjarke. "Freedom of Avatars (or rather, The Thingness of Dolls and Avatars)." *The Philosophy of Computer Games Conference*, Istanbul (2014)

Loomis, Roger Sherman. *A Mirror of Chaucer's World*. Meridien, CT: Meridien Grayure, 1965,

Lorrin, Shona and Marc Lorrin. *The Half-Doll with Related Items, Makers, and Values. Walsworth Publishing, Volume 5, 2006.*

Mahmoody, Betty and William Hoffer. *Not without my Daughter.* New York: St. Martin's Press, 19911.

Martin, F. Diaz, et al. "The Origin of The Acheulean: The 1.7 Million-Year-Old Site of FLK West, Olduvai Gorge (Tanzania)."
https://www.nature.com/articles/srep17839. Dec. 2015,

Martin, Anthony F. (2016) "A List of Racialized Black Dolls: 1850–1940," *African Diaspora Archaeology Newsletter*:
Vol.15:Iss.1, https://scholarworks.umass.edu/adan/vol15/iss1/14

Martin, Sylvia. *I, Madame Tussaud.* Harper & Brothers, 1957.

The Mascherade. http://themascherade.com/contents/en-us/d5_Page_5.html

The M'Naghten Rule.
https://legal-dictionary.thefreedictionary.com/M%27Naghten+Rule

Mitchell, G. and M. Templeton. Ethical Considerations of Doll Therapy for People with Dementia. Nursing Ethics. journals.sagepub.com, 2014.

Morely, Jacqueline. William Shakespeare: A Very Peculiar History. The Book House, 2012.

Nutter Susan Emerson. "Legendary Doll Collection Sells Strong at Theriault's."Antique Week. 7 November 2016. Vol. 48. Issue No. 2462. pp. 1+.

Oates, Joyce Carol. *The Corn Maiden.* New York: The Mysterious Press, 2011.

Pearce, Susan. *The Collector's Voice: Volume 2,*

Early Voices. New York: Routledge, 2016.

Plato. "The Allegory of the Cave." *The Republic.* New York: Dover Thrift, 2012.

Puppeteer.org

Pruis, E.C. "Dolls Illustrate History of Nursing." *AJN The American Journal of Nursing,* 1935 – journals.lww.com

Rinker, Harry. "Entrepreneurial Spirit Index Wanes." *Antique Week.* Vol.51

Issue No. 2535. pp.2, 12.

St George, Eleanor. *The Dolls of Three Centuries.* New York: Charles Scribner's Sons, 1951.

The Dolls of Yesterday. New York: Charles Scribner's Sons, 1948.

Old Dolls. Gramercy Press, 1940.

SSatyendra Kumar Mishra and Satyaki Roy. Conference paper

First Online: 11 February 2017. Part of *the Smart Innovation, Systems and Technologies* book series (SIST,volume 66)

"Saudi   Arabia   Doll." https://www.youtube.com/watch?v=Ujkp_VamLwk

"Saudis Ban Female Dolls and Toy Bears." *Telegraph.* 18 December 2003.https://www.telegraph.co.uk/news/worldnews/middleeast/saudiarabi a/1449775/Saudis-ban-imports-of-female-dolls-and-toy-bears.html

"Saudi Religious Police say Barbie is a Moral Threat." *Fox News.* 9 September2003.http://www.foxnews.com/story/2003/09/10/saudi-religious-police-say-barbie-is-moral-threat.html

SSchaefer Charles E. *Play Therapy with Adults.* Wiley, 2002.

SSchroeder, Joseph J., Ed. *The Wonderful World of Toys, Games and Dolls.*

Digest Publishers, 1971.

SSchulz, Charles. *Charlie Brown's Super Book of Things to Collect.* 1984.

SSmith, Patricia R. *Modern Collectors Dolls Series 1.* Collector Books, 1972.

Modern Collectors Dolls Series 2. Collector Books, 1975.

Modern Collectors Dolls Series 3. Collector Books, 1976.

Modern Collectors Dolls Series 4. Collector Books, 1979.

Modern Collector Dolls Series 5. Collector Books, 1989.

Modern Collectors Dolls Series 6. Collector Books, 1993.

Modern Collectors Dolls Series 7. Collector Books, 1995.

Modern Collectors Dolls Series 8. Collector Books, 1996.

Patricia Smith's Doll Values: Antique to Modern: Collector Books, 1996.

Spiering, Frank. Prince Jack; *The True Story of Jack the Ripper.* (1955). Jove, 1981.

Taylor, Alice. "Dolls". *World of a Slave Encyclopedia.* Vol. I. 20ll.

"Tlingit."*Warpaths.*https://www.warpaths2peacepipes.com/indian-tribes/tlingit-tribe.html

Treleven, Ed. "American Girl Astornaut Doll Draws Lawsuit from Astronomer claiming Likeness was Stolen." etrevelen@madison.com. Google.com/amp/s/madison.com.

Tsagaris, Ellen. *A Bibliography of Doll and Toy Sources*. Rock Island: American Doll and Toy Corp. 2011.

"He's not one of Them: The Interpellation of the Self in Anne Rice's The Witching Hour." The Gothic World of Anne Rice. Bowlling Green, OH: The Popular Press. Ed. Gary Ranstand and Ray Brown.

Sappho, I should have Listened. LeClaire: 918studio 2011.

The Subversion of Romance in the Novels of Barbara Pym. Bowling Green, OH: The Popular Press, 1998.

With Love from Tin Lizzie: A History of Metal Dolls.

Rock Island: American Doll and Toy Corp., 2013

Vintage Halloween. http://www.vintagehalloween.com/halcostume.html

Von Boehn, Max. *Dolls*. *(*1927). Trans. Josephine Nicolls. New York: Dover, 1970.

Wada, K et al. "Robot Therapy for Elders affected by Dementia."

IEEE Engineering , 2008. ieeexplore.ieee.org

Wade, Nicholas. "A Host of Mummies, A Forest of Secrets." *The New York Times*.https://www.nytimes.com/2010/03/16/science/16archeo.html.

"WaylandFlowers."*Wikipedia,*   *20*
https://en.wikipedia.org/wiki/Wayland_Flowers

White, Gwen. *Dolls of the World*. (1962) Newton Centre :,MA: Charles T. Branford Company, 1963.

Wilder, Laura Ingalls. *Little House in the Big Woods*. New York: Harper Trophy, 1971.

Young, Helen. *The Complete Book of Doll Making and Collecting*. New York: Abrams, 1967.

Yung, Judy *Unbound Feet: A Social History of Chinese Women in San Francisco*. Berkeley: University of California Press, 1995.

CPSIA information can be obtained
at www.ICGtesting.com
Printed in the USA
BVHW060124240221
600896BV00010B/1503